CUT MY HAIR

CUT MY HAIR

by

JAMIE S. RICH

AN ONI PRESS PUBLICATION
PORTLAND, OREGON

Front cover art by MIKE ALLRED
Colored by LAURA ALLRED

INTERIOR ILLUSTRATIONS:
Character designs and chapters 1, 10, 11, 12, 15, and 25 by
ANDI WATSON

Chapters 3, 5, 6, 8, 9, and 20 by
CHYNNA CLUGSTON-MAJOR

Chapters 8, 9, 13, 14, 19, and 24 by
SCOTT MORSE

Chapters 17, 19, 21, 22, and 23 by
JUDD WINICK

Misc. illustrations and author portrait by
RENÉE FRENCH

Book design by JULIE E. GASSAWAY
Copy editing by JEN VAN METER
Published by SCOTT MORSE & JOE NOZEMACK
e-mail the author at cut_my_hair@hotmail.com

QUOTES:
"Not For This World" by Lara Michell © 1998 Lara Michell
"I'm One" by Pete Townshend © 1973 Fabulous Music Ltd.
"Please Please Please Let Me Get What I Want" by
Morrissey/Marr, © 1984 Morrissey/Marr Songs Ltd.

*The author thanks all the various other writers whose lines I have sampled
for my own use. Please don't sue me. It was meant with love.*

PRINTED IN CANADA
Oni Press, Inc. • 6336 SE Milwaukie Ave. PMB30 • Portland, OR 97202 • www.onipress.com
ISBN 0-9700387-0-4 • FIRST ONI PRESS EDITION, AUGUST 2002

3 5 7 9 10 8 6 4 2

ACKNOWLEDGEMENTS AND THANK YOUS

Special big-up to Scott Morse for finally pulling this thing out of my hands.
Second that emotion to Mike and Laura Allred for the amazing cover and unparalleled
encouragement; Andi Watson for the character designs and illos; and Renée French,
Chynna Clugston-Major, and Judd Winick for lending their brushes, as well.
Buy copies of their comics, because they are all amazing and talented people.
Thirdly, Jen and Julie, you helped make this look great so that people would read
it and not think ill of me for anything except the writing. Seriously, thanks.

Other acknowledgements of all kinds - be it inspiration, hands-on
support, discouragement, or whathaveyou - (in no particular order) go to:

First up has to be Pete Townshend and The Who, whose music has been fueling this
project from the word go; from there - The Sex Pistols; Kristan Strong; Thane Tierney;
Dead Kennedys; Dr. Stephen Cooper and English 407 Spring '93, CSULB; Dr. Charles
Webb and English 407 Spring '92; Joanne James; Muriel Mouring; Michael Druce; Mike Light
(I hope wherever you are, you've regained your shine); Kelley McCrory; Rachelle Gardener;
R.E.M.; Sean Lewis; The Jesus and Mary Chain; Ian McCulloch; Joy Division; Dr. David Peck;
Dr. Charles May; Dr. Gerry Riposa; Dr. Wilhelmina Hotchkiss; Ken Rugg; The Ramones;
Violent Femmes; David J and the other lads in Bauhaus, etc.; The Glove/The Cure/Banshees;
Morrissey and The Smiths (Johnny, Andy, Mike . . . there is always something there to remind
me . . .); Social Disortion; Diana Schutz; Bob Schreck; Paul Heaton and The Housemartins;
Bow Wow Wow; Fear; The Clash; Nick Cave (and his Bad Seeds); Black Flag; Primal Scream;
The Stone Roses; The Charlatans; The Sundays; Trash Can Sinatras (a full pocket is a happy
pocket); Benrus Madlangbayan (the boy who introduced me to the work of Marisa Tomei, whose
film *Untamed Heart* inspired much of the romantic directions contained herein); Harlan Ellison;
my old man, Scott Lee Rich; Brett Anderson & co. (me and the stars stay up for you); Elastica;
Dave Cooper; Pat McEown; Paul Pope; Lynn Adair King; Suzanne & Toby Taylor; Sara Kaine;
Lara Michell (thanks for meeting me out here on the fringes); Darko Macan; Christopher
McQuain; Tynan Wales; Ariel Schrag; Shirley Manson and Martin Rossiter, for being the two
genuinely nicest pop stars I have been fortunate enough to meet; Sara Gilligan; Steven
T. Seagle; Stan Sakai; Nancy Hess; Joe Nozemack; Rebecca Bieberly; the kids at Ozone
Records; Greg Rucka; Ben Abernathy; Jim Mahfood; Sean Konot; Guy Major;
Cara Niece; Maryanne Huntzinger; Steven Birch; Matt Wagner; Sophie
and everyone at LeBonFon-Quebecor; Ben Holcomb; James
Lucas Jones, and I am sure many, many more.

Think what you will of the list. Be it pretentious or whatever, there it be - all
those who were there in person or on vinyl, as I sat in a bubble and nudged this book
towards completion. Above all, remember, there is music, and in this is everything.

For SADIE
who never lets me down

"free fall
dream for the stars
say you love me
they burn above me
and I stand alone"

- LARA MICHELL

"Every year is the same
And I feel it again.
I'm a loser, no chance to win.
Leaves start falling,
Come down is calling,
Loneliness starts sinking in.

But I'm one."

- PETE TOWNSHEND

SUMMER
1990

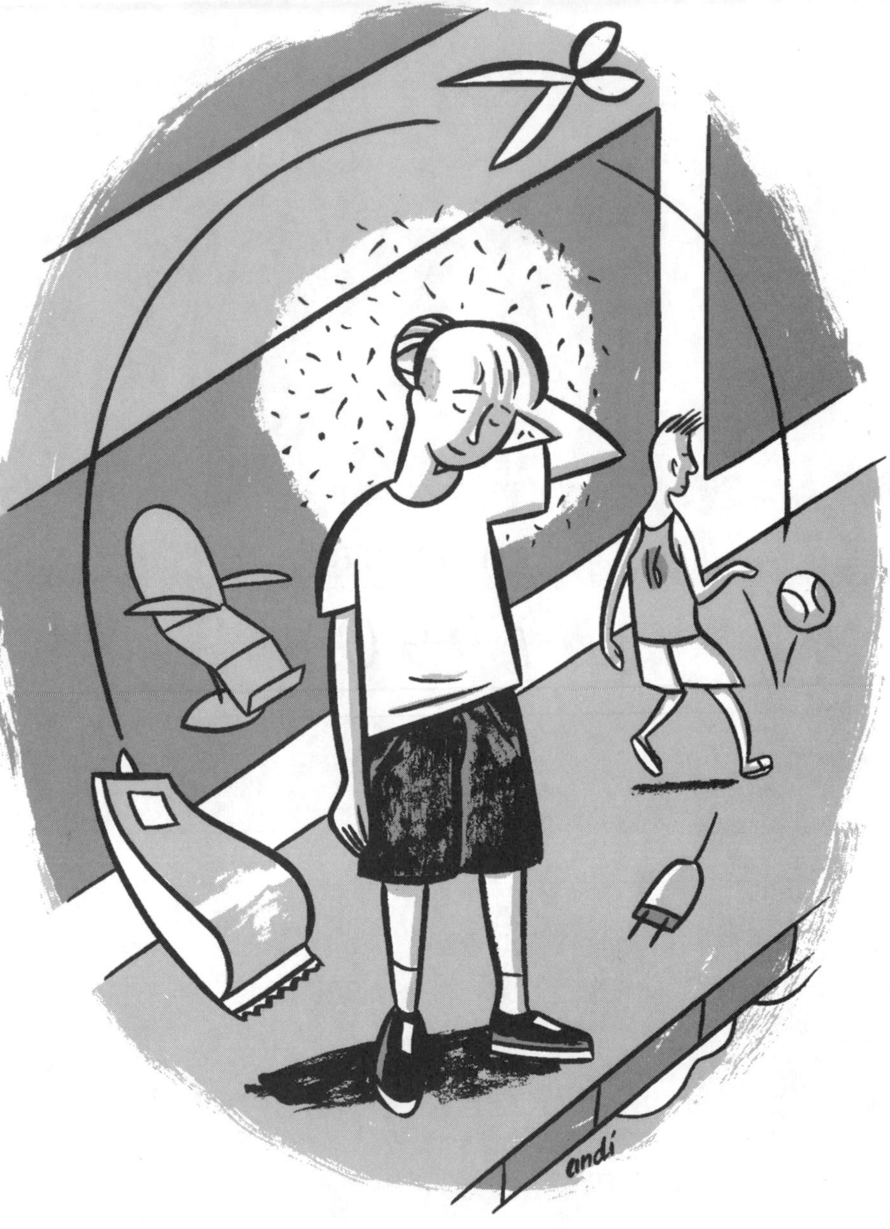
16
andi

1. HOLIDAYS IN THE SUN

The clippers scraped against the side of my head. They scratched and were hot and the buzz tickled my ears, but each piece of skin they touched ended up free and cool.

"You're all set, son."

I reached up and rubbed the shaved areas as hard as I could, shaking away the loose hairs and getting rid of the leftover sting. I checked the cut in the mirror. The sides of my head were freshly bald, little prickly hairs blending up into the clump of blonde that remained on top. I sneered at myself and laughed.

I paid the barber the six bucks and jumped out onto the street, hoping to feel the crisp summer air on my newly exposed scalp. No such luck.

It was probably the hottest summer I've ever lived through. All the punks were wearing cut-offs and ripped shirts and shaving their heads just to survive. I didn't have any cut-offs because I never wore holes in my knees. I couldn't justify cutting jeans without holes in them because I couldn't afford any new pairs to replace them. So, Jack and I stole me some shorts from his sister. They had a big, fat Jimmy Z logo on the back, which was annoying, and they were a little tight in the waist, but they did all right.

Besides, you did what you could to fight the soaring heat. Up in the nineties, up in the hundreds. Not to mention California was having a drought. It hadn't rained since winter, and even that had been slight. It was killing me. Everywhere I walked, the air was dry and hot and made me sluggish. To just get across the street was a major effort. My whole body was a mess of droopy, melted skin, like a huge blob of tar.

I spent most of every day ducking in and out of stores to drink from their air conditioners and stomping through the gutters and the piddling amount of water that could be found in them. Jack didn't seem to be bothered by the heat, which was strange, because usually people with bulk overheat easier.

"You should wear a bandanna on your head," he'd say. "Like me." He'd point to the blue hankie tied over the top of his head—like a pirate would wear. "Protect your melon from the sun, Mason. Don't fry your brain."

"I don't like things on my head," I'd say.

"Awww, you just don't want to mess up your hair."

Which was only partly true.

"It would also probably help if most of our clothes weren't black," Jack'd say.

I had to agree with that one. So, rather than killing myself for fashion, I tried to mostly wear my white T-shirts. Jack, however, would still wear his T's with flannels overtop, saying, "When you're well protected, nothing can get through." I swear, if the sun fell from the sky and landed on Jack, he'd just shrug it away, wipe himself off, and walk on—leaving the sun the worse for the encounter.

I was never sure why Jack hung out with me. I mostly felt

pretty useless, just a tag-along. Jack was something like 6'5", and I'm only 5'7", which usually means I'm just in the way. Sometimes I did okay, though. Like once, when a friend of ours locked his keys in the car, my arm was skinnier than everybody else's, and I was able to reach through the crack in the window to unlock the door.

Sometimes, too, it's hard for tall guys to see everything. Certain details can fall below their normal vision. For instance, I was the one who spotted the flyer for Like A Dog. Most of them had been covered up with posters for *Pretty Woman*, but some were peeking through down at the bottom of the posting board:

LIKE A DOG
— *with* —
UFOria
On Your Last Nerve
@ NoWay Home 8:00pm Thurs.

We hadn't seen any of the guys from the band recently, and we had been wondering when they would be playing again.

"Oh, man! Are they headlining?!" I exclaimed.

"What? What are you talking about?"

"Like A Dog. They're playing NoWay Home. *Tonight!*"

"No shit?"

"No shit. It says right there."

Jack crouched down. "Ah, yeah! Cool."

Like A Dog were some guys we knew from high school. They were a postpunk-type punk band, which, yeah, is pretty vague. They mainly played a slightly deranged guitar pop, twisting bouncy tunes, juxtaposing them with melancholy lyrics. They gigged at the smaller, seedier clubs around town, sometimes underground parties, trying to build their name. NoWay Home was the best club. They played all the different kinds of music punk had become. Thrash, rave, ska, goth, techno—all the disparate channels punk had traveled. Punk was the only real word. "New Wave" wasn't new anymore. "College" and "Alternative" were too self-conscious, too music journalist. We were punk. We were attitude. We were agony.

3

The rest of the day after that was tedious. It was Thursday, and on Thursdays we got the new comics for the week. This meant that we had to stay late so we could sort them out of their boxes, put them in alphabetical order, and set them up on the display racks. This meant, too, that we had to move last week's new comics from the new rack and into the recent rack, while also removing comics from the recent rack and setting them aside to be filed in the back issue bins. This was all so that the fans could come in on Friday morning and get the latest issues of their favorite titles. They may have gotten their fix right away, making them all blissful and happy, but it made my life hell. There were a couple of comics shops on Melrose and that made for rough competition. Normally, I only worked the morning through evening, and that was on Sunday, Tuesday, and Wednesday. Thursdays were tough. I got there when the store opened and stayed after it closed. Thankfully, I had Fridays off and didn't have to deal with the onslaught, and the rest of the week was pretty light. I could spend most of the days just reading comics and listening to the radio.

When I got off that night, Jack was waiting for me outside the store. He worked pasting up posters around town. I could tell he had gone home and showered. He smelled like cheap soap, not paste, and he didn't have crusty white streaks on his face and hands. When I said, "Hello," he handed me an envelope.

"We got mail today," he said.

The envelope had been carelessly ripped across the top. I took the letter out and opened it. The paper was an off-white color, and the texture was gritty. It had the blue masthead of a real estate company. It said they had bought our apartment building. We had until the first of the year to find a new place to live.

"Oh, my God," I said. "They can't . . ."

"Yeah, they can," Jack said. "It's finished, and there's nothing we can do about it."

"But the apartment . . . it's *ours*."

"There's nothing we can do, Mason." Jack stuck his hands in his pockets and stepped out of the doorway onto the sidewalk. "No sense worrying about it now. January is six months away. We'll deal with it when the time comes."

He took the letter back, crumpled it up, and threw it into the street.

"Come on," he said.

There may have been no sense worrying about it, but all the way to the club, I couldn't get it out of my head. Jack and I had gotten that place when we graduated. We saved money from jobs and stockpiled graduation checks from relatives we didn't know and put down first and last month's rent and the deposit. I had thought we would stay there forever. Or at least long enough to make it a real home. We had only been there a year. That wasn't enough. We'd barely had enough time to figure out what posters we wanted where.

A car came whining around the corner. An orange Gremlin. Its tailpipe spit and made a loud BANG! Jack howled and stuck his arms up in the air, as if in victory. "*Yeahhhhh!*" He loved the sudden noise. He loved the surprise of it. I laughed at his excitement and forgot my worries.

"Hey, wanna hear a joke?" he asked.

"Sure."

"What do you call a lesbian dinosaur?"

"What?"

"A Lick-a-lot-o'-puss."

"Gawd."

"Ha!"

Jack punched me in the arm and skipped ahead. I chased after him and we ran down the street screaming and kicking at trash and generally being nuts.

When we got to NoWay Home, the line was halfway down the block. The bouncer at the door was new, and that was slowing things up. It took us almost half an hour to get to the front. Usually, we didn't have to flash I.D. to get in, either, because we went often enough that the guys normally running things knew us. As per usual, Jack walked in no problem, but the new guy pushed me in the chest and said, "Where's your I.D.?"

"Hey, man, let him in," Jack demanded. "He's old enough."

"He don't look no eighteen to me," the bouncer said. "He looks more like twelve."

"What's holding it up?" someone shouted from the back of the line.

"Hey! It's Jailbate. Hey, Jailbate? Wha'samatter? Tell 'em you just

5

want milk in your bottle."

It was Steve and Burton, some guys we hung around with sometimes.

"Hey, shut your face!" Jack yelled at them.

"Here, here, I got my driver's license," I said. "Look . . . I'm nine-teen, okay?"

The bouncer took the card from me. "Is it real?" He smirked.

Jack shoved him in the shoulder. "Yeah, it's real. Let him in, you pud."

"Don't be pushing me."

"It's real! It's real! I'm nineteen."

The line was getting restless. It pushed forward, sucked together, all heads and eyes down on me. People started grumbling. Mumbling. Someone was going to kick my ass, someone was going to do it to the bouncer, a third would take us both.

"Baby with the bathwater!" Burton jeered. "Baby with the bathwater!"

"I think I'm going to keep this," the bouncer said. "It's fake."

"Like hell!" Jack exclaimed. "Give him his fuckin' I.D.!" Jack's face was turning all red, and his fists were opening and closing instinctively.

"Dude, just give me my license and I'll go away, all right?"

"No, Mason. You're coming in. You always come here. Just 'cause this pud . . ."

"Jack . . ."

Somebody threw a bottle, and it popped against the wall above the bouncer's head. He stood up and looked around. "Who threw that?" he shouted. "Who was it?" His lips were pursed.

"Shut the fuck up, asshole," somebody replied.

"Look, no one's gettin' in till I'm ready . . ."

"Eat dick."

By this time, Lenny, the head bouncer, had noticed something was going on and came outside. "What's up out here?"

"I don't believe this kid's I.D. is real, Lenny," the new guy said.

"*This* kid?" Lenny asked.

The new guy nodded.

"I've been letting *this* kid in for almost a year now. I *think* I would have noticed a long time ago if his I.D. was fake. *Don't you?*"

Lenny was a veteran bouncer. He had worked at CBGBs when it was hoppin' in the early eighties and, most recently, The Whiskey on Sunset. He was fired from there for beating up Axl Rose before Guns 'n' Roses hit it big. Axl kept pissing on the floor backstage, and, after several warnings, Lenny let him have it. When Axl got famous, he also got Lenny canned. Not long after, Lenny's brother opened NoWay Home, and Lenny took over things there. Me and Jack sometimes came early and listened to him talk about being a roadie for Sid Vicious and breaking up pits at Germs shows.

"Sorry, Mason," Lenny said. "New guy. Bouncing always boosts the testosterone when a guy's starting out. Makes 'im dumb."

"'s okay," I said.

I snatched my card from the guy's hand. I stuck my tongue out at him and waltzed inside.

About half the club was already full. People were dancing to Public Image Ltd. and beginning their search for the cool confines of oblivion at the bar. Jack and I went straight to the stage to grab a spot on the barricade. Waiting, we compulsively hunched over—both because we were used to having hordes of people at our backs during shows and because NoWay seemed to be designed to make you feel like you had something heavy on your shoulders. The walls were slanted in, and the ceiling was domed. Below it were fat beams—practically whole trees—that criss-crossed one another, creating a dizzying web of wood. Ropes were wound around the beams, their ends dangling down toward us. Some nights, when I looked up through the web, I thought maybe I saw shapes of things moving around up there, but they always moved too quickly for me to catch focus.

The walls were covered with layer upon layer of music posters and flyers and ads from fashion magazines, one pasted up over the other, another over it, constantly changing as new things came in, were ripped out, and taped up. Lights were few and dim. Darkness was the ambience. The goal was doom. The place smelled like cigarettes and incense, and when it was empty, it was very cold.

People filed in, filling the dance floor, crowding the bar. More die hards came to the stage and packed up against us. It was beginning to warm up. By the end of the show, we'd be covered with sweat and ready to pass out. By then, though, the heat wouldn't be oppressive any longer. There was freedom. The music. We could let go. *I* could. It was just me and the music, if I liked. No one else mattered.

The DJ played The Dead Kennedys' "Holiday in Cambodia," and the pit moshed and slammed wild. The crowd was getting restless because it was a quarter after nine and still no band. After I took someone's elbow against my ear, Jack moved behind me and became my shield. Few dared to slam into Jack, and the ones that did were slammed back, usually not making their way back over again.

Out of the corner of my eye, I could see guys leaving the ground, being tossed up into the air by their friends or leaping off of somebody's shoulders. Some would fly over and land on top of the crowd, rolling over heads and bending necks till someone would finally get mad and throw them back down or just break under the weight. I always hated doing that. You got people hitting you and hands where you didn't want. If Jack wasn't around, guys bigger than me would lift me and throw me up there. Once I got sucked down into the pit and couldn't get out. All I could see were people's legs, their jeans pressed against my face, stepping on my hands with their boots. I screamed and screamed and finally got to my feet and shoved my way out. The guys who had tossed me saw me, laughed, and threw me up again.

Since the stage was empty, some of the punks decided to expand the dance floor. They climbed up and pogoed around and gloated, flipping everyone the bird and hocking gobs at us. The bouncers came out and took their positions behind the barricade. They grabbed at the punks on the stage, who dove over the bouncers' heads and into the crowd before anyone could nab them. They turned it into a game, climbing up again and diving out, flirting with being 86d from the club. One time, a guy tried to stage dive, but the crowd scattered. He dropped like an overturned rocket and smashed hard into the floor with his face. Blood spurted in every direction, and his nose caved in, and when he got to his feet, there were a few teeth on the floor. He just started slamming some more, blood running down his face and onto his chest. There was no pain. There was no care. Only the music. Only the drive—the grind of guitars and the pound of the drums, propelling him forward, throwing us all ahead.

After The Dead Kennedys, they played Fishbone's "UGLY." Then Like

A Dog came out. We were surprised because we had expected On Your Last Nerve to open because they were on the bottom of the poster. Yet, hearing the familiar strains of their opening song, a charge shot through me. Anticipation. Like the moment after you hear the rumbling of thunder and you wait for that flash . . .

The band came on without their singer. Enshrouded in darkness and dry ice, they began to play. The music was slow at first. Acoustic guitar, a light brush against the cymbals, faint keyboards. Then came a great surge as guitars flared up and Mike pounded down on the drums. On cue, the lights came on. Tristan, who had slipped out after the rest, was there at the microphone. He enjoyed the mystique, sneaking out last, cloaked in the black, to magically appear in the spotlight—each time a revelation—his slender form in place, wide shoulders leading down in a diagonal direction, like a knife blade, to the edge of his cuffed, black jeans. White T-shirt gave way to pale, skinny arms. A long face and coif of hair—sandy blonde bangs rising from his forehead and cresting over like a wave. He had on small, round sunglasses, and I wondered if his eyes were closed behind them.

The music was swirling around Tristan, and he paused, waited a second, stood in it. Then he reached out and held the microphone with both hands, leaning forward, tilting the stand toward us, and then whispering, singing, thrusting out his life—his words. Over and over,

Sleeping on a hill all alone
Light of the moon moves by me
I've come home.

The words were far back inside me. I could feel them. It sounds stupid when I say that . . . but I could. His words. Words that come into you soft and leave their mark without you realizing it. Words that crawl under the covers of your mind without waking you, letting you know they are there by little, gentle taps on your ears, touching ever so slightly, but enough. Tristan's pain fell from him. Pain I understood. Pain he and I alone shared.

I guess it was what confession must be like. Only I didn't have to say anything to be cleansed.

Behind us, the crowd was growing even more restless. This wasn't going to placate them. They wanted to slam hard, but the music was too soft. They began to shove to the front, smashing the Dog fans—or Doggies, as I called them—who had gathered there. Angry boys started shouting things over our heads. "C'mon! Move it!" "What fuckin' is this?" "You pussies!" They gave Tristan the finger and spit at him. The band took a couple of steps back, except for Tristan, who stayed. Tristan persevered. He had to give the words.

After fifteen minutes, Lenny's brother, George, pulled the plug, and they brought out UFOria. The audience had gotten too hostile. Lenny had to come out to help hold the moshers back, and they were about to pull the guys from the doors. Leaving the stage, Tristan's head hung low.

UFOria was a hardcore band, and the crowd got excited and screamed and yelled and started to really mosh. Jack and I stayed for the beginning of the set. It was all pretty basic, nothing special, but the punks in the pit trampled over the top of it like it was the best thing they'd ever heard. A guy with a mohawk sailed above everyone, holding himself straight, spinning like a drill. He came down and people crumbled beneath him. I saw a few of the Doggies—girls mostly—ripped from the barricade. One girl clung to it and refused to let go. The punks grabbed her by the ankles and tugged as hard as they could, scraping the skin from her hands and releasing her into the shuffle. A skinhead got shoved into the empty space she left behind, hitting the barricade so hard that he almost puked his guts. He was bent over and coughing, and I thought blood would squirt from his eyes, his face was so red and contorted and horrid.

But no matter how violent or mean the pit got, or how many people ended up bloodied and broken, Jack was not shaken once.

Bored, we left the pit and went to the backstage door. We were permanently on the guest list.

The backstage was accessed through a drafty brick corridor covered in graffiti. There was one central room with a couch and a TV, and it was full of guys from bands lounging around smoking and drinking. A few people had scribbled their philosophical and poetic breakthroughs on the walls, probably etched at the moment of enlightenment, when whatever they were on really kicked in. Mike Ness and Dennis Danell had signed their names next to a drawing of the Social Distortion skeleton; John Doe had put in his hancock; Lux Interior wrote something foul about young girls and heavy artillery. Tristan had even lent his hand, composing many couplets directly on the brick, a lot of throwaway phrases like "Perversity is the better part of squalor" and "Taste the Plague." His pockets were always filled with scraps of paper, all containing quickly jotted thoughts, lines, sayings. His room was littered with them. He was constantly writing. Every time I saw him, he'd be grabbing something and scribbling down words. He just had to get it out, he told me, just had to get it out so he could move on to the next one.

Sean, Like A Dog's keyboard player, was on the couch watching "Green Acres" with one of the members of On Your Last Nerve. Tristan was standing in the corner, staring blankly at the tube.

"Jailbate! Jack!" Sean said. "What'd you think of the show?"

"Short," Jack said.

"But intense," I added, sneaking a look at Tristan. He didn't visibly acknowledge whether he was listening or not, his glasses fixed and unwavering, the image of the TV shimmering across his lenses.

"No shit." Sean half rose up off the couch. He was getting incensed. "'Too rowdy,' they said. We said, 'No shit, they're a punk crowd.' They said, 'But rowdy in the wrong kind of way. We were scared they'd hurt you. We were scared they'd damage the equipment.' Well, it's their own fucking fault for putting us on a bill with thrash bands. They always put us on bills with thrash bands. We don't belong there."

"It's your name," the Nerve guy said. "Like A Dog. It says beat me. Hurt me. It says *thrash*. You've gotta change the name."

"No name change," Tristan blurted out. "Name stays the same. Like. A. Dog."

End of argument.

The name issue was a sore spot for Tristan. One day, I had found him in Johnny Rocket's on Melrose. He was at the counter, head in his hands, elbows propped on a stack of flyers for a show. He looked despondent. I sat next to him.

"What's up?" I'd asked.

"They want to change the name of the band," he said. "Everyone says nobody understands it. They all misinterpret it. But it's Kafka. It's from Kafka. They tell me nobody reads Kafka. I can't be expected to change the name of my band because the world is full of idiots."

I wanted to tell him I liked the name. I wanted to say to him that it said something to me about the nature of music, about the relationship between star and fan, both dependent on the other. Both give to each other, but ultimately take, ultimately treating the other like crap. It says something about the way we beat each other into submission. How we crawl to our heroes on all fours and lap at their feet, scared to lift our heads and be found unworthy. How music pets us, subserviates us, and coddles us. We are all dogs. Yet, even still, in those greatest pop moments: *release*.

I said none of it. I hadn't read Kafka and didn't want to get it wrong. I didn't want him to think *I* was one of the idiots.

"Those who are meant to get it," I told him, "will."

Tristan took his head from his hands and looked at me with a big grin on his face. "Exactly," he laughed. "That's it exactly."

I had never seen him really smile before. His whole face rose with it.

Only now, in the back of NoWay, his features were sagging, and his mouth was sad. He ran his hand through his hair and stomped his foot to bring a high cuff on his pants down closer to his ankle. "We were on tonight, Mason?" he asked me.

"Very," I said.

"Yeah, we *were* into it, weren't we?" Sean said.

"What about you, Jack?" Tristan asked. "What do you think?"

"I'm too disappointed to think," Jack replied. "I think you were starting a great show, but . . ." He shook his head.

"So do I," Tristan said. "They seemed determined to ruin us."

"Where the hell were our people?" Sean demanded. "We advertised. Why didn't they come?"

"We even thought you were headlining," I said. "Your name was first on the poster."

"That's 'cause I made them," Tristan said. "I figured if I did the work, I might as well invert the order."

"Shit, if our people had come," Sean said, "they couldn't have yanked us. The swell would have been on *our* side."

Tristan looked scornfully at Sean. "There is no swell for us," he said. "We have no people. We're nothing. We'll never be anything, because we're no good. *I'm* no good . . . just a mediocre talent . . ." His voice choked off. He pulled at the hair on the back of his head, groaned, and stormed out the back exit.

"Oh, shit," Sean laughed. "There he goes, in one of *those* moods again."

"I'm telling you," the other dude said, "you've gotta dump that guy. He's too fickle. He's like a girl. You never know what he'll do. He runs off and kills himself, and then where's your band?"

I wanted to yell at him, tell him he was a moron. Of course there was no band without Tristan. Like A Dog *was* Tristan. He was the band because he was pure, because his words were true.

But I couldn't do it. I balked. I was embarrassed of myself, and I stuck my hands in my pockets as deep as I could push them. My cheeks burned.

Jack asked if maybe we'd better go, and I said I thought maybe we should.

"Well, see ya later, then," Sean said.

"Yeah, see ya later," the Nerve guy said.

I waved to them, quietly, and left.

2. TOO DRUNK TO FUCK

Steve came to the door barefoot. He wore a ripped white T-shirt with "Jesus Christ presents . . . Christian Death" printed in red and black on the front. There had been a picture on it once, as well, but it had been faded by too many washings and I couldn't make it out.

The apartment belonged to a guy named Chuck. A skinhead. He had gone to Mexico on some crazy expedition–to see some temple and get some pure peyote from the inner-Mexican jungle. He'd asked Steve and Burton to hold onto his keys, afraid that he'd lose them across the border. He felt safer knowing where they were, and since the guys lived one floor below him, they could also keep an eye on the place. Rather than taking the responsibility offered them and playing the great guardians of the homestead, they took it as an opportunity to eat his food, drink his beer, and blow the speakers on his stereo.

"Welcome to the pleasuredome," Steve said, giving a half-baked bow and flourish.

The apartment was pretty sparse. The carpet was the color of creamed coffee and was dotted with scattered stains. In the center of the room,

15

Chuck had a green divan with a hole in the back, and the stuffing was falling out of it. Directly to the right of that, he had his stereo and records on milk crates. An overturned cardboard box in front of the couch served as a table, and in front of the box was the TV on more milk crates. The TV was turned to "Full House," but the sound was off and "Ants Invasion" was on the stereo.

Steve dove face first onto the couch. More stuffing spilled out the back. "You've *got* to see these magazines," he said, grabbing one off of the box. He rolled over onto his back and waved the mag' at us. The cover had an overly-endowed woman with a leather biker's cap on her head. She was squeezing her hands between her crotch and sticking her tongue out like she was trying to lick herself. She was looking straight at the camera as if she were challenging it. "Where he gets some of this shit, I'd *love* to know."

"From your ma," Jack said.

"Fuck you, Jack," Steve snapped back. "C'mon, you've got to *see* some of this stuff. It's whacked."

Jack vaulted over the couch. The leap scared Steve, who stiffened, grabbing the sides of the couch and dropping the porno. Jack laughed and slapped Steve's cheeks. He took a magazine and plopped down on an orange beanbag over by the stereo.

I looked around the apartment. Immediately behind me, there was a "dining room," a small space connecting the room we were in and the kitchen. In it, there was a round table. The top was white, and it was all scratched up. Four vinyl chairs surrounded it, all of different makes and colors. On the wall was a poster of Madonna, of all things. It was a black-and-white photo with sepia tints. She was bending over, mouth wide open, holding her exposed breasts together with both hands, as if they were about to spill onto the floor wildly out of control.

"So, what's this guy like?" I asked.

"Just your average," Steve said.

Burton came out of the bedroom through a small doorway just to the right of Madonna. "Man," he said, "you've got to check out Chuck's closet. You would not be*lieve* some of the things he's into."

"Like what?" Steve asked, excited.

"Oh, man, it's just out there."

"Out there?" Jack laughed. "I'll show you out there. Look at *this*."

He held up the magazine, open to a double-page photo. It was of a Mexican woman. She was on all fours, facing away from the camera, tossing a knowing look over her shoulder. She was wearing a flower print dress, and it was pulled up over her waist so her bare butt was exposed. I didn't know what was so unusual about it until I looked a little closer.

The woman had a dark, thick patch of hair on her ass.

It went from the pubic hair on the front side of her vagina, and extended all the way around the back and up through her buttcrack, stopping in a small circle on the small of her back.

It was one of the nastiest things I had ever seen. Jack was obviously revolted, but amused. His face was all scrunched up in a toothless grin. "Is this gross or what?"

Steve moaned and fell back on the couch in a giggle fit.

"No way!" Burton exclaimed. He bounded over to Jack and knelt down, moving his face in close to the magazine. "No way!" He stared at it in drooling awe, and then took it from Jack's hands. He stood and held it out in front of him, turning it this way and that way, and just stared. "No way. This is *so* cool. Oh, man. Guys, guys, I've got to show you something."

He ran back into the bedroom, squealing.

Burton was into perversion. As Steve was into pharmaceuticals, Burton was into kinky sex. His favorite boast was about this girl he had balled who had a clitoris ring and how it scratched him all over and the heat and sweat of it all made the wounds burn. He imagined himself quite the charmer with his devil-blue eyes and I-don't-care brown pompadour and sideburns. His face was angular and smooth, and he spoke with a husky voice that came deep from the hollow of his stomach. He was into all the nudie mags, body piercing and tattoo books, freaks. He claimed his best fantasy was double-teaming a midget and a bearded lady, which I always thought was corny as hell and definitely trying too hard to be weird, but he swore it was true.

Still, Burton said even if he achieved his circus-freak fantasy, that girl with the little silver ring would still be the best, that there would be nothing like that. Ironic thing was, Burton could never pierce anything himself. Not even his ear. He went to a drugstore once to get it done, but before they could get the gun to his lobe, he passed out. He never liked to admit it, but Jack had gone with him and wasn't going to let him forget. Mention a nipple ring, and Burton would cringe from you, chills running through his body, goosebumps decorating his neck and arms. Guys who knew this weakness would pull up their shirts just to piss him off, and they'd pinch and tug at their nipples. Burton would be gone, straight away.

Burton came back out of the bedroom, accompanied by a loud buzzing sound. In his left hand, he had a black dildo about a foot long and half-a-foot wide, with blunt spikes all around the head. "Check it out, man!" he shouted. "What do you think Chuck does with this?

"I don't *want* to know," Jack groaned.

"Go put it back," Steve said. "Chuck's gonna murder us."

Laughing, Burton stumbled out. Jack changed the tape, and we did an impromptu mosh to Nine Inch Nails' "Head Like a Hole." Steve started to feel weak and was coughing near the end, so we stopped. He excused himself to the bathroom. When he came back out, his eyes were bright and he was smirking, but he moved and talked kind of slow. "Deadbeats," he said. "What th' fuck you just sitting around for?"

Burton got out the beer. He and Steve had wrangled a whole case of Lucky Lager, the beer with the puzzles on the inside of the bottle caps. After my second bottle, I was totally buzzed and became hopelessly occupied with the letter B, an eye, and two little men in tuxedoes posing suavely with guns. I wracked my brain into frustration trying to figure it out.

"I'm still bored," Steve complained.

"How about a porn flick?" Burton suggested. "Chuck's got tons."

"Screw that," Jack said.

"Why not?"

"Screw *you*, Burton. I ain't sittin' here watchin' porn with a bunch of guys, all of 'em gettin' hard and not being able to do anything about it. I hate that. It's stupid."

"Man . . ." Burton looked like he wanted to spit. "You suck."

A movie of some kind seemed agreeable, so we decided on *Bladerunner*. Chuck had a rented copy with the receipt still inside. He'd checked it out six months before and never returned it.

Fifteen minutes into it, I had finished my third beer and was feeling blessed with a new sense of humor. At least, *I* thought everything I came up with was extremely funny. I always did when I was drunk. My best joke ever was once during a game of quarters. A guy named Frank, dismayed at frequent misfires, declared, "Damnit, I can't get it in," to which I replied, "I know. Your girlfriend told me." I laughed really hard. Of course, I puked, as well.

So, that night being no exception . . .

"Hey, if he's having sex with a robot—is that, like, getting plugged in?"

"They'd better not do it in the shower. He's liable to get electrocuted."

"Oh, a snake on a naked woman. Like we don't know what they're trying to say!"

"Hey, shut the fuck up," Steve said.

"I can crack their code. I eat vegetables. I got brain power."

"Shut up." Steve was getting mad.

"No," I laughed.

"I'll kill you, you fag."

"What if Princess Leia finds out he's stepping out on her? She'll be pissed."

"That's it!" Steve exclaimed. He threw an empty beer bottle at me, and I swatted it away with my hand. It bounced unharmed on the carpet a few feet away.

"Lay off," Jack said, low in his throat.

"Hey, Jailbate," Burton jumped in.

"Huh?" I grunted.

"You never solved the puzzle on your bottle cap. Why don't you focus your brain power in that direction?"

It made sense, and so I was occupied anew. Lying on the floor, I held the cap over my head, staring up at the little men and their guns. I knew the "B" and eyeball: *buy*. But who were the men?

Rutger Haur was putting his head through plaster when it hit me. It was James Bond! And there were two of him! It was so simple. I started laughing uncontrollably and rolling around on the carpet in the ecstasy of it.

"Goddamnit!" Steve yelled. "Couldn't you make it to the end, for fuck's sake?"

"What the hell is it *now*, Jailbate?" Burton snapped.

"*Buy Bonds*," I said, trying to catch my breath. "*Buy Bonds!*"

"Jee-*zus*," Steve moaned.

I laughed until there was no more laughter in me. I flopped over on my stomach, pressing my cheek against the coarse carpet. I was tired and ready to rest and felt like maybe watching the rest of the movie. Only it was over.

It was about eleven, and the guys, buzzed, wanted something more interactive. Burton ordered a pizza, and Jack produced a deck of cards. We sat down at the dining room table for some poker. Jack was across from me, Burton on my left, and Steve on my right. The big poster of Madonna was behind me. Jack dealt first, and every time he spun a card my way, his eyes caught her there, holding her breasts. He would look at her quizzically and then move on to Steve. He did it every time, and I thought about saying something, but then thought better of it. Within a few hands, Jack was winning, and I wished I *had* said something just so I could have given him crap before he started making the rest of us look like fools.

Steve got up and hit play on the Nine Inch Nails tape again. Sitting back down, he lit up a Salem cigarette. He blew the smoke up the inside curve of his bottom lip, and it curled up into his short, black, spiked hair. I noticed his hair was oily, but then, after catching a glimpse of the rings around his collar and armpits, I realized that it was sweat. Steve was sweating. He was always sweating. Perpetually sweating. Eternally sweating. No matter what the weather, his shirt was thick with it, his body dripped of it. That was Steve. Times when he was short and needed a fix, he sweat blue and his skin became doughy. Large bags puffed out under his eyes—eyes with a slight slant that gave him a cat-like look. They, and his pale brown skin, were because his father was in the Air Force, and he met and married Steve's mom in Okinawa. She was full-blooded Japanese.

I was slightly distracted from the game because Steve kept pumping his left arm, like he was lifting dumbbells. There was a reservoir of sweat in the joint of his elbow, and he had five dark bruises, the size of dimes, in and around the joint, as well. Little map markers along the path of the vein. My eyes kept wandering to those. They were somehow more interesting than the spades and Queens and Jacks. With him pumping his arm like that, they rose up to me, and then away, up and down, me with them.

20

Steve smelled like old sheets.

I took another beer. Its cap was easy. A screw and a ball. Not challenging at all. I didn't want the beer, and I didn't want the easy puzzle. I wanted something more complicated. I wanted something more interesting than Steve's arm. Halfway through the bottle, the beer started tasting bad and making me sick. I was smashed.

"You want the rest, Jack?" I asked, offering it across the table.

Jack took it and sniffed it. "Still cold?" he asked.

"I think so . . ."

"Good thing we didn't get you the hard stuff, eh, One-and-a-Half-Can Sam?" Steve said.

"Too bad alcohol's the only *hard* stuff you can get," I said.

Jack and Burton laughed.

"Listen, Teenie Weanie, half my salami will fill more sandwiches than your Farmer John any day."

"Sounds like a lot of baloney to me," I chortled, pounding the table.

"You're stupid," Steve said.

"What?" I asked, pretending not to hear.

"You're stupid."

"What?"

"I *said*, 'You're stupid.'"

"Wh--*?"

"Shut up! God, you're a fuckin' twat."

"What?"

"A fu–*shut up!*"

"You're the one who falls for it," Jack said.

"The squirt's pushing it, regardless," Steve replied.

"What?" I asked.

"I said, 'You're *pushing* it!' . . . Oh, fuckinay!"

That was too much. I laughed so hard, I almost fell over backwards in my chair.

"Sure, Jailbate, so funny," Steve said. "You and your stupid pussy Social Distortion band. Damn poseur music."

"Huh?" I asked, this time really meaning it, hoping he'd said something different.

"You heard me," he said, his face all hot and red, a drop of sweat balancing itself on the tip of his nose. "You listen to that pussy stuff, that wannabe hard music, when you know you can't even piss straight. Now *that's* funny!"

I sat up. "Are you saying Mike Ness isn't tough?"

Jack was scowling at Steve.

"Well," Steve said, softening, "he used to be. I just think the new stuff is kind of weak. I mean, 'Ball and Chain' just isn't hardcore. It's just an old man . . ."

"That's not true," I said. "That's not true."

And I remembered Tristan. *He's too fickle. He's like a girl.* I had been sober, and I said nothing. About my friend. And here, now, drunk . . . My cheeks burned. Tristan should have hated me.

The doorbell rang. "Thank Christ," Burton said. "I'm starving."

"No shit," Jack said.

Burton went to the door, and Steve started to collect our money.

"Hey, guys," Burton said, "I think you should see something."

We got up and went to the door. We looked at the Domino's guy. He was just a kid, really. A high-schooler, maybe a little taller than me. He had his cap on backwards, and bleached hair poked out on either side, curling down to his forehead, framing an oval patch of pimply skin. He wore a brown flannel over his uniform and had on Converse high tops, one green and one red.

"Why, what's this?" Steve laughed, putting the money down on the couch. He moved to the door and stood on the left, opposite Burton. "Isn't he cute?"

"Oh, yes," Burton agreed. "Tell me, do you think he's a skater?"

The kid smiled uneasily. He wasn't sure if had found friend or foe.

"Yeah, I'd bet he's a skater," Steve said. "You a skater, son?"

The kid started to answer, but Burton held up his hand. "Don't say anything. Not necessary. We have an expert here. Can divine a skatefuck from a mile away."

"You mean . . .?" Steve asked, batting his eyes.

"Oh, yes," Burton replied. "Jack!"

Jack stepped forward. He cracked his knuckles, one by one, beginning at the pinky and moving to the thumb. His body completely eclipsed the kid's, and I had to step to the side just to see him. Jack rubbed his chin. "Hmmmm . . ."

"What do you think, Jack?" Burton asked. "Is he is, or is he ain't, a skater?"

Jack wet his lips. He nodded. "Yup."

Steve grabbed the pizza from the kid's hands. Before the kid could react, Jack shoved him hard in the chest, knocking him back against the wall across the way. The kid's eyes were the size of hubcaps. Burton slammed the door and hit the lock. "Skate*fuck!*" he shouted.

Steve danced around and howled. "Oh, my God! Fuckin' shitass skater! Can you believe it? *Ha!*"

"Did you see his face?" Burton shrieked. "God, classic!"

Jack struck several exaggerated poses, flexing his muscles, and let out a great roar.

"Skate and die!"

They brought the pizza over to the counter, and we ripped it apart.

3. YOU ARE THE EVERYTHING

The next morning, I woke up with a stomachache. My head was okay, I didn't have a hangover or anything, but the pizza sat in my belly like a lump of tire rubber. I dreaded getting up, because it was yet another Thursday new comics day, and Thursday's were shitty enough without having to be eating Tums all day. The sheets were clinging to my body, attaching themselves to puddles of perspiration, and my hair felt matted and thick. Next to my bed was a poster for Social Distortion that Jack had snaked from his job. A thug was kicking down a door, rushing through to the crisis on the other side, suggesting (at least in my early morning haze) that maybe there was a necessity to action, much as I just wanted to sleep my day away.

I showered and got dressed and felt a little better, so I decided to go down early to look around and get circulating. Jack and I lived within walking distance of Melrose and were there quite often, but sometimes I liked to go by myself early in the day before all the people got there. It felt much more free when all the shops were empty. I could take my time and not get bustled around.

My wallet was a bit light that morning, but payday was twenty-four hours away. I could look around and see if there was anything I'd want to buy once the cash was flowing again. It's much more exciting to buy things when I've been anticipating them. Gives me a sense of accomplishment. I've made a plan and fulfilled it.

I stopped in at The Soap Factory—a sort of kitsch bookstore—to check out the art and movie books. I looked through the shelves and was a little disappointed that nothing new or tantalizing had come in since the last time I had visited. Sometimes things seemed to change so slowly—or, at least, it seems that way when you are waiting for the change to happen. It's the changes that you don't anticipate that slam you down like a speeding car.

On my way out, I passed the greeting card rack and spotted a card with a newspaper boy hawking the headline "Hell Freezes Over." It struck me as funny, because I figured, well, if it did freeze, wouldn't you know? What with all the impossible shit happening, wouldn't you be able to tell?

I opened the card, and it said, "Did it really take me that long to write?" It was a pretty lame payoff to something so full of possibilities.

The Soap Factory was adjoined to a clothing store, and they had a door connecting them on the inside. I cut through it and was heading out their exit for the street. I pulled on the door, though it clearly said "PUSH," and was feeling slightly stupid, when I heard my name called from the back of the store.

"Mason!"

There was jubilation in the first syllable, and the second tapered off into a growl.

I froze. I knew that voice. It was like the flow of hot caramel dripping from the pan, falling down in a line and folding in on itself, ribboning like an endless stream of collapsing S's. My ears tasted the caramel, and a remembrance of the smell of the breath behind it, of words it had sent to me before. I caved in on myself. I smiled despite my own efforts to remain cool.

It was the voice of the eternal girl.

Laine came up to me with a grin that puffed out her cheeks and sparkled her blue eyes. Her hands played with her necklace, small white sea shells strung along a thread. Her shirt was loose fitting, with sea green and blue and yellow and purple stripes. She squinted at me deviously and sucked her lips, pink against her tan face.

I clutched at my breath as if it were bubbles bursting to extinction.

"Whattaya doing, Mason?"

"Hanging out before work," I said.

"Yeah? I'm supposed to be in summer school, but fuck that. It's summer. I don't need English in summer."

"Well, you're using English now."

She socked me in the arm. "Okay, Mr. Genius. Mr. School. Just 'cause you graduated . . ."

"I never said I was a genius. You made me a genius."

"Oh, so you're saying that around someone as stupid as me—"

"No, no. You get me wrong."

She socked me again. "I know, you dope," she said. "You're so silly. So, what? You just working?"

"Yeah. Hangin' out."

"Hangin' out," she mocked. "I see you've at least managed to get a new cut. Let me feel the buzz."

She reached up to rub my stubble. I pulled back. "Hey, hey, hey," I said. "It's my hair."

"Gee, sor-*ree*."

"Well, what've you been doing, *smartass*?" I asked, playing it off.

"Hey, like I said, I've been doing something productive with my life. I *have* been going to summer school. Sometimes."

"Oh, is that right?"

"Yeah."

"Is that so? Well, if I still know you, you've been in school less than you've been out of it."

"Smart people like me don't need to go every day. We get bored with it. You know, like Einstein."

"Of course."

"I'm just bumming around now, waiting for some of the guys. You know. Resting my mind."

The store had a rack of long dresses along the wall—flowery sun dresses, velvet, sexy black. Behind Laine, there was a display of hats. Real floppy

ones in bright colors, bowlers, checkered golfing caps. I grabbed a black-and-white one. It had a round top and long sides that hugged the face. I put it on her head, stepped back, and examined the situation. "You look like you should be in *The Great Gatsby* or something," I said.

She smirked. "Yeah, sure. So, it's me?"

"It's you, my love. I'd buy it for you, but I don't have any cash on me."

She took it off and put it back on the shelf. "Silly," she said.

A blonde guy skated up to the window and knocked on the glass. I recognized him. He was one of the skaters we messed with when we were in school. He was sort of their leader because he was the craziest. The whole school was excited one day because he had skated an empty swimming pool. He took a spill and scraped up his legs and broke both his arms. His name was Otto. He was wearing sky-blue Oakley sunglasses with little clouds on them. No person in his right mind wore Oakleys. They were for skaters only.

"Oooops, the guys are here."

"I only see *a* guy," I said.

"Ah, you . . ."

"Well, I guess I got to be at work anyway."

Laine moved toward the door. "Bye, Mason."

"Say, want to do something sometime?" I forced the words out. With Otto there, I felt like a moron. But I pushed anyway. I knew I'd never have her and I'd probably die alone, but maybe if I said something, it wouldn't be true. So, I said it. "Say, want to do something sometime?"

She clenched her mouth down, and her bottom lip stuck out in a pout. "Sure," she said, smiling slightly. "I've got to babysit my step-brother and sister next Saturday. If you come by around ten, they'll be in bed, and I'll need the company."

"Great. I'll be there."

"See ya, Mason."

"Bye," I said.

The door swung closed. Laine smiled at Otto. His board was at his feet, and he stepped down on its tail. The board flipped up, and he caught the nose of it with his hand. He put it on top of his head, holding it with just the tips of his fingers, letting it teeter back and forward. He grinned and said something to her, and she laughed. They walked off together, Otto spinning the skateboard on his head as if it were a propeller.

I traced Laine's outline in the air with my finger, pretending she wasn't far way, but this tiny figure floating right in front of my eyes. Yet, soon, I had nothing left to trace, for she and Otto disappeared down the street, turning into some strange alley I didn't know or see. Maybe to meet others, possibly not. I couldn't know.

Laine was two years younger than I was. I had met her a year and a half before. It was my senior year in high school, and Jack and I took seventh period Journalism because we were friends with the teacher and he would let us slack. We'd just write these scathing editorials about stupid stuff every once in a while, and that would be it. An easy A. Laine transferred into the class in the middle of the fall. I figured her for a socialite, with her nice clothes and too-cool black shades, and she never talked much to anyone. I figured a girl like her wouldn't feel it was important enough to talk to a guy like me—because I wasn't in her clique or anything—and I never really gave it any more thought.

Then in the spring, I was going over one of Jack and my articles, and Laine was sitting at a desk next to me. She turned to me abruptly and said, "What do you think when a girl shaves her head?"

She was looking at me rather pensively, her lips puckered and her eyes squinted, the aqua blue of the irises peeking through the cracks.

"I think it's cool," I said.

"Really?"

"Yeah, well, I mean, how much you going to take off?"

29

Laine ran her fingers back through her hair. It was light brown, shiny—a fine bronze. She pulled it up from her skull. "Just the sides here," she said, "so when you put it in a pony tail, you see the fades."

I felt the side of my own head, which had been shaved all the way around some time before. It had mostly grown back and needed to be redone. "Yeah, I think that looks cool. Do it."

"Really?"

"*Yes*. I was going to get my own done again in a little while."

"Then we should go together."

It came so quick. I didn't really know what was happening, but I said, "Sure," without really thinking.

But we never went. She came to school one day with it cut. It wasn't shaved bald, as I thought it would be, but taken down to a fine fuzz. She had her hair pulled back and tied with a scrunchie. I thought it looked rather sleek, and I told her so. She perked up and said, "Thank you."

That seemed like a forever ago, and now the street outside the clothes shop looked so empty without her. The lady behind the counter asked if I needed any help. "Plenty," I said, and left for work.

4. KILL SURF CITY

We loaded into Steve's El Dorado for the Jesus and Mary Chain show in Ventura. Jack and I were in the back seat, and we had to sit amongst dirty clothes and cigarette butts and candy wrappers left over from munchie fits. We kept all the windows rolled down because of the smell, which Steve insisted wasn't that bad. "Of course you don't think so," Jack said, "because it smells like *you*."

We listened to The Sisters of Mercy's *First and Last and Always*, and Steve drove with his arm out the window, pounding the door to the beat and waving slow cars out of the way—first with a friendly hand motion, and then with a rude gesture if they didn't shuffle off to the side. He had to drive hunched over the wheel, with his face close to the windshield, because the glass was so dirty he could barely see through it. "A wet rag would do wonders for this heap," Burton said.

"I don't see you helping out, do I?" Steve snapped. "Shut the fuck up, whydon'cha?"

We got there in half the time it should've taken, but that was normal with Steve. It was only six o'clock, and the doors probably wouldn't open until seven. Still, there were about twenty people in line already, die-hard fans of The JAMC who were determined to get a spot in the front. The club was general admission, so it was a free-for-all as soon as they opened the doors. Fans could be particularly driven when it came down to finally being close to the ones they worshipped. I saw a girl at a Peter Murphy concert who had filed her nails into points and worked her way through the pit by stabbing people in the back of the neck. Double dots of blood marked her path all the way to the stage.

I, myself, preferred to show up early to avoid fighting in the pit, and I would have gotten there even earlier it if I was in charge. No one else seemed to worry about these things as much as me. The guys could get to the front any time they wanted to. They could make people get out of the way.

We got in line behind a pale girl in purple velvet, an Eddie-Munster-style suit. She had dyed her hair a bright red, and her lips were painted black. She smiled at Burton, but the suave fucker flipped her off and she didn't turn around again.

"I'm hungry," Jack said. "What you say to a burger run?"

It was agreed that this was a good idea, so we took up a collection of money. Steve scraped some measly change from his pocket. The coins were greasy and had lint stuck to them. There was barely even a dollar.

"That's it?" Jack asked. "That's all you got to contribute?"

"I'm broke, man," Steve said. "Shit. I don't see any of you guys driving or hustling to pay for no gas. I don't see why you can't float me."

"Damn bum," Jack grumbled. He shoved the money in his pocket, and he and I left. We didn't know Ventura, but we figured it wouldn't be too hard to find some sort of fast food joint.

The streets weren't very busy, and they weren't much different than any other street in any other town—cracked pavement and unkempt trees, mailboxes with chipping paint and houses with dying lawns. Yet, there was a whole different vibe to the place. Ventura is a beach town, and maybe it was because the air smelled like the ocean or the bright sun and clear skies. Whatever it was, it seemed to push me just off the center, keeping me slightly displaced. Occasionally, a car full of kids dressed all in black would go by, and I'd feel things shift a little in my favor. They were of my species, obviously not from this land of sunshine and rainbows. I was sure the more of us we piled on, the more the scale would dip. Once they passed, though, I slipped again, waiting eagerly for the next dark cloud to enter the brightness.

"Ten guesses where they're going," I said as a hearse with Alien Sex Fiend stickers rumbled around the corner.

"Beats me," Jack said, "but here come some more."

About five death rockers were in a little Honda, and Jack waved at them as they went by. They revved their engine. The car backfired twice, a double shot. "All right!" Jack shouted. "My kind of people!"

"Think they're here to get a tan?" I asked. "Do some surfing?"

Jack looked at me with a cock-eyed expression. "Why would anyone want to be doing that?" he asked. "I mean, what is the appeal of surfing, anyway?"

"I don't know," I said. "What's the appeal of skating?"

He shrugged.

"I don't understand why people do it," I continued, "largely because I don't see any *point* to it. For one, it's so defeatist—you go out, just to come back in, just to go out again. It never ends, you never win. It's always stronger than you.

"And, like, why isn't bodysurfing good enough? I mean, it's just another thing that people are perfectly equipped for, but somehow they can't convince themselves it's enough."

"Yeah," Jack said.

"I don't know. Maybe it's the illusion that you're mastering something. It's like wanting the biggest house or the fastest car. It gives you a perceived dominance over the elements, let's you pretend you're beating life even though it knocks you back every time. And then there is the idea that you're superior to other people, that you can do it the best, even though it's an extension of your body, something outside of you, that makes you think you're better."

"I never need anything to feel better than everyone else."

"That's because you're big. You're already above people."

"No. What good is being big if you don't *feel* big?"

"How should I know?" I laughed.

"Size is all in your brain, Mason. I don't feel so big because I can't think big. I'd give anything to have your smarts. I can't think like you do. You tell me things, and they make perfect sense, but I know I could've never come up with them."

"I'm not so hot," I said.

Jack ignored me. "Have you seen Laine lately?" he asked.

"No," I said, surprised by the question and quick change of subject. My voice cracked. I blushed.

Jack stopped. He shoved me in the shoulder. "You did! I've been wondering whether you were gonna go after her or just sit on your ass—"

"Yeah, yeah, yeah," I said, walking ahead.

Jack trotted after me. "Well?" he asked.

"What?"

"*Did you ask her out?!*"

"Not really . . . but kinda."

"Are ya or aren't ya?"

"I'm going to her house Saturday to keep her company while she babysits."

"Yeah?"

"But I don't think it's really a date or anything." I stopped him. "Don't tell the other guys, 'cause really, I don't think it's a date, so don't tell 'em, okay?"

He shook his head. "I won't tell," he said. "But, jeez, Mason, that's great. After all, it's something. It's a start. But you know, you've got to make your intentions known sometime. You just can't keep *kinda* asking her out."

"I guess."

I looked around. We had been walking for quite a while and had made a couple of turns. I had just assumed that Jack was paying attention to where we were going, but apparently he wasn't. The sun was setting and turning the sky red, and we were in a *cul de sac* by some park. We were behind a handball court or something, and there was a big wall made out of cement blocks. Written across it in black spray paint was, "Rip Curl Ocean Blue."

"Uh-oh," Jack said. "We be lost."

I spun in a circle to see if I could spot anything that was a slight reference to where we had come from. I found nothing. Jack mocked me by licking his finger and holding it up like he was checking the wind. I was about to tell him to piss off when I suddenly felt the bass *thwump* of a loud stereo from off in the distance. A black minitruck appeared at the corner. It rolled up to the stop sign. *Thwump thwump.* The bass was getting louder, and it shook my gut.

"What the . . . ?" Jack mumbled.

The truck turned into the *cul de sac.* The bass was now pinpointed on us–*thwump thwump*–like a tracking device, and the truck's tinted windshield vibrated with every hit. Beneath the drums, faintly, I could hear a furious rapper cutting loose–*thump thwump*–to the flow.

There was a speed bump between us and the truck, and the truck stopped just in front of it. The stereo shut down, and all I could hear then was the hum of the engine.

"Uh-oh," I said, under my breath.

Jack spit on the ground and smudged it with his shoe. I reached into my pocket for a piece of gum, but I didn't have any. I needed something to concentrate on, something to make me focus. My mind was running all over the place. I thought of Laine and thought of the concert and thought of being lost once when I was a kid. I couldn't stop and think of just one thing, it was a million things. If I had gum, I could just focus on the chewing, and let everything else become secondary.

The doors of the truck opened, and two blonde guys stepped out. The driver had curly hair, and he wore Oakley blade sunglasses, a tank top, and Jackson-Pollack paint-splattered shorts. He had wide shoulders and a tan. He tossed his hair about and reached back into the truck, turning off the ignition. His friend was smaller, with a bowl cut and Ray-Bans. He, too, had a tank top and shorts on.

"You guys lost?" the driver asked.

"No," Jack said.

"Then why're you here?"

I looked to Jack. He was staring hard at them.

"Do you know where you are?" the driver went on, moving closer. "Do you know where this is?"

"What do you think?" Jack asked.

"I don't think you two queers are from here. You don't look like it. You don't look like you should be here."

Jack threw a sideways glance at me. I nodded my head slightly to let him know I was ready, though it was a lie. I didn't see much choice in the matter. Things were going to happen, and there was no sense hoping they would not.

"So?" asked the driver, moving up to Jack.

Jack raised his fist and brought it down hard on the driver's forehead. I looked quick to the other surfer. He was charging at me, and I stuck out my arm. He ran into my flat hand. His head jerked back and his nose popped and there was a squirt of blood over my fingers. I took the space and kicked him in the nuts. He fell on me, and we both went down. He was heavy and crushed me on the asphalt. One of my hands was trapped underneath him. I shoved it again and again into his stomach. I used the other hand to pound on his back. My fists went on automatically, though I told myself it was useless. His forehead was against mine, and I couldn't see anything beyond us. All I could see was a black cloth stretched out before me, with a light shining on it from somewhere in the distance, miles away. I could hear the surfer breathing. Each exhalation pushed against my face. His breath was stale and prickly. His blood was dripping on my face in slow, careful dollops. It was thick like syrup. My arms kept up their movement but were becoming sore. The world felt like it had stopped spinning.

The surfer suddenly rose up above me and something smashed down on my face.

I remember dreaming. It was like whatever hit me had sent all of my thoughts to the back of my mind, and there they found my dream and let it out. Maybe not a dream. Maybe a vision.

I saw myself sleeping. I was much older, but not yet decrepit. I was the same, just bigger and gray. Something woke me. Nothing that was apparent, like a noise or some light. I just woke up. I nodded my head to myself and seemed to know what was going on, like I had been waiting for it. I rose out of bed and stood straight. It was a small room. I was wearing only underwear.

I went to a desk to the right of the bed. It was positioned below a window, and the window had dusty, off-white blinds. I cracked open a space in the blinds, and though I had thought it was night, outside it was day. A girl rode by on her bicycle, and a boy stood on the sidewalk across the street, bouncing a ball and wearing a paper party hat. I let the blinds snap closed, moving down to one of the desk drawers, inside of which was a gun. It felt like night again as I lifted the gun to my head, pushing the barrel to my left temple. I pressed my finger to the trigger.

The picture skipped like badly spliced film, and this is the image I remember most. My head was face down on an open spiral notebook, the blood smearing everything that was written there, except for a few spots. I couldn't read any of it but knew it to be my writing. My hand lay on the desk, just off the edge of the notebook, still holding the gun, which wasn't smoking or anything, but rather seemed as cold as if I had just pulled it out of a freezer.

And I know for sure that it *was* night, no matter what it looked like through the blinds.

The world spun. The truck was gone when I was able to rise and look up. Jack had moved me out of the street, over to the handball court. He was sitting next to me. I had to blink a couple of times because the vision in my left eye was webby, like a thick glue had grown over it. My head hurt. It was sort of like it was full up with water, and I needed to put a hole in my skull to let it all out.

"Hey," Jack said. He smiled down at me. He had taken the bandanna off his head and wrapped it around his right hand because he had hurt his knuckles. The cloth was stained with a dark liquid, but there wasn't a mark anywhere on Jack. His long brown hair fell loose, dangling in his face, which was diamond shaped, cut rough on its edges, but smooth in the features. His eyes were a placid green, and they, too, smiled. "You okay?"

"Yeah," I said.

"You mean it?"

"Halfly."

"Do you know what happened?"

"I was hit?"

"He gave you quite a bluey around your eye."

My eye winced at the mention of it. It felt puffy. I touched it, and the skin was raw.

"You hurt him pretty good, though," Jack said. "All the blood on my bandanna is his. I wiped it off your face. After he whaled you, he just rolled off and lay there. Sad thing was, he had to drive out. I messed the other guy up hardcore."

The sun had fully set, and the streetlights cast a foggy glow on the sky. I couldn't see any stars. I pushed my tongue against the inside of my teeth and let my head loll back. "See," I said, "my brains don't do me much good when I really need it."

"Pshhh!" Jack whistled through his teeth.

"It's true, it's true," I said, opening my mouth wide and sucking the air in deep. I tried to think where we were, and then all of a sudden, I remembered—"The concert!"

I fumbled my way up.

"Hold on," Jack said. "We got time. Take it easy."

I teetered. "No, man, we gotta go."

I felt my legs start to give away. I reached out for something. Jack jumped up and grabbed me, putting his arm around my back. I leaned my head against him, just below his shoulder. I shook myself to try and rattle out the dizziness.

"We can go if you really want," Jack said.

"Do we even know the way back?"

"Man, I *always* know the way back."

5. FAITH AND HEALING

Saturday night, I took the bus to Santa Monica. It let me off a couple of blocks from Laine's house, and I walked the rest of the way. Her street was always dark, but you could easily spot her house because it was yellow, not mud brown or dirty white like all the others. In the front yard, there was a Big Wheel and a green plastic pool with a slide shaped like an alligator's head. There was no water in it, only mud-caked leaves.

I checked my eye in the window of a car on the street. Despite all my hopes, a miracle had not happened on the ride over. There was still a purpley-blue crescent moon hanging over my left cheek, and my eyeball rested in its cup. I decided that this was just one of those things fate deals out, and it could have been worse, like a zit or some mouth sore. At least this had a story.

I knocked on the door, and Laine came right away. She was wearing a black T-shirt and cut-off shorts. "Hi," she smiled. She motioned me in. "What's up?"

"Not a lot," I said.

Then she noticed.

"Your eye!" she gasped. "What happened to you?"

"Surfers," I said.

Laine reached out to feel it. I pulled back, and she withdrew her hand, putting it to her mouth and biting on a fingernail. "I'm sorry," she said.

"No, no . . . it's okay. Go ahead."

She reached out again. I clenched my teeth and held myself. I expected pain, but her finger only touched it lightly and was gentle. It didn't hurt at all.

"It's squishy," she said, a little bewildered. "And warm. Does it hurt?"

"Not particularly," I said, wanting to add, "You make it feel especially better," but deciding against it.

She touched it again, like she couldn't really believe it was there. "Let me guess," she said, smirking slightly, "I should've seen the other guy."

"I don't know, 'cause I sure didn't."

Laine scrunched up her left eye and stared at mine for a few moments longer, as if she were trying to imagine what it would be like. She opened her eye again and glared at me.

"What?" I asked.

"You're late."

"Impossible. I'm never late."

Actually, I had been early, and I had waited down on the corner until it was just the right time. I didn't want to tell her that, though. I'd look pathetic.

"The brats have been in bed for half an hour."

"But you said come at ten." I looked at the clock on the VCR across the room. "It's ten-oh-one. I'm totally on time."

"Okay," she said, punching me in the arm. She winked and walked into the living room, coyly looking over her shoulder. I followed, though I felt all a mess inside, my guts a flipping coin of uncertainty.

"What've you been doing all this time without me?" I asked.

"Just listening to music and being bored," she said. "You've let me down so."

I hadn't noticed before, but Depeche Mode's "Halo" was playing softly in the background. "You can change it if you want," Laine said. "I know you probably think they've sold out and aren't cool anymore."

"Where'd you get that idea?"

"What? *You* like Depeche Mode?"

"Yeah! Don't you remember? This tape came out on the same day I took you to dinner for your birthday last year. I borrowed Steve's car, and he didn't have a stereo then, so I stuck a ghetto blaster in the back seat so we could listen to it. Remember? You made me take you to *Joe vs. The Volcano*, and it full on sucked. You were wearing this red shirt with paisley designs—"

"How do you remember all this stuff?"

"I don't know. I just do." I fiddled with the rolled cuff of my pant leg. "I remember . . . I didn't want to go home afterwards." I had kissed her hand in the garage when we said good-bye. I left that out, though. I was ashamed I hadn't kissed her on the lips. "I drove around for a while and listened to 'Waiting for the Night' like a hundred times."

"Jeez, Mason. You hold on to the oddest things . . ."

We sat there in an awkward silence, neither of us able to come up with what to say next. I flipped through her stepdad's record collection, but most of it was stuff like CCR and The Band and Blood, Sweat, and Tears and other shitty '60s bands. He had a few Who albums and some Doors, though, which were a saving grace until I found the Springsteen. Then I just gave up.

"I would put in a movie or something," Laine said, "but 'Saturday Night Live' is going to be on."

"Oh, I'm fine, I'm fine," I said. I nervously scanned the room. The wall behind me was covered with pictures of the family. There were some of Laine and her sister as kids, school photos, things like that. I had seen most of them before, but there was a new group shot. Laine had on a summery dress and looked like she was about to burp. I tried not to laugh. "Hey, isn't this a new family photo?" I asked.

"Oh, *gawd*," she moaned. "It's so horrible. I hate that thing. I look like a pig. My mother made me wear that. I *hate* family pictures."

"Hey, it's not all bad. At least you've got a family."

"*You've* got a family."

"Not hardly."

"What about your mom?"

"Yeah, sure. I haven't even talked to her since I moved out. Bitch."

I imagined my mother sitting in her apartment, alone at the kitchen table, clutching her "Forty and Still Alive" coffee mug, muttering–though no one was there to protest-"It's only coffee . . . It's only coffee . . ." It made me angry to think of her, but I also felt a little guilty about leaving her like that–drunk with no one to pick up after her. I tried not to think about her too often. It generally brought me down.

"No," I said, "you should be glad you still have a family."

Laine seemed to be bummed out a little by the talk. She stared down at the couch and picked at a loose button on a cushion. I think she felt bad she had brought up my mom.

"I'm not totally alone or anything," I continued, trying to lighten the subject a bit. "Jack's like my brother . . . and then there's music. I think music may be the only real family I'll ever have. It's like, when I listen to certain bands, certain singers, they say things that I thought, you know, only *I* felt–not that no one else has ever thought that, but you know . . . It's so comforting, because there's like this voice, out there . . . I sometimes get the urge to go into a record store–a real record store with real records–and start grabbing them out of the racks and spreading them out on the floor. I'd let them slide out of their sleeves or let the gatefolds fall open, and I'd just cover the room with them and lay down among the vinyl."

"Sort of twisted."

"Yeah, I guess so. Some people are into leather car seats, and I dig black plastic. It gets kind of obsessive. Like the way I have to have everything–every B-side, bootleg, whatever. I like to learn about the artist, hear the gossip. I like to be involved. Like I said, it's a kind of home."

Laine was silent for a moment, and then she said, "You are the strangest person I've ever met."

I was a little embarrassed, so I excused myself to the bathroom. I didn't actually have to go, so I planned to just walk around in there for a few minutes, flush, and leave. I checked my eye in the mirror and tried to convince myself that it wasn't as bad as I thought it was. Then, knowing that it was Laine's bathroom exclusively, I couldn't resist looking inside the medicine cabinet.

The cabinet door squeaked when I opened it, and I was scared she might have heard me. I stood still for a minute, listening to hear if she was coming, but realized that it was stupid and the thing was already open so I might as well look.

Inside the cabinet, there were bottles of cream and make-up base, some eyebrow pencils and eyeliner, lipstick, chapstick, eye shadow and blush, a bunch of bottles with some different colored liquids. In the bottom-right corner, there were a couple of cigar-sized tubes wrapped in plastic. I picked one up to see what it was, and I suddenly felt my insides flatten out. It was a tampon. I put it back and slammed the door. Frightened that she heard me that time and nervous with guilt over what I had done, I panicked, flushed the toilet, and got out of there.

Laine was watching some show with comedians on it and didn't let on if she had heard anything. I just sat down on the floor and kept my mouth shut.

"You can come up on the couch with me," she said.

My stomach was still doing a jig, and my hands felt sweaty. "That's okay. I'm fine here."

Just before "Saturday Night Live" came on, Laine got up and went into the kitchen. I heard her get out some silverware and go into the refrigerator. "Do you want a snack?" she called out.

I went in. "What do you got?" I asked.

"I'm having a peanut butter and sugar sandwich."

"Peanut butter and *sugar*?!"

"Yeah, it's good."

"Sounds kind of weird."

"Do you want one?"

"I guess so."

She took out a slice of bread and spread some creamy peanut butter across the top. Then she took the big jar of sugar off the counter and spooned some out onto the sandwich. "You put on a lot," she explained, "because some of it falls off."

"Whatever. You're the expert."

Laine put the sugar and the peanut butter away and then poured us each a half glass of milk. "Come on," she said, grabbing up her plate and glass. "Let's go."

This time, she laid down on her stomach on the floor. I sat next to her, Indian-style. She set the plate in front of her and didn't touch it. I picked mine up. Some of the sugar did slide off and landed on the plate. I gobbled the snack down in about three bites.

"Gosh, did you like it? she asked.

"Yeah, it was really good. Sugar makes it sweet."

"*Duh*. Do you want another one?"

"No, that's all right."

I actually did want another one but didn't want to be greedy or put her out. I tried to make my milk last, but it was gone before the next commercial had finished. I drank too fast, and I was still thirsty.

The show started, and Laine ate her sandwich. When she finished, she sat up and set her dishes aside. Deciding to be chivalrous, I jumped up and took them, carrying hers and mine into the kitchen and putting them in the sink.

Laine was lying on her back when I returned. "Thank you," she said.

I sat back down next to her. Her hair was stretched out along the floor behind her. It shined in the light. Laine reached a hand back and started to stroke it, down from her forehead and across the length of the hair. She did this several times, and then noticed I was watching her. "Do you want to feel my hair?" she asked, her voice low. "It's so soft."

My throat felt pinched and hollow. I was nervous, like my touch might make her hair fall out or something. I reached over and felt it with the tips of my fingers. It was very smooth, like silk bedsheets. I ran my fingers back over it. After a few times, I stopped, afraid that if I kept going she might get mad.

"Didn't you think it felt neat?" she asked.

"Yes, I did."

"Then why did you quit, silly?"

She turned on her side and closed her eyes. I felt my breath getting short, and I moved closer to have a better reach. I began to stroke Laine's hair again, moving in the rhythm of her relaxed breathing. Soon, my breathing fell in line with hers. Across and back, across and back, nice and slow. I began to feel drowsy. I wanted to lay down next to her, hold her, and feel our stomachs moving together, feel us each take a single breath. Her hair smoothed out under my hand. The reflection of the light bent and curved with the motion, and I felt I was being hypnotized.

Just when I was thinking it would never end, a "Wayne's World" skit began, and it was like an alarm had gone off. Laine's eyes popped open and she immediately sat up. "Yeahhhh!"

We laughed together through the entire sketch, but Laine laughed hardest. The main gag was Wayne and Garth going over some of the movies they had seen recently. I could tell it was a rerun from a couple seasons before because one of them was *Batman*. Laine clutched her sides and wobbled with giggling. When the skit was over, she let it all out and rolled around on the floor, letting the laughing take its full course. As she regained her breath, she sat up and said, "Man, I wish I'd taped that. I could watch that stuff all the time and never get tired of it. My friend Michele tapes them all the time. We like to watch it and drink Coke and see who can get it to come out of their nose first."

"It must be a real pretty sight," I said.

"Oh, but it is," she said, winking.

I stared into her eyes and felt her smile, and I wanted to tell her how much I loved her, because I really did.

I really did.

Her parents came home not long after. "I think it's time you asked your friend to leave," her stepdad said.

"Fine," Laine groaned. "*God.*"

"It's okay," I said.

She walked me to the door. "I'm sorry," she apologized. "He's a dick. My mom likes you, though, which is weird. She never likes my friends, but

46

she always says she thinks you're neat."

"Neat, huh? Well, I guess it just proves she has good taste."

"I don't know. Look who she married."

We shared another laugh, and then she said good-bye, letting the screen door slam shut, then following it with the main door. When I heard it lock and the porch light went out, I left.

It was too late for the bus, and I had to walk back to Melrose. It took a couple hours, but it felt like minutes. I sang to myself and thought about Laine and wondered what it would be like to be with her all the time.

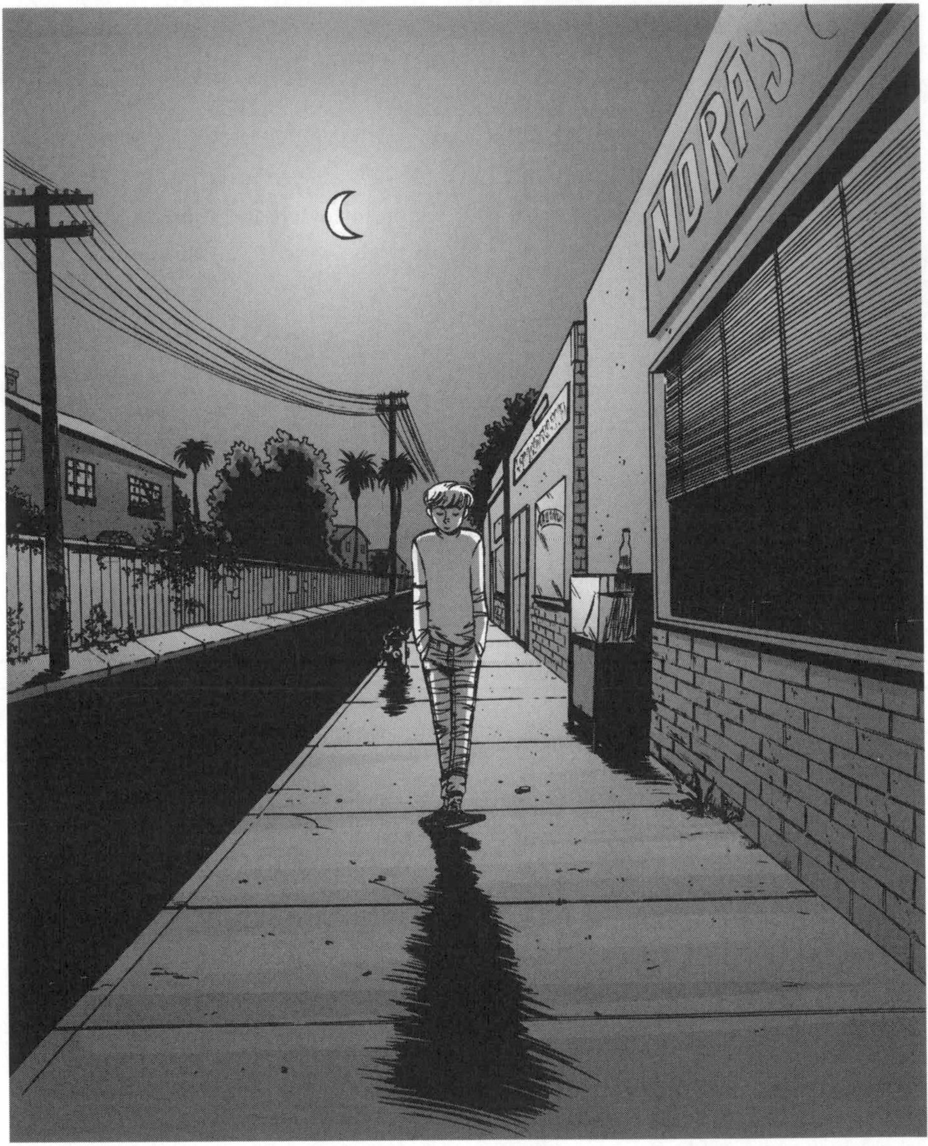
NORA'S

6. LOVE WILL TEAR US APART

I had an unusually happy week following my night with Laine. Every morning, I made a peanut butter and sugar sandwich for breakfast. Jack thought I had wigged out something fierce. "Don't worry," I told him, "my life is fully in control."

"It's scary, Mason," he said. "You bound around here with a huge smile on your face, you're eating crazy things. I've *got* to wonder about you."

"It's love," I declared. "Pure love."

Occasionally, Laine would skate past the comics shop with her friends, and I often found myself daydreaming and watching for her to come. I wondered if part of her appeal was the talent with which she bridged the chasm between being with skaters and being cool. She hung out with them, but she really wasn't one of them. She never adopted their attitude, but rather, managed to stay pure.

On Thursday, I was able to catch her before she got by.

"Hey, Mason, what's up?"

"My spirits," I said. "How'd you like to go dancing at NoWay Home with me tonight? Jack and the guys will be there, too, but we don't really have to stick with them."

"Oh, Mason, I'm sorry, but I really can't."

I nodded. "That's okay, then. Just wondering."

"Thanks. I'd really love to . . ." She pouted and crinkled her brow. "Forgive me, please?"

"'s okay. Really. I understand."

"Yo, Laine, come on!" All the skaters had stopped down the street and were waiting for her. "Yeah, quit talking to the fag and come on!"

"Shut the hell up!" she shouted at them. "I'll be there in a fucking minute, assholes." She looked back at me. "I'm really, really sorry, Mason. They're jerks. Please, don't be mad."

I waved her off. "No, no, no, go on. I understand."

She gave me a little tap with her fist and said, "Thanks, Mason, you're the best of 'em. You're a true pal."

"Go, go, before I cry."

She hopped on her skateboard and caught up with the group, and they all started off down the street. One kid, a guy named Pete who I had gotten into a fight with in tenth grade, waved daintily at me. I flipped him off and went back in the shop.

I wasn't joking when I told her I'd cry. I really felt like I would, and I desperately wanted to. The store radio was on KROQ, and they were playing "There is a Light that Never Goes Out," and I thought how cruel radio stations were. Just when you didn't need a depressing, romantic song, they'd play one.

I didn't really feel much like going to the club after that. I had whipped myself into a rather glorious depression by the end of work and just wanted to sit in my room listening to sad music in the dark.

"This is bullshit, Mason," Jack said. "You don't honestly think I'm going to let you not go, do you?"

"Why not?"

"Because I remember how you used to tell me how miserable your life was when you had no friends, and you'd stay home alone all weekend listening to The Smiths and watching the phone in hopes someone would call. Do you think I'd let you start that up again? I'm your friend, for fuck's sake."

"But—"

"Listen, Laine's your friend, too, right? You just have to trust that she meant what she said."

That made me feel like a major heel, so I told Jack he was right and got dressed. I shoved my copy of Kafka's *The Metamorphosis* into my back pocket in case I got bored or needed a distraction. I had bought it only that morning because I felt it was about time I read it. I didn't want to be one of the ones who didn't know Kafka. I just hoped it was the book Tristan had meant.

There were no bands at NoWay that night, which meant that the dancing would be tamer and the drinking heavier. I took a table off to the side to watch, and the guys cruised around the club, sizing up the action. I tried to read, but the light was too low and the music too loud. A sweaty guy with curly hair spotted me and asked, "What're ya readin'?"

He was drunk. I showed him the book's cover, and he leaned in real close. His breath reeked of fish and beer.

"What're ya readin' dat shit for? Not ta say dat it's shit, but dis is a club, motherfuckah!"

"I'm just feeling mellow, and I want to read."

"Yer not gay, arrr ya?"

"*No!*"

"Okay, okay. Ah know what ya need, dough, if ya wanna get on top ag'n, if ya know what ah'm sayin'."

I stood up. "I think I got it," I said, "but thank's anyway."

"Okay, but lemme know if ya wanna pahty."

I went out through the back exit, into the alley. Some nights, people used it to make out or procure harder stuff than NoWay

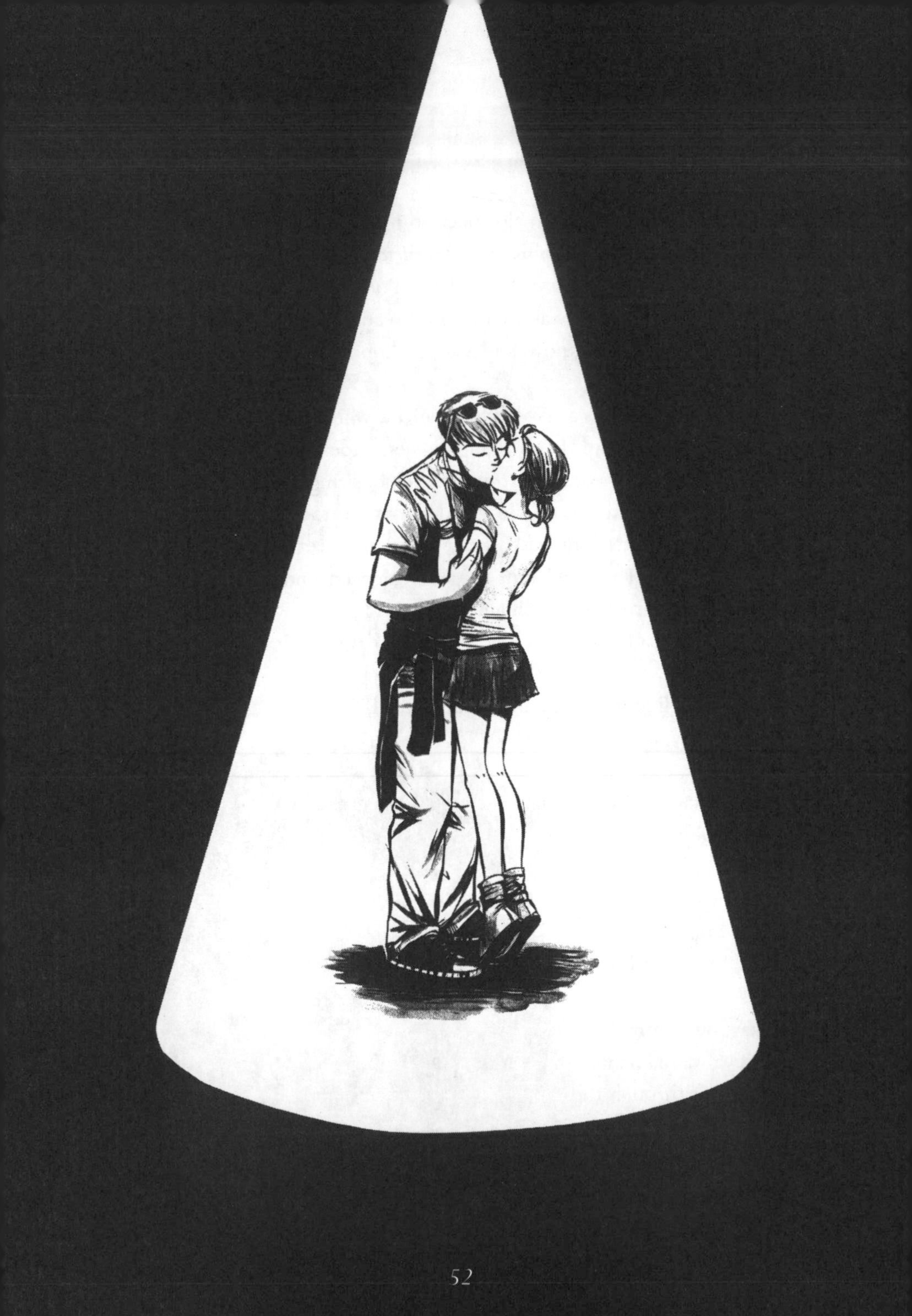

had to offer, so I was glad to find it empty. I sat down on a railroad tie by the wall and thumbed through my book for where I left off. A couple was passing by the mouth of the alley, down by the street. When they walked under the streetlight, I thought I recognized the girl, and when I heard her laugh and say, "You're such an idiot," I knew it was Laine.

I got up and ran down the alley. I peered around the edge of the building. Laine was walking away from the club, holding hands with Otto. I saw him say something, and she stood on her tip-toes to kiss him. The moment got stuck there, and I could feel it filling me like thick oil, hard and burning, catching in my throat. I watched their lips meet and come apart, her smile as she remained still for a moment, her face almost touching his. She settled back on her feet, smiled again, and clutched his hand.

"Bitch!" I screamed, and ran back down the alley into the club.

I stopped short inside the door. A wave of heat rising off the people in the pit slammed into me. I was choking. I wanted to be angry, but wasn't. I was just sad again, and the air was hot and foul with body odor, beer, and piss. I cursed myself as stupid. I was having trouble swallowing. My breath was curdled. I was starting to feel nauseous. I ran over to a corner and puked.

Wiping my mouth, I stood and turned to find Steve waiting behind me. He was laughing at me. "You shouldn't play, Jailbate, if the game's too rough."

"Fuck you," I said, and I spit some of the leftover vomit at his feet.

"Little shit!" he exclaimed. He grabbed me by the shirt. "I've been letting you get away with your crap for too long. It's about time you got thumped."

He hauled off to hit me, but before he could bring it down, Jack pounded him in the back of the head. Steve's knees

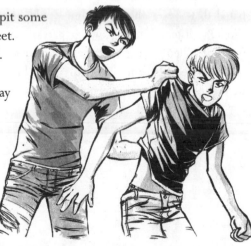

53

buckled, and he let me go. He steadied himself before he could fall and rubbed his eyes like the pain was coming out through them. "What the fuck, man?" he whined.

"I've told you, hands off Mason!" Jack shouted. "You mess with him, and you'll feel it."

Steve stumbled away and collapsed on top of a table.

I moved from the puke and went back outside to the railroad tie. The image of Laine stood on its tip-toes in my mind, and I wanted to retch again, all over it. Jack came out and sat down on the ground in front of me.

"What went on in there?" Jack asked.

"He was making fun of me because I threw up," I said. I kicked the dirt. I couldn't bring myself to look up at him. "I got mad and spit at him. I had just finished heaving it up and wasn't thinking. It was my fault."

"Nah," Jack said. "He brings it on. What made you yak, though?"

I finally looked at him. "Real reason?"

"Real reason."

"I saw Laine kissing Otto."

"Otto the skater?"

I nodded.

"Shit, I'm sorry, man."

The night air was cool and felt soothing compared to inside the club. I felt so incredibly dumb now that it was all winding down. I hated myself, hated that I ever thought Laine would have anything to do with me. I should've listened to the smarter part of my brain when it told me my life would be filled with nothing but loneliness and spared myself the misery.

Jack traced his name in the dirt with his finger. When he was finished, he drew a line through it. He lifted his head. His eyes were serious.

"We'll fix it," Jack said. "We will."

7. BLITZKRIEG BOP

We went to a skating rink with a couple of guys we knew and had partied with once or twice. One was named William, a black guy with bleached blonde hair cut real short. He wore a green velvet fedora and square sunglasses and never smiled.

We rented skates and rode around the rink for a couple of songs. Steve had a real hard time staying up. He did a lot more stepping than rolling, clomping loudly on the floor. When he'd finally get going, Jack would skate up behind him and punch him in the back of his knees. He'd bend backwards and windmill his arms to try to keep from falling. Usually, though, his legs would spread or kick out from underneath him, and he'd fall on his butt, his limbs shooting out in every direction. "Fuck you," he'd spit. "You're an asshole."

I felt pretty good on the skates and got over my shakiness right away. I had a pair when I was a kid and would go skating around the local high school because it had a lot of bumps and small hills. I never knew how to stop, though, and would either just fall in the grass or put my shin down, eventually burning away the laces with the friction.

Jack whistled and moved to the front of the pack, and we followed as he went around the rink once more. On the final curve, Jack slammed into the emergency exit and threw the double-doors open. A harsh alarm began to buzz, and we all skated out under a spinning red light. Burton was waiting outside with a pick-up truck that this guy named Dean loaned to us. (We would later have to do some roadie work for Dean's band, Gene Larkin's A Bum, in return.) We all piled into the back. A balding man wearing suspenders came running out after us. "Hey! Hey, you kids! Get back here! Goddamn!" He threw his cigar, and it landed in William's lap. William picked it up, very calm and slow. He held the offending shaft with his thumb and forefinger, dangling it and letting it go over the edge. His face was stone. Burton hit the gas, and I watched the exploding orange ash dance on the concrete behind us, getting farther and farther away, smaller and smaller. The bald man stood over the hot debris and shook his fist at us. We all gave him the finger and laughed.

"Fuck you, fatass!"

"Cocksucker!"

"Fuckin' geezer!"

There were baseball bats in the truck bed with us, enough for everyone. Steve picked up an aluminum bat and started swinging it around, chanting, "Beat on the brat, beat on the brat, beat on the brat with a baseball bat, oh yeah, oh yeah, oh oh oh," over and over.

We knew a place where all the skaters hung out—an abandoned minimall with a fairly large parking lot. They had built a ramp going up the front of the empty 7-11 and painted their names and dirty pictures on the sandwich shop and the Laundromat. "Otto will be there," Jack had said when he informed me of the plan. "Things'll get fixed."

Some of the guys smoked out and others just drank beer. I hugged my bat and watched the road behind us, the divider lines snaking out from underneath us, almost as if we were laying them down. Steve's chanting was stuck in my brain. *Beat on the brat, beat on the brat* . . . I let my head hang heavy over the tailgate. It felt as if I could fall out and explode like the cigar, scattering all the pieces of myself over the road. I had a brief flash of myself, older, rising out of bed in the middle of the night. I was in my underwear, and I held the sheet for a few moments, pulling it slightly off the bed.

Burton made a quick turn. The tires screeched, and I rolled over into William. He didn't move. I pulled myself up, and before I knew what was happening, the truck was stopped and everyone was getting out. I looked over the side of the truck. About ten skaters were in the parking lot, just as predicted. They stopped what they were doing and stood still, staring at us. There was a little ghetto blaster on the curb, playing Suicidal Tendencies, and the first thing someone did was smash it. It sprayed silver sparks everywhere, and suddenly everything was abuzz with movement. Steve leaped over me, slapping me in the back of the head. "Let's go, Jailbate."

I went over the side and rolled right into the middle of everything. It was chaos. About three guys were circling in and around the perimeter of the lot, keeping anyone from skating off. One kid was making a mad dash for it, but Jack caught him in the stomach with his bat. The kid rose up off his board, and it kept going right out into the street. He hung there in the air, his body bending in the middle as if the bat were a hinge. His gum flew out of his mouth and hit Jack in the face. Jack laughed. The kid dropped.

Jack saw me watching him. He tapped his head, I think telling me to get mine together, and then extended his arm, pointing with the bat to a blonde skater with sky-blue Oakleys. Otto.

I remembered that kiss in the streetlight, as I had been remembering it since it happened the night before. It had come to me again and again, all through the day, and each time, I felt more and more foolish. Now, I felt anger. A hot anger that said I was a fool only because Otto existed, and I wanted to destroy him.

I started toward him, the wheels of my roller skates clacking on the cement. Otto took off on his board and managed to slip past the guys guarding the sidewalk. I followed and chased him around the back of the building. I swiped the bat down, cracking the tail of his board and sending him tumbling off the front. He was used to crashes, though, and rolled with it, ending up on his ass without much of a scrape. He balled himself up, pressing his face into his knees, readying himself to take a hit.

I tilted my leg, skidding to a halt with the side of my foot. His shirt was yellow, and his back curved over like a smooth stone. Or maybe he resembled a cowardly turtle.

My bat was wooden and felt rough in my hands. I hit it on the concrete to see what sort of sound it would make. A solid crack echoed through the alley. Otto didn't move, even though I hit it really close to him. This made me madder, because the guy who made a fool of me wasn't fighting, but rather rolling himself up like a pill bug. I at least wanted to be thrown over for a guy that amounted to something, not somebody worthless like me.

Seething, I rose the bat above my head and prepared to swing . . .

. . . but something rushed out of me. My muscles froze and spasmed, and I looked at Otto's back and thought how brittle it must be, how easily it could be smashed. I remembered taking a hammer when I was little and pounding pebbles on the driveway until they were powder. It was all so simple and easy. Even *my* small muscles could do it.

Otto stirred, and I got ready to drop the bat on him. He turned his head around, possibly confused by the pause, and looked at me. His face was clear in the light. I didn't recognize him. He wasn't Otto. His hair and glasses were the same, but it wasn't Otto at all. I clenched up and let out a little scream. It was the wrong guy! The fact hit me hard. Not like finding out you've been wrong about a famous date or a song lyric, but much more damaging to the system. Finding out you were just about to beat some guy's spine to dust, and it's not the right guy. I thought I'd break apart myself.

The skater realized that this was his chance and scrambled over to his board. He clumsily hopped on it and skated away, not even looking back to see if I was coming after him. I let my arms hang limp and watched until he was completely gone, the tip of the bat nuzzled gently against the ground.

I stood without moving for several moments afterward, the whole time feeling something more was wrong, that somebody was there with me. I looked to my right, and William was standing in the shadows by the wall of the building. He smiled at me without showing any teeth, and then he skated away.

I was terrified. My belief in the situation drained away, almost like I had hooked it onto William and he had dragged it out of me when he rolled off. I remembered Steve singing, *Beat on the brat, beat on the brat with a baseball bat, oh yeah, oh yeah, oh oh oh*. I remembered myself sitting at a desk in the middle of the night, orange sparks flying from a gun and scattering me everywhere. The face of the brat was very clear, shining under electric lights.

Everything was pretty much finished out front. Most of the guys were already in the back of the truck, taking off their skates and getting some more beer. I climbed in and sat next to Jack. "Did you get 'im?" he asked me.

I couldn't tell him the truth. This whole thing had been for me, and I blew it. I couldn't let Jack know that. I couldn't. So, I said, "Yes."

BANG!

I jumped, nearly tumbling backwards out of the truck.

William had dropped his bat on the floor of the truck bed and was picking it back up. He shrugged to me.

"No," I said. "I mean, I caught the guy . . . but it wasn't Otto."

"Dammit," Jack said. "I thought for sure he would be here."

"It's okay," I said. "No big deal."

Jack looked at me like he didn't know what language I was speaking. I crawled over to the other side and made like I wanted to look at the carnage. There were a lot of shattered skateboards, and the skaters were starting to pick themselves up, clutching the various parts of their bodies that had been clubbed. A few were bleeding, a couple from the head. I was devoid of any feeling. I was lost.

Burton started up the truck and pulled out. As we left, another skater rode up and looked at the parking lot, at all his friends. The ramp he had probably helped build was torn down and totally dismantled. He looked at the truck, seemed to look right at me. It was Pete, the guy who had shouted at me when I was talking to Laine outside the comics shop. He knew her.

And worse . . . he knew me.

My eyes followed him and his followed me as the truck drove away. I began to panic. What if he told Laine? Maybe she knew more of the guys who were beaten. Maybe she hung out at this place, too. What would I tell her? I swear I didn't hit anyone, you can just ask the guy who looks like Otto?

I was doomed.

Then I thought maybe it wasn't me that Pete was looking at. He could've just been checking out the truck. Maybe he didn't see me at all. But, no.

He was looking right at me.

I was doomed.

I sat back down in the truck before I got any more urges to toss myself over the side. William was sitting on one of the wheel wells. He was staring at me, smiling with his lips closed tight, showing no teeth. I turned away and forgot him. Once more I saw the kiss in the streetlight, this time followed by the face of the boy who was Otto but wasn't. Then I saw the image of Pete watching me slide away.

No one had made me a fool. Not Otto, not anybody.

I was just one by nature.

8 . NEVER TELL

The entire week after the incident at the minimall, I was totally nervous morning to night. Every time I saw a skater, I worried that perhaps he would recognize me and that he knew Laine. Things were made worse by the fact that I didn't see Laine anywhere, and I could never manage to get her on the phone. It had always been hard to get a hold of her, but now it was impossible to convince myself that this was just like any other time.

I spent most of my time reading, trying to keep my mind occupied. I got through *The Metamorphosis* rather quickly and wasn't quite sure if I had gotten the right book. "Like a dog" didn't appear once. The edition I had was rounded out by a lot of essays by critics, and I decided to read those in case I missed something. There was a letter from Kafka to his father, writing from the father's point of view, saying that Kafka was worthless and had ruined his father's life by his own inability to live. This particularly struck me. I thought all the academics that wondered whether or not Gregor Samsa was a real bug were totally out of it. What did it matter if he was a real bug or not? I could totally believe he was one, that all the dignity and life were sucked out of him by his parasitic family. *They* turned him into a parasite that, ironically, could not suck back. They were already empty, and there was nothing for him to take.

In the middle of the week, Tristan actually came into the comics shop. He was carrying a ratty old backpack with only one strap. "Hi, Mason," he said. "Can I hang a flyer in your window?"

The window was bare except for a painting of Spider-Man and the word "COMICS" in big, yellow letters. We had never accepted flyers before.

"Sure," I said. "I don't see why not."

"Great," he said, and started digging in his bag. He pulled out a pink piece of paper and a roll of tape.

"Can I have one?" I asked.

Tristan took out another and handed it to me. The band was playing at some outdoor bar in Pasadena on Saturday night. There was a picture of a drenched sheep dog, dripping with water, looking very cold and pathetic. In the corner, it said, "With The DiscoTents."

"This is our own show," Tristan said, sticking the flyer in the lower corner of the glass. "We all put our money together and set it up. Sean knew some of the DiscoTents, and they gave us a third of what we needed to be our opener."

"Cool," I said.

"This won't be like last time. Now, we're in charge."

"Well, Jack and I will definitely be there," I said.

Tristan smiled shyly and looked around the store. "What's hot these days?" he asked. "It's been so long since I've been in one of these places."

I had never imagined Tristan picking up a comic book. He wasn't the type. It seemed they'd be too low for him.

I shrugged. "Wolverine. Anything X-Men," I said. "Probably the same as last time you looked."

He nodded. "What about *Love and Rockets*?" he asked. "Anything new from them?"

"Not for a couple of months. And Jaime peaked with 'The Death of Speedy.'"

He noticed the book in my hands. "What've you got there?"

I held it up so he could see the cover.

"Ah!" Tristan laughed. "Great. Try *The Trial* next. That's my favorite."

"Oh, I will."

Tristan lifted the pack over his shoulder and pushed the hair back from his eyes. "Thanks, Mason," he smiled, and left.

My boss most likely wouldn't notice the flyer for a couple more days, too late for him to figure out who was responsible. And if he did, it would be worth whatever he did to me. Giving Tristan the plug was more important.

As soon as I got off work that day, I went down to the bookstore and picked up a copy of *The Trial*. I used it as an excuse to stay in nights, not admitting to Jack that I really didn't want to go out because a skater might see me and rat.

The Trial was a long book, and it read like a dream—slow and seeming to take forever, though if you looked at the clock, it was only minutes. The cover had a man with a triangular face who was being stared at by a row of men with blank, but somehow derisive, eyes. The characters seemed small and claustrophobic, not even fitting into the tiny frame surrounding them. As I read, I felt sorry for Joseph K. not being able to figure out what was going on, and I hoped he would finally settle down with the girl with webbed hands. No such luck.

In between chapters, I tried to call Laine and felt particularly sunken every time she was out. The phone lines were an indecipherable web, just like the justice system Joseph K. had to deal with. I felt neither of us would ever find our way to the end.

The book's final chapter was particularly engrossing, as poor Joseph was led to the middle of nowhere by two goons. As they were about to kill him, a person from a nearby farm house leaned out the window and reached for him, and I thought, "Finally, Joseph is being saved!" but then the goons plunged a knife into his chest. The last sentence tied it all up for me, knocked me dead in the eye. *'Like a dog!' he said; it was as if the shame of it must outlive him.* He *was* saved! He was! In those final moments, Joseph K. had a chance to scream and reach out, and in so doing, to finally see

clearly. In the face of death, he saw life was truly lived beyond its normal bounds. Knowing the moment of death made that clear. I wondered if the shame was a separate entity now, a disgusting residue he shed and left behind in his transcendence, or if, perhaps, it was the shame that set him apart, made him different, able to take that step beyond. If that shame continued, he'd continue. His strength would continue.

I could see why Tristan had chosen Like A Dog as the band's name. It was so powerful, said so many things. Perhaps that was why his lyrics dealt so much with fear and cowardice. The lyrics were *his* way of reaching out, gaining power through the mutual hurt. Perhaps that was why there were Doggies. It created a community–the banding together of the shamed.

With *The Trial* finished, Tristan appeared even more fantastic to me. I often fantasized about being in a band, and in those fantasies, I was always just like him. It's kind of funny, I guess. You'd think I'd lean more towards a Social D-type image, full-on rough and tumble, but I suppose what really appealed to me was the alluring figure cut by someone like

Joy Division's Ian Curtis or Morrissey—or Tristan. I knew it was an impossible idea, though. I didn't have the voice or the writing talent. I didn't have the need for success that is so essential to a messiah, that reluctant yearning to be loved. Tristan would survive and prosper because he had to. It was that strong.

I was only weak.

On Saturday, Jack came home from work with a really cool Guess? poster. The model was sitting at the bottom of a stairway that led up to the door of a small airplane. There were a bunch of photographers snapping her picture, but she wasn't looking at them. She was looking out at the audience, at us, smiling. She knew who the show was really for.

Jack put it up on the living room wall.

We got ready to go to the show and were halfway out the door when the phone rang. We let the machine get it, hoping it wasn't anything urgent that would keep us from going.

It was Laine.

"Hello, Mason. Sorry it took so long to call back, but now that I finally have, you're not—"

I bit my lip. Jack started to close the door and go back in, but I shook my head no. "Forget it," I said. "Let's go."

I had been trying to talk to her—it seemed like an eternity—and now that I finally could, I no longer wanted to.

"—there. Call me if you can. I'll be around all night."

No, I wanted to. I knew I wanted to by the way hearing her say she'd be in the whole night made me shrivel. She still had me, and there was nothing I wanted more than to rush back to the phone and have her—have her from then until dawn.

But I was scared. I was scared to talk to her. So, I ran.

We made our way to Pasadena by bus. We didn't say much. I think Jack understood that I wasn't in the mood to talk and let me have my time. Every once in a while, he would point out something on the street or make a crack about another passenger, enough to assure me that he was still there and open for conversation, though not pushing it.

But I wallowed in self-pity.

After we got off the bus, Jack and I had to walk up a hill to get to the bar. It was called The Garden, and it was modeled after some architect's vague memory of a Spanish villa, a memory that many misguided Californian architects shared. There was a heavy wind that pushed against us and made it a fight to climb up to the top.

The Garden had two buildings—a bar and a cantina—and an outdoor stage. We entered through an arched corridor that led to where the stage was. Behind the stage was a small little house, probably for the bands to store their equipment in. In front of the stage was an open floor made out of red tiles with white trim. It probably had tables for dining on normal nights, with a mariachi band using the stage. Tonight, the fancy red tile would support a mosh pit. About fifty people had already arrived. They sat in scattered clumps around the place, claiming a few leftover picnic tables as their own.

The stage area separated the bar and the actual garden that had given the place its name. The edges of the garden were marked by tall hedges that were trimmed to form pathways and were dotted with red and pink roses. It was a fairy-tale creation taken from an archaic time when, just to get a date, some fine, upstanding boy would have to find his way through the maze to the love of the princess, only there was no way through and there was no princess and many a lovesick fool starved himself to death on the inside just to find that out. The only thing waiting for him was the gooey, dark center that exists in all fairy tales. Still, there must have been a feeling of incredible promise upon entering the maze, enough of a promise even to keep you happy up to the end.

Jack and I went through, following the flowers and the hedge walls and the young trees to the center. Waiting for us there was a fantastic fountain made of blue marble. We sat on its edge and listened to the waters. There were a lot of punks hanging around, and it was strange to see all the bad haircuts and leather among the delicate plants. It somehow soiled the magic. Diminished it.

Sean and Emery, Like A Dog's bass player, were in there as well. When they saw us, they came over. "Hey, glad you guys could make it," Sean said. He was wearing blade sunglasses that made him look like someone out of Devo.

Emery, who never liked us, pretended we weren't there. He played with his ponytail, undoing it and redoing it, not once looking at us. I suppose in the beginning he wasn't a bad guy, before being in a band went to his head, before he became convinced he was in a rock 'n' roll dream and when the people screamed they screamed for him—especially the girls.

"Glad to be here," Jack said, standing up. He moved close to Emery, tilting his head back so he could look down his nose at him. Jack was trying to piss Emery off, knowing that Emery always resented the fact that Jack was a couple of inches taller than him. Emery had a delusion that he was best in *all* things, and Jack couldn't resist reminding him that six-foot-two wasn't enough.

Emery tried to act like nothing was happening and was doing an okay job until the rubber band he was using for his hair broke. He became irritated. "Really wouldn't have made a difference if they *hadn't* made it," he said. "Plenty of people without 'em."

"Catch me after the show, fucker, and we'll see who really matters to you." Jack took a rubber band from around his wrist and shot it at Emery, hitting him in the chest. Emery picked it up and walked away, pulling his hair back and fixing his ponytail.

"Sorry," Sean shrugged. "Some guys can't help being pricks."

Sean followed after Emery. It wasn't clear who he meant.

We went back to the main area, and The DiscoTents were just about finished setting up their equipment. There were a larger number of people now, but they still stuck to their small groups all around the floor. No one seemed interested in much of anything.

The DiscoTents were a synthesizer band, following the example of

Depeche Mode and Erasure very closely, with maybe a little Kraftwerk in their finer moments. I had seen them before and had thought they weren't too bad, but most of the people were there to see Like A Dog and didn't care one way or the other about who was opening.

Jack went into the lounge to try to scam his way into a drink. I grabbed a spot at the center of the stage. The sun was just a red bar in the distance, descending behind the mountains beyond the city, and when I turned, I could see the half-moon behind me. A roadie did the final microphone check, and The DiscoTents came out. The band consisted of two keyboard players, one of whom doubled as the singer. He was a skinny guy in a skin-tight leather jumpsuit with a turtleneck collar that went all the way up to his chin—which I'm sure was just awful to wear—I'd probably die from the heat, myself—but it looked kind of cool. He also wore square-rimmed sunglasses and had his hair slicked back with at least a pound of grease.

There had originally been three keyboard players, but the third now sat behind a drum kit. I guessed that they were trying to go for a more "authentic" sound. Yet, they hadn't abandoned electronic percussion completely. The drummer had three different drum machines next to his actual kit, and they had been programmed to serve different functions, to add a second layer of rhythm to certain songs.

The band had also added a fourth member I had never seen before. A big guy with a bald head. He wore a leather vest with no shirt and cut-off jeans, and he had an extremely large bass. It was almost as tall as he was, and it looked exaggerated, almost like he was shrinking and regular instruments had become too big for him.

They opened with a psychedelic, instrumental jam that lasted about ten minutes. I could see why they had added the bass player and switched to real drums. The DiscoTents were adapting their sound to be more acid house, a new trend that was just hitting with The Stone Roses and Happy Mondays—sort of a dirtier dance sound, with more elements of funk and rock than most eighties dance acts. I kind of admired their hipness and ability to get on the bandwagon so quickly.

After the initial jam, The DiscoTents broke into a techno version of Gang of Four's "I Love a Man in a Uniform" that was actually pretty cool. Their own stuff wasn't as tight, however, and it made the show drag quite a bit. They sounded like they needed a lot of practice.

I started to feel bad for ignoring Jack on the bus ride over and totally stupid for not answering the phone. A heavy wind had started and was blowing dust and paper around. A lot of the trash went under the stage or blew out of sight, over the fence. I watched one piece of paper blow up and away and become so distant, so small in the open sky, it blended in and disappeared.

Jack came out of the bar toward the end of The DiscoTents' set, and he was slightly buzzed. He stood behind me. I turned and smiled.

"Thank you," I said.

"For what?" he asked.

"For blocking the wind. My ears were getting cold."

Jack smiled back.

The DiscoTents finished and they helped their roadie remove and change the equipment. I chewed on my tongue and could hardly stand still. The rest of the crowd was beginning to pack in. Looking behind me, I realized that the audience had gotten a lot larger. The girl who'd had the skin ripped from her hands at Like A Dog's NoWay gig was there among them, and I was pleased to see that her hands looked all right.

I was all excited by the time the lights went out and I heard the first chords. This show began like the last show, like all of their shows. It was a signal, and it made me feel safe, like I had gone somewhere that was mine. *I've come home . . .*

Tristan seemed particularly possessed with the desire to perform. He leaned his mike stand so far forward that I had to look up to see him, like I was in the front row at a movie theatre. His voice was soft, but newly assured, as if he had finally been convinced that what he was saying was the absolute truth. I wanted to reach out and touch his leg or grab his hand.

The set took no breaths, each song flowing into the next. Tristan kept refining the song list from gig to gig, and he even fine-tuned the songs so that everything appeared to spring from the same thought, just as you'd expect from a good album or movie—the sense that it was all made along the same linear groove without pauses or second guessing. My stomach was pressed against the stage, and the sound hummed through my body like little electric pulses bouncing between my nerves. I felt a tingling in my lips.

When the last song was finished, Tristan stepped back, letting his mike stand rest flat, and said, very low, "Thank you."

He walked off.

The lights came on. Everyone started milling about. I rushed back behind the stage to find Tristan. He wasn't anywhere I could see, but Eleanore, the guitarist, and Mike, the drummer, were behind the little house, standing around a steel tub full of ice and beer. Eleanore was fishing through it. "Where's Tristan?" I asked her.

"I think he's out in the garden," she said, pulling out a bottle of Corona. "How'd it look from the front row?"

"Fuckin' so cool," I said. "Thanks." I waved and dashed off to the garden.

The lights along the path had been turned off, I imagine to discourage people from going in. It was my guess that the owners of the place wanted us weirdo kids out of there as fast as possible, and knowing the way things usually worked, I knew they wouldn't have much luck.

I found Tristan sitting on the edge of the fountain, which had been shut off. He was trailing his fingers in the water, chasing the frightened fish. I watched him for a few long moments, sitting there, content. He seemed ageless. One of the fish brushed his finger, and he pulled his hand back with a giggle, splashing water everywhere. He looked around, laughing to himself, like someone who thinks

70

he's alone always does, as if he is looking to the imaginary people who share his sphere to show their approval, to laugh with him. He saw me off in the dark and jumped in surprise, almost falling into the water. He regained his balance and chuckled self-consciously.

"How long have you been there, Mason?" he asked, a tremor in his voice.

"Just got here," I lied.

"I was just looking at the fish," he explained.

I walked over to him. "Eleanore told me you were here," I said. "I wanted to tell you I've read *The Trial*. Like you suggested."

He swiftly moved aside to let me sit down. "Great, great! What'd you think?"

I took a seat next to him. "It was the best."

"Wasn't it?" Tristan laughed. "Kafka's such a total genius. I mean, *The Trial* was him. Nobody ever encouraged him to write. In fact, people like his father were always against it and would try to arrest him in his goals—but he could *see*. He could see beyond that gate, like K. at the end."

Tristan turned away. He tried to grab a fish in the water but only wrinkled his own reflection.

"If only I could write like that," he said, watching the rippling image. "To so perfectly, so creatively, set down all your experiences, everything you feel . . ."

The water settled, and Tristan's reflection became clear again. He turned from it as if disgusted.

"I think you can," I told him. "You say a lot to me."

"Thank you, Mason. That's very nice." He paused. His expression was almost blank, like he was chewing on something in his brain. "What'd you think of tonight?" he asked finally.

"It took me away. It was something else."

"It felt *weird*. These things are so hard. You've got to be so *set*. One crack in your confidence and these people . . . these people will swallow you. And if you do give them what they want, if your conviction holds, they come after you anyway. They *still* gulp you down. They feed on you, Mason. You can never let them have it all. You can never let them suck you dry. If they had their way, there'd be nothing left."

The moon was high, and its light rolled down on Tristan. He kicked a

pebble and watched it bounce across the garden floor. His delicate complexion, so pale, blended in with the whiteness of the light. For a moment, I could have sworn I was watching him fade. Then he turned on me suddenly, and this time I was startled. This time *I* nearly fell in the water.

"Mason, do you want to know my secret?" he asked.

I looked at him. I was confused.

"Do you?"

I nodded. "Yes," I said.

"I don't know what I'm doing. Every minute I am out there, it's just one guess after another. I'm thinking, 'It's only seconds before they see I'm a fake, that I'm a big joke, and laugh me right off the stage.'"

"I wouldn't laugh," I said. "You'd never be a joke to me."

Tristan tried to smile, but I don't think he really had it in him. So, we sat there awkwardly while he occupied himself with the fish once more.

We were saved by a crash and some shouting from back at the bar. A fight. Tristan and I got up and ran through the garden. Most of the people had formed a big circle around the perimeter of the dancefloor, and in the center of it there were about fifteen punks fighting. I saw a couple of bus boys and cooks in the brawl, as well. Right at the core of it all were Jack and Emery thrashing on one another, with Emery taking the most. I had a sinking feeling that they had probably started it.

When a bus boy put a skinhead through a window, the management decided they'd had enough. A Mexican guy with a thick moustache got up on the stage and shouted out that the cops had been called and anyone who was still here when they arrived would be arrested. Most of the observers ran for the door, knocking things over and yelling as they went. Eleanore came over and grabbed Tristan. "The gear's loaded up, and we're leaving," she said, "so come on. You can catch a ride, too, if you want, Mason."

"I better wait for Jack," I said. "But thanks."

"Suit yourself," she said, and took off.

Tristan put a hand on my shoulder. He leaned in to my ear and whispered, "See? It's just like I told you. They'll destroy you. Only you and I know. No one else ever will."

He ran off after Eleanore.

Jack, having heard the announcement, put one last good one into Emery's face. He pushed his way out of the fight zone, through those who really didn't care about being arrested, who actually got a kick out of this sort of thing. He made his way to me. We ran out of the place and were heading down the hill to catch the bus, when the cops arrived. One car broke from the pack and put their spotlight on us.

FALL
1990

9. SONGS FROM ANOTHER SEASON

The Garden was the last great hurrah of the summer. August went by like a melted strip of film, gumming up the wheels of its projector so that the movie goes by slower, slower, slower—and the air conditioner in the theatre is broken and you're forced to sweat and bake and live through each moment till the absolute end.

Labor Day was the day before school was supposed to start for all of those still in school, and it came like an exclamation point on the tail of the summer sentence. Walking down Melrose, it seemed like everyone from everywhere was in the street. I imagined it was a giant count-the-jellybeans game like they used to have in drugstore windows. Just how many can be packed into the space?

Skaters weaved in and out of traffic, and people crossed the street wherever they pleased, keeping the cars at a standstill. A few guys just gave up and got out, locking up their cars wherever they happened to be stuck. Goths and death rockers huddled in packs outside the record stores, showing off the rare singles and imports they had blown their summer savings on. I saw Eleanore selling some Like A Dog demos. I asked her where

Tristan was, and she said he had spent eighty bucks on a twelve-inch of The Smiths with Sandie Shaw and had rushed home to listen to it. She was try-ing to get enough money to buy a Joy Division *Ideal for Living* EP on col-ored vinyl and asked if I wouldn't mind being a dear and buying another tape, to which I graciously declined. She smiled and gave me a wink. Some guy asked her, "Hey, what's a chick like you doing playing guitar?" She started shouting at him and threatened to kick his ass, and I figured it was a good time to leave.

Channel 7 came down to film the Hollywood freaks for a fluff story like the ones they do on stoned frat jocks in Palm Springs on spring break. The camera crew climbed up on the roof of a trendy Italian restaurant so they could get a good view without getting too close to the animals. I stood across the street and watched as punks flipped them off or shouted the names of their favorite bands. I went over, zig-zagging through the stalled cars, and paced up and down in front of the restaurant, chanting, "Like A Dog! Like A Dog! Like A Dog!" I went faster and faster and was soon run-ning around in circles on the sidewalk, chasing my own tail. A technician came down. He asked me to leave and take my kinky worldview with me. Somebody spit on him, and I totally cracked up. He went back up to the roof without a word. As far as I know, we never made it on the air.

By this time, Burton was gone. He had actually decided to go to col-lege and had moved to the dorms at San Diego State. Steve was bummed and had started getting high even more often, though he was toning down to pot and doing less of the hard stuff. William and a clothes fag named Phil moved into Burton's room. Phil did drugs only if they were trendy, so he was on ecstasy a lot. William never seemed to do much at all.

All of this switching around reminded me of *our* coming move. The months were disappearing, and we only had four left. The thought of it scared me. Every time I had moved, it meant something different, and that wasn't always good.

I was born in Agoura, a community an hour out of L.A. I lived there till I was ten. When I was a kid, it was a real small town; when I left, it was practically a city. I didn't really notice the change, as I was growing up at the same time it was, and since we never realize we are getting bigger, I guess the growth of the town just seemed natural, too. Besides, I spent most of my time outside of the main drag, getting lost in the more rural areas, away from everything and everyone.

When my dad left, my mom got a job with a collection agency in Santa Monica. It was the first different place that I lived in, and there were no longer any big backyards or grassy mountains for me to hide in. There also wasn't my dad for my mom to fight with, and since she needed someone to take it out on, she turned her energy on me. That move was bad.

My second move was after graduation. Jack and I cashed in like all greedy kids leaving high school, getting money from relatives we didn't even know and using it to get our apartment. There was no one to yell at me anymore. That move was good.

I was frightened that there was a cycle to these things, that it would go bad-good-bad-good, this one falling on bad. This one miserably on bad.

Deciding to go home, I pushed my way through the crowd, slipping in and out of the tiny spaces between, making my way down the street. I stopped at the shop next to the comics store. It had been vacant for almost six months. The old man who had rented there had lost his liquor license for selling to a minor, subsequently losing his liquor store—a bad move. Now, finally, someone was coming in. *Sew What – Tailoring & Fabric*. I thought it was funny that they painted the window but hadn't any stock in the store. I thought that it would probably be a good move. Good to follow the bad.

The comics store was closed for the day. My boss didn't want to work a holiday, and he didn't trust any of us to run the place. We all got paid anyway because it was the law, and no one really thought of complaining.

When I got back to the apartment, Jack was coming down the stairs with Steve and his new roommates. Phil looked a little bit like a horse. The slope of his nose curved out like a slide and his jaw followed the same line. His hair was long, combed over to the right, hanging down to his chin, bleached blonde with red roots. His skin was splotchy with freckles, and he wore a denim jacket with zip-on leather cuffs and a zip-on leather back. The back was black with REVENGE printed in white. Phil didn't like me because I didn't get excited about clothes like he did, and I once told him an earring he was wearing—a dagger on the end of a chain—looked stupid. I wonder how he got along with Steve, the perennial jeans and T-shirt man.

"Everyone's going down to Venice for a bonfire and to get ripped," Jack said, excited. "You wanna go?"

I looked at Steve. He gave me a snotty look, like "What the fuck you think I care if you go?" Phil saw and snorted, and Steve socked him in the stomach. Of course, he didn't want Jack to know he was being a dick. William saw it all, though, and he just stared at me and smiled.

"I don't think so," I said. "I think I'd rather stay here."

"Okay," Jack said, sounding a bit down. "Don't know when I'll be back."

"All right."

"We'll miss you, Jailbate," Steve said, patting my head.

"Don't call us if you get arrested," Phil added.

I went up to the apartment. It was hot and smelled a little like dog food, so I opened a window. Somebody had put a little red dart—about an inch long—into the Guess? poster, right into the model's chin. She had been betrayed in her exhibition. Her over-excited audience had marked her.

I went into my room and put on Love and Rockets' "****(Jungle Law)," cranking the volume as high as it could go, and danced around on my mattress, throwing myself into the walls. By the end of the song, I was overheated and sweaty and fell back on my bed. I had been listening to Love and Rockets a lot lately, anxious to see David J at McCabe's the next day. I took the tickets out of my dresser drawer and looked at them, just to make sure that they were there, to check again that they were real, that the date was right, that nothing was off center.

David J was Love and Rockets' bassist. The band's first album, *Seventh Dream of a Teenage Heaven*, was the first music I had bought that could be classified in any way as punk, though it was pretty melodic and full of strings. Punk had exploded by then, and classifications were no longer strictly nailed down. I had been curious about the band because they had taken their name from the comic book *Love and Rockets*, which I liked very much. I was trading in a lot of Top 40 tapes at a used store and bought the album with the credit. It was my start, the opening door that let me into this place, saving me from loneliness and depression. There *were* knowing voices out there.

To cool off, I went and sat at the open window in the front room. I looked out over the houses to Melrose and the dark crowd moving back and forth down the street in a steady stream, unconstipated, unlike the cars in the street, unlike normal Los Angeles traffic. I drank a Bartles & Jaymes and ate crackers and reread some of *The Stranger*, which, apparently, Jack had been reading and left out on the table. I hoped he wasn't having trouble understanding it. He tries so hard to read stuff and get into things he knows are supposed to be quality, and he beats himself up if he doesn't get it right away. The thing I can't make him see is that nobody gets it right away, he's not any different from anybody else and is a lot smarter than he gives himself credit for. In the background, Love and Rockets sang about motorcycles and speed, wind and being free.

I fell asleep in the sun, my head pressed against the chipping paint on the windowsill. It was a peaceful sleep, except for a short dream—just a flash, really—of a hand pulling a gun out of a desk drawer.

Jack woke me up when he came in. It was dark. I ran my fingers across my forehead, over the large crease that ran from one side to the other, made by the windowsill. I felt terrible. There was a kink in my neck that I could hear squeaking in my head. Every time I moved, someone somewhere had left open a rusty gate.

Jack sat cross-legged on the floor behind me. "What've you been doing?" he asked, his voice timid. He was at that point of drunkenness when he became quiet and sad. I was glad he had come home, because it was best not to leave him alone when he was like that. He had once walked all over the city, up and down nameless streets at five in the morning wearing nothing but a pair of shorts. The guys had abandoned him at a party, and he got depressed. When I found him, he said he was "just trying to figure things out." It made me scared. He said, "I don't think the answer would have been very promising."

Again he asked me, "What've you been doing?"

"I fell asleep," I said. "How was Venice?"

I got up, taking the snacks and the book from the sill and putting them on the coffee table. I sat down next to him.

"You've been reading my book," he said.

"Yeah, skimming over some parts I liked. I read it before."

"I don't get it. Why'd he shoot that guy?" Jack picked the book up and examined the cover.

"He was just fed up," I said. "Everything was making him sick, beating on him. He had to do it. He needed the release. The gunshot was like a wake-up call to him—the big boom was his alarm—and it sends him on his way to finding out who he is."

"Is that what the Cure song is about? 'Killing an Arab?'"

"Yeah."

"Shit. Really."

"Yeah."

"It's messed up, though. He gets all in trouble 'cause that other guy's messing around with what he shouldn't. It's the other guy got the Arabs pissed."

"It works out in the end, though."

"No, it doesn't. He gets fucked. He gets executed! His goddamned head is chopped off."

"It's a more philosophical thing, Jack."

He sighed. "I guess," he said, "but I don't get it."

"How was Venice?" I asked again, trying to change the subject before he got frustrated and down on himself. Camus wasn't the best author to discuss with him while he was drunk.

"F'king cool, man," he giggled. "The fire was *so* big. We listened to The Beastie Boys and Black Flag, and Steve and a couple other guys got so

blasted they went out into the goddamn water. In their underwear! They went goddamn swimming. *Nobody* swims at goddamn Venice beach, *especially* not in their underwear. Too much motherfuckin' trash."

He fell over on me, laughing, and I laughed, too. He rolled onto his back and clutched his stomach, still laughing hard. "Oh, shit, I can't breathe," he gasped. "Ohhhhh, man."

Finally, Jack calmed himself. He lay there, panting heavily. He must have looked at the Guess? poster, because he said, "That wuss Phil put a dart in our poster. Had it in his pocket. I clocked him in the shoulder and wouldn't let him have it back. Steve thought it was funny, so I belted him, too. Puds."

I took a cracker off the table and ate it. "You want anything to eat, Jack?" I asked.

"No," he said, and then suddenly sat up. "Hey, NoWay's having a no-cover night for Labor Day with Church & Skate and On Your Last Nerve. Why don't we go?"

"Sounds cool," I said.

We walked down there, neither of us saying much. Jack watched his feet, watched each step, and I wondered what the distance between the ground and his eyes looked like to him. Was it like driving a long road with another car in front of you, keeping your pace, and no matter how far you went, you never got any closer to it? Or did it seem like nothing at all, no different than the distance to the tip of his nose? We passed a van stopped at a light, and when the light changed, the van squealed its tires and back-fired. I waited for Jack to let out a shout, but he didn't even notice.

It was so late when we arrived at the club, there was no line outside. We had missed Church & Skate completely, and On Your Last Nerve was halfway through its set. NoWay was packed, and the pit was raging hard. Jack felt like slamming, and I told him to go ahead, I'd hang at the back. He bounded out into the middle of it, and I saw his fists pumping up and down above everybody. I felt sorry for the poor guys who would end up on the bottom of them. Then again, a lot of them would be skaters, and I really couldn't have cared less whether those guys got pounded or not.

I went to the bar and ordered a Coke. I sat on one of the stools and swiveled around to watch the stage. The guy who had insulted Tristan at the beginning of the summer was at the microphone. A song had just ended in a burst of guitar feedback and bass drum, and the band was at a pause. The singer was breathing heavy. He growled into the head of the mike. "This song is called 'Gainwaves.'"

There was a rush of abused guitar, and the singer screamed,

> *Moneyyyyy!*
> *I work, I toil, I collect!*
> *Moneyyyyy!*
> *I spend, I buy, I'm in debt!*

I shook my head. There was very little originality in thrash anymore.

I turned back to the bar to have my drink. I noticed a picture on the wall I hadn't seen before. It was of a boy sitting at a desk. On the desk, there were some scattered books, a sandwich, a glass of milk, and in the center, an open composition book. The boy had one hand on top of the empty paper, and he was holding a pencil. The other hand was below the desk, out of sight. The boy was looking at the viewer. His face was sad, but not really imploring. The caption above his head said, "Are You **Sure** He's Not Thinking About Suicide?" I thought the other hand was probably reaching for a gun.

10. LOOKING GLASS GIRL

Melrose was naked after that. Everyone was back at work and back at school and didn't have much time for hanging out anymore. All the leaves had abandoned the tree.

The comics shop was real slow during the day, and my boss sent me out to run errands a lot. I took my time because he never questioned me, assuming a good job didn't go quickly and it was better if I went slow and didn't screw it up. It had cooled off considerably since July, and I now liked meandering along the streets and smelling the air.

Coming back, I passed by Sew What. They had been open a few weeks now, and it seemed they were doing okay. I figured the fall wouldn't be too bad for a shop of their kind. Maybe a lot of fabric was sold for Halloween costumes.

It's normal for me to look in stores as I pass by them. You never know who you'll see or what might be on display, and when you're all alone, people-watching can aid the illusion of being some great power, of being a separate observer to the crowd. On this day, looking in Sew What, I saw her.

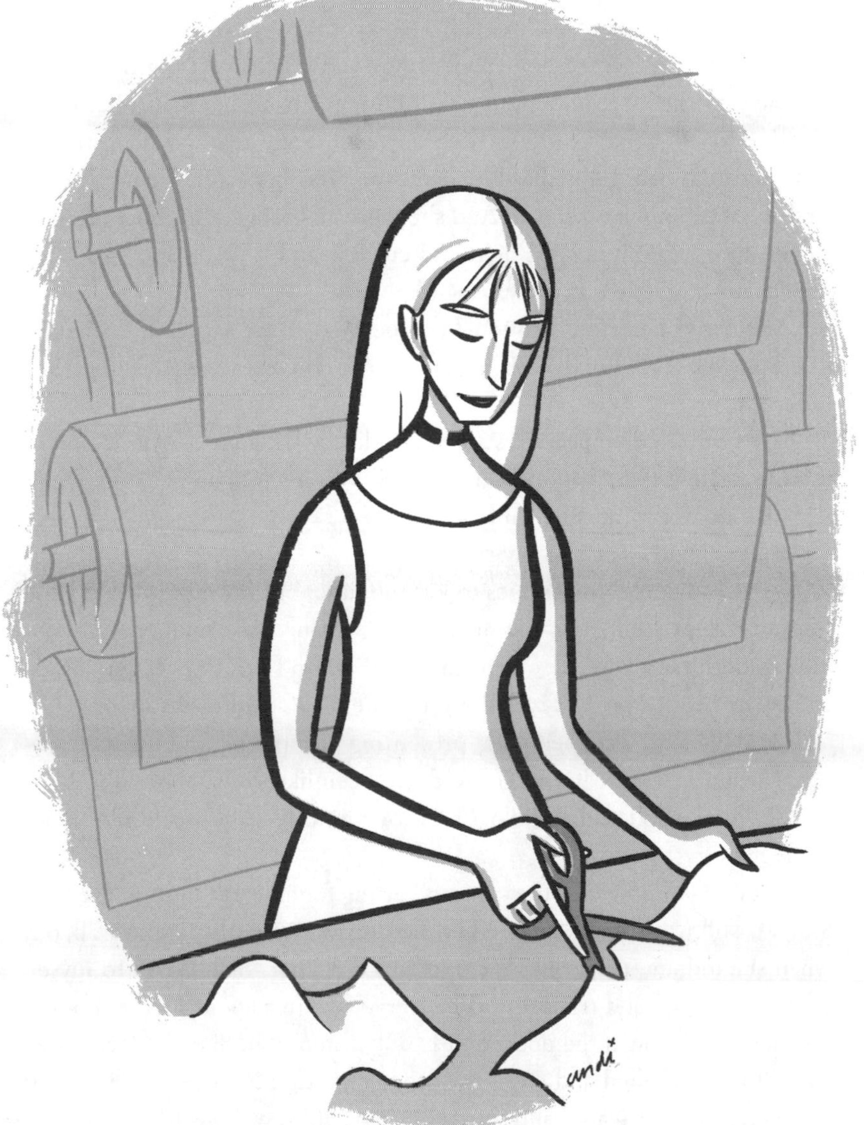

She was standing behind the counter, cutting a piece of cloth. I stopped at the door, in front of her, because I had to take more than a quick look. Everything around her fell away, and she stood there amongst the blur, soft but sharp with detail. Her eyes were down, spying the line that she cut. Her hair was long and blonde and silky, and it was hanging in her face, to the side, floating just a millimeter from her skin like it was afraid to touch it and disturb the delicacy. Her face was long with a straight nose and pink-laced lips that blended away into her natural complexion. And she was hourglass shaped. And she wore an orange sundress that went to her knees. And it hugged tight and cut low and it was made of a yarn-like fabric—knit, like a sweater.

She lifted her face. Around her neck was a brown leather choker, like a cat collar, closed with a gold snap. Her eyes left the line. She looked at me.

My stomach disappeared, sucked up like a washcloth caught in a bath-tub drain. I felt like I had a chunk of tinfoil on my tongue.

She looked at me. She smiled politely.

I waved and went into my store.

I tried to read some comics to kill the time, but my mind wasn't in it. Instead, I kept seeing her—her angled face, strong nose, and straight hair. Her smooth neck rose up out of the band around her throat, curving up to display her features. It was there for me, this sculpture, supported by an invisible hand, a cupped palm presenting her to my mind for its pleasure. I wondered what her voice would've been like, how it would've been had she spoke and said, "Hello," and for me to feel the world die under my feet.

When I got off work, the sun was setting for an early autumn evening. She was still working, so I waited in the doorway and planned to walk out when she did and play it like a coincidence. I sang "Sick Boys" to myself to stay occupied and tried not to be nervous. After about half an hour, I saw her step through the door, and I took a step, too. She was facing me, about to spin around and go in the other direction. Our eyes were about to meet, but I got scared and went the opposite way as swiftly as I could, feeling stupid when I tripped over a high crack in the sidewalk.

Over the next week, I told myself to walk slow when passing by her work, so she could see me, but I'd always get panicky and go by real fast and awkward.

Jack came by on Thursday to bring me dinner. We sat on the curb in front of the store, and he noticed that I couldn't help looking over my shoulder to see her.

"What's going on?" he asked.

"Nothing," I said.

"No, I don't believe that," he said. "You've been fidgety lately. And giddy. It's sick. Tell me what's going on."

"I . . . nothing."

I flashed a look to the store window. Jack craned his neck around to see. She was measuring some silk from a roll mounted on the wall.

"Ahhhh . . ." Jack said. "A new girl, is it? I should've seen the signs. Your cheeks get all glittery."

"They do not," I insisted. "You know so *much*."

"I do, Mason. Little glitter boy. Is *she* for whom your palms sweat?"

"Nnn—"

"Ahhhh . . ."

"Okay, they're mildly moist."

Jack smiled. "What's her name?"

"I don't know."

"What? Haven't you talked to her?"

"No *way*, dude."

"Come on!"

"I haven't."

"I don't believe it."

"Quit torturing me. I haven't."

"Well, let's fix that . . ."

Jack got up and untied the bandanna on his head.

"What're you doing?" I asked.

"I suddenly have an urgent need to purchase some material," he said, feigning a lisp.

"Oh, no, Jack, Jack, Jack . . ."

He went inside the store and went up to her. She greeted him, and I heard him say real loud, "Do you have anything softer than this?"

Jack held out his bandanna, and she felt it. Her hands looked so small compared to his, and so smooth and white, like seashells. She and Jack talked for about a minute, and she took the bandanna into the back of the store. Jack looked out the doorway and stuck his tongue out at me. I flipped him off. I wanted to kill him, he made me so nervous.

She came back out carrying a couple squares of cloth. She handed them to Jack, and he felt them between his fingers. He nodded his head, gave her some money, and came back outside. I looked past him in utter fright, scared that she might make the connection, realize what was going on. She was going about her duties as if he had never been there.

Jack sat down next to me. "Got me some fancy new headdresses," he said. "Softer, for those days when I need that extra comfort."

"I can't believe you," I said. "I oughta smash your head."

"I suppose you want to know her name, huh?"

"What is it?"

"Forget it. You gotta find out on your own. *Haaaaa!*"

Jack jumped up, slapped me on the back of my head, and left. "I'll never forgive you!" I shouted after him. He shrugged, knew I would, didn't worry about it at all.

Now that the question of her name had been introduced to me, now that the curiosity had been injected into my head, it became the thing I *had* to know most. I wondered what it could be, ran through a list of favorite names, classical romantic names, names of other people I knew and could call to memory. None of them seemed to fit. None of them were right. I would have met her after work, asked her, just so I would know, just to get the answer, but it was Thursday and I worked later than she did. There was no chance.

I decided to wait until Sunday and not ask Jack. I didn't want to give him the satisfaction. Besides, I knew he wouldn't tell me anyway. I'd just be humbling myself for no reason. Unfortunately, she didn't work Sunday, and I couldn't take it any longer. I broke down and *begged* Jack, said, "Please, please, tell me."

He laughed loudly and said, "No."

So, Monday, I made a special trip in the afternoon. I walked across the street from the store, hid behind a lamppost until I saw her and was sure

she was there. Then, in the evening, I went back just before she was supposed to go home. This time, I waited around the side of the building so I
could cross her path on the corner and turn with her. Chewing a piece of
gum for good breath, I listened for the little bell on their door, and after
two false alarms, it was finally her.

She reached the corner before I did, and I ended up coming in behind
her. I stepped loudly, though, and she glanced over her shoulder at me. I
followed her at her own pace across the intersection, unsure of what to do.
I thought maybe I had blown it by not saying anything right away and
should abandon the whole idea. I just about swallowed my gum when *she*
turned around. "Aren't you friends with the big guy who was looking for
soft stuff to wear on his head?" she asked.

Her voice was like taking a bath in a waterfall. It came to me so sweet
and easy, as if soothed over to me, nudged by her tranquil green eyes. I
wanted to fall down and cry.

"Yes," I said, barely audible.

"And you work at the comic book place, right?"

"Yes," I said, even lower than the last time. I was scared she didn't
hear me, so I cleared my throat. "Yes."

Either she slowed down a bit or a sudden rush of wind pushed me,
because I was suddenly walking next to her.

"My name is Jeane," she said,
extending her hand.

I knew. Now, I
knew. It was so
clear. Jeane. I
could see it, knew
how it was spelled.
It had to be that
way. That was all
it could be.

"I'm Mason,"
I said, taking her hand.
"Pleased to meet you."

Her grip was light. Her skin

was like the surface of a marble—the kind with the little flare inside.

We walked a few steps in silence. "Live around here?" I asked, unable to think of anything more original.

"Yeah," she said. "Westwood."

I nodded.

Jeane turned at the next corner, and I did, too. "My car is down here," she said. "You going up this way?"

"No," I said. "I'm just a lemming. I follow whoever is in front of me."

"Straight to your death, huh?"

"In a manner of speaking . . ."

It *was* kind of like I was rushing to my own destruction. There's always a cliff in love. That's why you fall into it. You land and are smashed flat. That's why they call it a crush.

She stopped at a little blue Dodge with a New Order sticker in the back window. "This is it," she said.

"Nice."

"Thanks." She smiled. "See you later, Mason. It was good to finally meet you."

"Yeah, you too. Hope to do it again sometime."

Jeane laughed and climbed into her car. I stood on the curb and watched her drive out of sight. I imagined my hand waving to her, long after she was gone. My head lilted to one side, like I was a puppy who knew of nothing else to do.

I took a walk around the block. There was an initial surge of excitement, and I got all buggy. The Mary Chain's "Head On" was running though my head, and I felt like jumping around and screaming. Then I sort of took a step back and felt foolish. I was being pretty presumptuous assuming that just because I talked to her it would mean anything. I mean, who was I to suddenly insinuate myself upon her life? I had no idea what she had or did outside of Sew What. How could I assume that she didn't have a whole circle of friends? That she didn't have a boyfriend? With my luck, it was almost certain she would. You could line up every girl in the world and tell me I could have my pick of all but one, because outside of that single exception they were all available, and I'd zero right in on the one with a boyfriend. Every time.

No, I had no right to think I could have any place in her life, that I could even enter it. I should've forgotten the whole thing.

But I didn't.

Every night that week, I met her again and walked her to her car. I figured I was being a total nuisance, and so I was shocked when Jeane came into the store looking for me on Thursday night. I was waiting for the new books and basically figured I would have to forego the walk. The ding-dong sensor on the door announced her entrance. She was smiling, and she said, "What's up?" She was chewing spearmint gum, and it made her breath cool.

"What're you doing in here?" I asked. "Don't you know it could be very dangerous for you?"

"How so?"

"Some of the guys who come in here have never seen a girl like you so close. They might freak."

"I'd better watch out then," she laughed. It was a very quiet laugh, coming out just underneath her smile. "How come you weren't outside?"

"Thursdays we work late." Damn Thursdays suck.

"Oh, I was beginning to think you didn't like me anymore. I would've been sad."

"Weep no more. What they said was just a lie."

"Well, I guess that's that, then."

"I'm sorry. Would it make you feel better if I told you my heart was broken, too?"

"It is?"

"Like the bones of a man tossed from a 12th story window."

"That's broken."

"You bet."

"Good-night, Mason."

"So long, Jeane."

She left, the bell ringing again, ushering out the memory of minty gum.

Putting out the comics was dull and tedious. I resented the task because it was responsible for making me miss my time with her. Kevin and Roger, the goons I worked with, were excited because some dumb superhero comic had The Punisher guest-starring in it. I was suddenly embarrassed that Jeane had seen me in such a den of social inadequacy, and I was mad at Kevin and Roger for being walking proof of the joke I had made to her. I wanted to avoid guilt by association. I wanted to kick their faces in.

When I left, I felt hot and was glad that the night had a crisp wind. Someone called my name, and I was again shocked to see Jeane outside a yogurt shop across the road, waving at me. "Mason, over here!"

I sprinted across the street and was a bit out of breath when I got to her. Jeane was holding the remains of a vanilla yogurt with Reese's crumbs on it. "Want the rest?" she asked.

"No thanks," I said. "What are you still doing here?"

"I decided it was my turn to wait. Now I know what you go through every night. No fun, is it?"

"Ah, things make up for it."

"Like what?"

I just laughed.

We walked together, and when we got to the corner where we normally turned, she kept going. "You park somewhere else today?" I asked.

"Uh-uh," she said. "Since the tables are turned, I'm walking *you* home."

"This is a little unexpected . . ."

"Don't worry. I'll ignore it if it's a mess."

When we got there, the outside walls of the building looked filthy. I thought it was funny I had never noticed before that the stucco was supposed to be white, but the dirt made it the color of peanuts. I hoped she meant it about being able to ignore a mess.

Inside, however, I was happy and a little proud, because it was my place and I loved it. Jack was there, looking over the *L.A. Weekly* and smelling like paste. He got up off the couch and walked over to Jeane with his hand outstretched. There were a couple of splashes of white on it, but he said, "It's all right. The glue's dry."

She laughed and shook his hand. "Jeane," she said.

"Jack. Nice to meet you. Sorry I didn't properly introduce myself last time." He shot a self-satisfied smile in my direction. The schmuck had lied to me.

"You're not wearing one of your new bandannas."

Jack felt the dirty blue cloth on his head. "No, ma'am," he said. "Save those for when I'm on social engagements. They go more with my stepping-out clothes."

We laughed. Jack rolled up his newspaper and hit me on the head. "I'm going to jam down to Steve's and see what's running tonight, okay?" He winked and slipped out the door.

"He seems nice," Jeane said.

"Yeah, he is." I knew he wouldn't really be going to Steve's, but hanging out around the corner or grabbing something to eat, letting me have my time.

Jeane looked around the room. She laughed when she saw the band-aid we put over the model's chin on the Guess? poster. I offered her a drink or some food, but she declined. She seemed both amused and genuinely interested as she made her way through the apartment, checking everything out. I opened the door to my room and put some Replacements on. Jeane came in after me. She looked at my Smiths "This Charming Man" poster, with the fresh-faced boy dead on the ground, staring at his own reflection in a puddle, like Narcissus, but his eyes permanently closed. Like sleeping close to a lover.

"This is cool," she said. "Where'd you get it?"

"A shop in Venice. They have a lot of old stuff."

She also noticed my Social Distortion poster. "They're my favorite band," I told her. "I'm going to see them this Sunday."

"Really? You must be excited."

"Yeah, you could say that."

The message the poster always gave to me—action is inevitable; *take it!*—was particularly frightening in these circumstances.

Jeane decided it was late and asked if I'd excuse her, she needed to go home. I told her only if she let me walk her to her car. "I know it defeats the purpose of you coming here, reversing the roles and all," I said, "but I'm the host now, and it's only polite."

She laughed and touched me on the arm. "Of course," she said.

It was a really dark night and the streetlights created circles along the road, like a strip of candy dots. I wanted to peel one off and offer it to

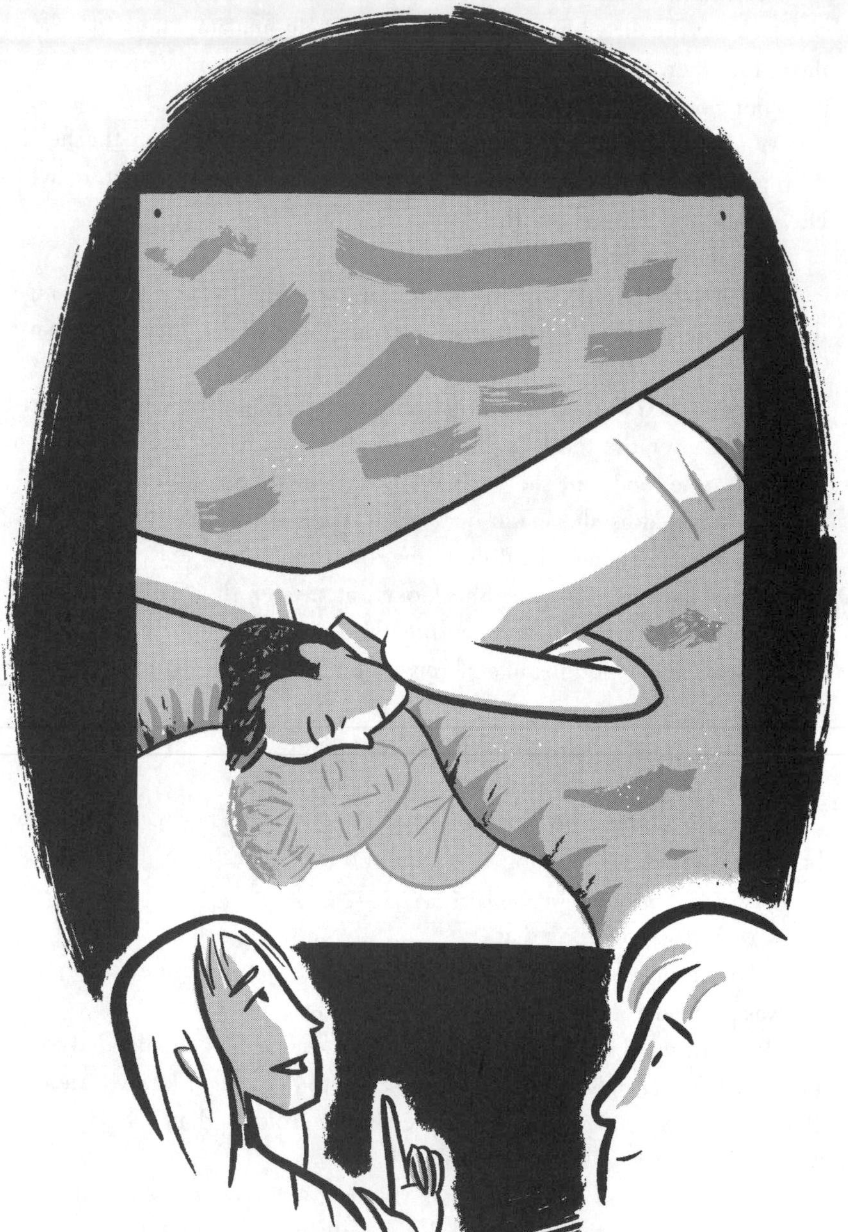

her—the tradition of giving candy amplified to a grotesque level. I considered telling her this idea, but then thought better of it. I didn't want to seem too silly, and besides, my stomach was full of erratic excitement and my nerves were jangly. I thought I'd probably bite off my tongue if I tried to speak, and then I'd sputter the words with a severe lisp while squirting tongue blood all over her, and that wouldn't create the right kind of impression.

I opted for a piece of gum, and I offered Jeane a piece. My words were thick, coming out like slugs trying to slither through a straw. My lungs felt empty of air.

"Thank you," she said.

I didn't speak the rest of the way. I figured it was better not to make a fool of myself, and besides, I needed to be giving myself a pep talk, build my confidence. What I was going to do had never worked for me before, and I wanted so bad not to screw it up again. I imagined kissing her under one of the streetlights' big circles. I wanted to run back to my apartment and rip the Social D. poster down off the wall and tell it action wasn't necessary, that you get hurt . . . but it wouldn't understand.

Finally, we got to her car. She went over to her door and opened it. "Good-bye, Mason," she said. "See you Monday."

Well, that's it, I thought. She doesn't expect to see me until Monday. Doesn't *want* to. She's just being nice to me.

But I caught myself. I had grabbed the excuse and was going to run, but I remembered how Jack had left the apartment to give me time and the guy on the poster kicking down the door, and if I couldn't do it for myself, I should at least do it for them—but I should do it primarily because I needed to, because I would never be satisfied with myself or my life if I didn't just *try*.

"Hey," I said. "If you're not busy sometime, do you think we could go out . . . and do something?"

"You mean like a date?"

"Yeah . . . I guess."

"Sure. It'll be fun."

"Okay. Wow. I'll call you."

"All right."

"Okay . . . bye."

"Wait. Wouldn't my number be helpful?"

"Oh, yeah." I laughed.

Jeane grabbed my wrist and pulled my arm up. She took a pen out of her purse and very gently wrote her phone number on the back of my hand. It tickled, and I watched the pen's movements intensely. It was very quiet between us, very still. I could hear her breathing, and I'm sure she could hear me, too. She let go, and my hand floated in mid-air for a second. I looked down at the number, her very own writing etched into my skin.

"Be sure not to wash it off."

"No problem. I have really bad hygiene."

"Don't start giving me second thoughts."

"Oh, right. Can't show you the real me until at least the third date."

Jeane wrapped her arms around me, and for a too brief second, hugged me tight. I felt her shoulder blades, her hair on my face. I was flabbergasted. I couldn't move. Like an idiot, I just stood there, smelling her flowery shampoo, not saying anything, barely even returning the embrace.

She stepped back and looked into my eyes. She was smiling.

"Good-night, Mason," she said.

For a moment, all the lights in heaven blinked.

11. WONDERFUL WOMAN

I wore a black turtleneck. On the bus, I pulled it up over my face and looked at my reflection in the window, mimicking James Dean.

I was going to pick Jeane up at her apartment, which was kind of ridiculous since she would end up driving anyway. I just wanted to do everything right, to make it all romantic. As the guy, *I* was supposed to pick *her* up—besides, I wanted to see where she lived.

The bus dropped me off

one street away from her building. I stood on the corner, afraid to move, in the center of a streetlight all by myself. It made me nervous. I felt like I was under interrogation–scrutinization. My hands were heavy, like I was wearing gloves of thick rubber.

A building across the way had a rosebush in front of it. I ran over to it and twisted one of them off. The effort mangled the stem, and I thought, "Oh, God, this looks real cheap," so I threw it in the gutter. I noticed some lights on in the building's windows and took off before anyone saw me destroying their plants.

Jeane's building was three stories high and white. She lived on the second floor. There was no open court, all the apartments and hallways were completely contained inside the structure. Her doorbell and peephole were in a box on the door, at about head level. A clear strip of plastic across the top housed a piece of cardboard with her name–JEANE–typed on it, and there was a flower drawn in black pen after it.

I pressed my ear to the door. I could hear some music–The Sundays–but no other sign of life. No human movement. I didn't have a watch and it suddenly occurred to me, "I may be late. I may be early. What if she isn't ready? What if she's been ready forever?" I hastily pressed the doorbell, my hand shaking.

The door opened. Jeane smiled. "Hello." Her hair was up on her head in a single knot. She was wearing a black dress that went down to her knees, black stockings, and shiny, black, pointed shoes. "Come in."

I stepped inside. The room smelled like flowers. It was small, and it appeared that she had gone to great care to pick out the furniture and delicately place it so as to get the most out of the space. There was a glass coffee table and a silky blue couch, the kind that after you've sat on it, there's a mark indicating where you've been. In the far corner were a TV and a stereo and small bookshelf. On the wall was a framed poster for New Order's *Power, Corruption, & Lies* album and a Maxfield Parrish print. I thought if I threw a pebble into the center of the room, it would send ripples out across the entire space and prove it to be only an illusion.

"I still have to do my make-up," she said. "You can watch if you like."

"Am I early?" I asked.

"No, right on time."

There was a Bullwinkle clock on the wall. The numbers were in reverse order, and the hands moved backwards. It said it was six o'clock exactly.

"It's so hard for me to keep track of time sometimes," she said. "The clock seemed funny when I bought it, but now it just bugs me."

Her bathroom was in two parts—a small room with a toilet and shower, and an area in the hallway by the closet with a mirror and sink. I sat down against a closed door and watched her as she applied powder and blush to her cheeks. She looked at me in the mirror and asked, "So, what's the plan?"

"Well, I thought dinner first, since, you know, chicks give top priority to their stomachs."

"Oh, of course," Jeane laughed. She brushed on the last bit of blush and put it away. She took up a toothbrush and ran it along her eyebrows, making sure each hair was in place. Then, she took her eyeliner, pursed her lips, and twisted the pencil back and forth between them as if they were a pencil sharpener. She leaned in toward the mirror, arching her back like a crisp wave of water, and opened her eyes wide, running the pencil along the lower lids, the tip of her tongue poking out of the corner of her mouth. When she finished, her tongue slowly rolled back in. She glanced at me in the mirror, again, and smiled.

"Having fun?"

"Loads."

And I was.

She closed one eye and put a line across the edge of the lid. Then the other. She did it effortlessly, almost carelessly, just a whip across and that's that.

Mascara followed, her hand applying it with

little flicks of the wrist, her mouth wide open. Then, she took a needle and began poking it between the lashes.

"Yikes! What are you *doing*?"

"Getting out the clots, what's it look like?"

"I don't know . . . just don't poke yourself."

Jeane laughed. "Why do boys think it's all so dangerous?"

"It is, it is!"

"Please, Mason, I've been doing this since I was eleven, and not one injury yet, okay?" She smirked at me in the mirror and went on with it.

When she was done with her eyes, she moved to her lips, rubbing a streak of wine red lipstick over each lip. She sucked on them, spreading the paint. Then she looked in the mirror, pressing her tongue against the inside of her lips, touching up the spots that weren't covered, cleaning up the excess with Kleenex. She looked over at me, her tongue making her bottom lip fat. "Yuh wike dis?" she asked.

"Intensely."

And I did.

I felt I was being allowed to watch some secret, private thing. Something totally alien to me and completely female. I couldn't understand how the machine worked, but just watching it was enough to know it was incredible. It was perhaps the single most beautiful thing I had ever witnessed.

And the sexiest.

It was as if Jeane was letting me glimpse all of her.

She finished up her lips and leaned into the mirror one more time, checking everything over. A quick tug on the knot of hair caused it to fall, the hair splashing down around her face. She looked at me in the mirror. "How's that?"

"Amazing. Do it again."

Jeane giggled and turned around. The lights of the mirror created a halo around her, made her magical. She took a black and gray checkered suit jacket off the doorknob of the bathroom door and slipped it on. "All set," she said.

Since Jeane lived in Westwood, we decided we might as well eat and go to a movie in town and then decide where to go from there. We ate at

Johnny Rocket's. I ordered a double cheeseburger. Jeane was making me so nervous, I ate the burger in two bites, and then had to sit there feeling foolish and disgusting. Jeane just laughed at how quickly it disappeared. I ordered a vanilla malt to pass the time with, rather than just having to watch her eat, but I was too full to properly drink it. I only took a couple of sips and then sat there with the straw in my mouth, fondling it with my tongue.

The Mann Bruin down the street was showing *Welcome Home, Roxy Carmichael*, but we had about half an hour before it started, so we went to Penny Lane to look at the used CDs. Jeane found The Primitives' "Out of Reach" single. "Tracey Tracey is so cool," she said. "New Order's my top band, but I *really* like bands with female lead singers–Transvision Vamp, Go-Go's, Sundays, Shonen Knife . . ."

"Bow Wow Wow?" I asked.

"*God*, of course," she replied. "I remember when MTV just started, they were all over it."

"And on 'MV3.' You remember that show? They always played Duran Duran, Adam Ant, Golden Earring. I didn't like all the music at the time, but I didn't have MTV. All the other kids did, and it was necessary that you watch videos of *some* kind."

"My older sister liked Journey and Styx and all that, so she wouldn't let me watch 'MV3.' We shared a room and kept fighting over the radio. I'd switch it to KROQ every time her back was turned. I'd drive her insane playing my Madness 'One Step Beyond' 45 on repeat for hours."

"The first seven-inch I ever bought was Appolonia 6, 'Sex Shooter.' I was in the thick of puberty and it drove my hormones bananas. I still have it. It cracks people up when I pop it on."

"I'll bet." She chuckled.

"I mean, jeez, thirteen years old and Prince and Madonna were just hitting it big. Every girl in my junior high was wearing lace shirts and underwear–that was it. It was a good time to be a boy."

"Oh, you would have loved me," she said. "I wanted to be Annabella Lwin so bad that, in an act of sheer rebellion, I took scissors and a razor to my hair and gave myself a mohawk. My mother made me wear a scarf over my head until it grew out, which, of course, I took off as soon as I got to school. This was Woodland Hills and all the little new wave girls thought I was the coolest."

"If they could only see you now. So proper . . ."

"In my heart, I'm still last of the Mohicans. Besides, my boyfriend's a punk rocker."

I almost swallowed my tonsils.

"Your boyfriend?" My voice cracked. "You have a boyfriend?"

"Well, if you play your cards right," she said, spinning on her heel and going to the counter to buy the Primitives, leaving me standing in the most intense state of elation humanly possible. I felt like jumping up and bouncing the moon off my head like a big soccer ball.

Throughout the movie, I had a terrible time. I wanted to turn and just stare at Jeane, look at her face outlined by the dancing pictures on the screen. I'd glance at her out of my periphery, praying for just a second, just a little bit of time that she wouldn't notice. She seemed to be enjoying the movie, because she only looked straight ahead and didn't pay me any attention at all. So, I extended my stares, a second at a time, until I was up to about ten seconds.

Finally, I lingered too long and she caught on to what I was doing. She glanced at me for only a moment before turning back to the film, a smile on her face. She reached over and put her hand on top of my hand. Her fingers slid between mine and squeezed them tight for just a fraction of an instant, grinding her fingers' bones against the bones of mine, and then released. A surge of energy washed through my pipes, hot and fast. Her hand was soft and her veins bulged from the effort of holding. I felt my own veins crushed beneath her palm.

I sat back in my chair. From that moment on, the movie passed something like a speeding car on the freeway. A streak of color in my line of vision for a split-second, then nothing, not even a real memory of what type of car it was. It wasn't important. Not like her hand on my hand. Not like the smile curling her lips.

When the closing credits began, I became afraid. I didn't know what to do, if I should slide my hand out or wait for her to take hers off or if maybe I should try to hang on and walk out holding it. I tried to see if Jeane was starting to move or was waiting for me. She watched the credits contentedly. I worried my hand would become clammy with nervousness and gross her out and decided I'd better make a move real fast.

I turned my hand around carefully and felt my way back through her fingers. This time, *I* squeezed. Jeane didn't look at me, but she squeezed back. Her smile was fighting to become more pronounced. She was holding it in, but she couldn't keep it from dancing in her eyes.

We left the theatre hand in hand. I wanted to lean over and rest my head on her shoulder, but was scared I would break the moment. When I was a kid, I once threw a half-filled carton of ice cream through our kitchen window. The ice cream had been really hard, and I could not scoop any out. I got angry and hucked it. As soon as it hit the glass, the whole thing split in several directions. I was amazed by how easily the glass had shattered. I quivered at the thought that this, too, could be that delicate. Something built so easily couldn't have a very strong foundation. I could see it exploding with a loud bang, like a bullet from a gun.

"What a cool movie," Jeane said. "Didn't you think so?"

"Oh, yeah," I said.

"I wish when I was that age I had painted my walls black and had black carpet, and had a little boat to go to when I wanted to get away. A place where I could be all by myself and create my own home, have my own family."

"That would be nice."

She swung our hands back and forth and laughed. "It would be *perfect*," she said. "A place all our own."

I wondered how the "my" had become "our."

"Look," I said, "let's not go home just yet. Let's get in your car and drive up PCH. There's a beach up there called *El Matador* where you have to walk down a mountain path to get to the water, and there's never anyone there. It'll just be you and me and no one else."

Jeane turned away. She licked her lips, and her tongue pushed them into a grin, a big grin, the grin that had been fighting to come out since the movie.

"Okay," she said. "That would be lovely."

Jeane drove us up the highway. We had the windows rolled down and the air coming in was cold. It made my teeth chatter.

She played 808 State, and I rested my head against the doorframe, letting the rush of the car whip my bangs back. The speakers were down in the door, and I could feel the beat through the metal banging lightly against my temple. The world going by me seemed almost confrontational, the telephone poles and streetlamps coming at me between the eyes, appearing to almost strike before disappearing behind. I imagined a man rushing out from the bushes, running into the headlights with his mouth open and arms stretched out in front of him like he was trying to stop us. He disappeared just before we smashed him. I imagined it was me.

The Hawaiian king keeping watch over Zuma waved to us as we went by. I sat up and watched the road more carefully. *El Matador* was just a few miles down and its turnoff was hard to see, one of the reasons why it was never very crowded. I spotted it and told Jeane to turn.

A two-foot high gate was blocking the entrance, locked for the night. "Park on the embankment a little bit down," I said, and she did.

We walked from the car to the gate and easily stepped over. The parking lot was all brown gravel. Jeane giggled at the way it crunched under her feet.

"This is meant to be a campground," I told her. "You park and stick a couple bucks in a box over there, and some camping cop checks to see if you paid. If you didn't, he fines you. I don't think it's running anymore, though. Or, at least, business is slow."

From the edge of the hill, we could see the waves crashing on the beach. I picked up a rock and threw it. It fell well short of the water, landing noiselessly somewhere on the sand. I remembered telling Jeane that I was a lemming, but the ocean seemed to promise so much more than that.

The initial trail was a dirt path that wove a crooked pattern down the mountain. It was a fairly clear night, well-lit by the moon, but we still held hands to keep from slipping, somehow thinking the simple grasp of the other would hold us up. The path met up with some wooden steps that creaked when stepped on. Jeane stumbled on one and fell against me. We looked in each other's faces and laughed. "Almost lost me there," she said. "You need to be more careful."

"Sorry, won't let it happen again."

We stepped on the last step and huddled close together. Jeane counted down, "One . . . two . . . three . . ." and we leaped off, sinking down into the sand. It seeped into my Vans, so I kicked them off and carried them the rest of the way.

I removed my leather jacket and laid it down on the sand. "You sure we should sit on it?" Jeane asked.

"We won't hurt it," I said. "Don't worry."

We sat down, but not too close. We stopped holding hands. Suddenly, it seemed we had both become frightened of the other, afraid to touch. I fingered the sand, spinning a whirlpool pattern into it. A seagull was digging for something in the soft mud about ten feet way. Salt filled our throats and noses.

"How did you meet Jack?" Jeane asked.

I thought it was a strange question to come out all of a sudden like that, but then realized that she was trying to get the conversation going again.

"We were in high school," I answered. "We had health class together. We both sat in the back. I didn't have any friends and didn't talk to anybody. I just did my homework and hoped not to be bothered. One day, Jack hadn't done the homework and asked if he could copy off of me. He was so big, I was scared to say no.

"Well, it wasn't the last paper he copied from me. Pretty soon, I was whispering the answers to him during the tests. It was actually kind of frustrating because he'd always get better grades than me. He'd just shrug and say, 'Guess sometimes I know better than you is all.' Then, during one test, the teacher heard us. She came to take our papers, but Jack wouldn't let her take mine. He said, 'I asked him for the answer and he told me to shut the hell up. He didn't do anything.' I was pretty surprised. I figured he wouldn't really care one way or the other if I got busted or not, he was just going to use me as long as he could. It made me realize that he actually appreciated it.

"After that, Jack tried to talk to me more, and I made an effort to talk, too. Sometimes he'd find me at lunch, in the corner where I sat alone eating and reading comics, and he'd hang with me, telling me about what he and his friends did on the weekend and stuff. I'd tell him about my comics or a record I'd bought. I'd even help him with his homework. He eventually invited me to tag along one weekend, and it sort of went from there . . ."

"It must be something to have a friend like that," Jeane said. "It's obvious Jack thinks very highly of you."

I stretched out on my back and looked up at the sky. There was some fog off the ocean, but through it you could see a zillion stars. "Some day," I said, "I'm going to reach my arms out and gather up all the stars. Then I'm going to bring them all down here and tell everyone in the world that they can have any star they want, as many as they want, just tell me. But it's really a trick, see. I'm going to have my eye on one special star—the smallest star, the one gasping for breath, barely able to keep alight. The dimmest star that sits at the edge of the sky in constant fear of going out. The one who asks for that star will receive everything. I'll refuse all others."

Jeane rolled over onto her stomach and propped herself up on her elbows. Her face was above mine, so close that her straight nose was almost touching me. "Why is that?" she asked. "Why would you do that?"

I could feel her warm breath on my face as she talked. It smelled sweet. Like candy.

"Every star is a soul. Each of us has our own in the sky, that lives our life with us and falls when we die. Mine is that little, struggling star. You can see it off to the left there, all by itself in that dark patch of sky where there are no other stars. The person who picks that star will be my one true love, the one I've always dreamed about."

She rubbed her nose back and forth across my cheek, her hot breath making my skin tingle. "I'd like to be given a chance to pick," she said, so close that I could feel the vibrations of her voice. "I know I'd pick it right."

Jeane leaned over and kissed me. Her lips were soft, and her breath rushed into me and chased away the cold. It tasted like late in the day, like comfort. The smell of her fell over me like a shower of feathers. A homey, safe smell. A smell like love. Love that keeps you warm, that holds you, and takes away memory and fear. I wanted to live behind her eyes.

She rested her chin on my forehead. "There were nights where I would sit alone in the dark," she said, "and look out my apartment window over Westwood, look at Hollywood and L.A. way off in the distance. For as far as I could see, there were lights. First individual dots, then a blurred blanket covering the horizon. In all of that, I couldn't find one note of solace. No emotion, nothing to ease the loneliness. If it really was a blanket, I thought, your feet would probably stick out the bottom when you tried to pull it over, so you could never escape the cold. I never wanted to leave the dark. There was too much security in it. Yours is the only light I've ever felt that made the darkness seem inadequate."

I tried not to cry but couldn't stop it. Jeane lifted the first tear away from my face with her finger. "Why're you crying?" she asked. "Don't do that."

"Someday, I'd like to build a cabin. I want to cut the logs myself and put them together and make a home. We could forget the world in it. We could."

"We'd have our own blanket."

She kissed the bridge of my nose. The imprint of her lips lingered there. I decided that the man in the headlights had nothing to be afraid of.

12. LIKE AN OUTLAW (FOR YOU)

She sprayed my hair with water from a small purple bottle. She pushed it back with her fingers, so that it tugged at the roots. The tension stretched my scalp, and when she released, the skin relaxed and felt good. Her fingers went through again, lightly, tickling the top of my head.

I had returned to Jeane's that morning with a box of donuts and a carton of chocolate milk. She was still asleep. We had left the beach near four, and she got home after me, having dropped me off at my apartment. I didn't sleep well. I was too excited—and I was afraid that if I went to sleep, when I woke up, it would all be gone. Or, perhaps, that I wouldn't wake up at all.

Jeane came to the door with a pink bathrobe on. Sleep was still in her eyes. I traced the black rings under them with my finger. They were soft. "They are beautiful," I told her.

We sat around and ate the donuts and listened to some old Duran Duran twelve-inch singles. We didn't speak much, only looked at each other between bites and giggled. I was afraid of making a mess, so I held my hand under my mouth when I took a bite, catching the crumbs in my palm. I asked Jeane where I could throw them away, gesturing with my open hand out in front of me. She closed my fingers over the donut residue and kissed my knuckles, and taking hold of my wrist, led me to the trash basket herself. When I had thrown the crumbs away, I held her close to me for a long while.

I told her I wanted to stay all day, but I couldn't. Jack and I had tickets to see Social Distortion that night. I had to leave early to get ready.

"What get ready?" she laughed. "You mean like pick-out-your-outfit and do-your-hair get ready? Who's going to be there that you want to impress?"

"I have to look my best. After all, it *is* Social Distortion."

"Oh, yes, after all . . ."

"If you're gonna tease . . ."

"You'll what?"

"I'm just saying don't make me get ugly. I can, you know."

"Get ugly?"

"Very."

"Can't have that. After all, it *is* Social Distortion," she said. "Why not let me help you stay pretty? Let me do your hair."

She took me back and sat me down on a small, green stool in front of the vanity mirror. After wetting my hair, she began to brush it out, careful of the snags, trying to take it through without hurting me too badly. I tried not to make any noise or faces because if it did hurt I didn't want her to know. I didn't want her to feel bad.

After she brushed my hair, she squirted Aussie Sprunch Spray on it. It smelled fruity. She leaned in close and began to brush it around some more, moving my hair to where she wanted it. Her touch was soft, and soon I began to totally relax. My eyes drooped, and I wanted to go to sleep right there, my head resting in the care of her hands. Her robe fell open a little, revealing a freckle on the curve of her pale breast. I tried not to look, but my eyes kept drifting back for another illegal glimpse. Every once in a while, Jeane would look down to see how I was doing, and I tried my best to look innocent.

"Have you ever thought of doing my hair professionally?" I asked, trying to cover my sins.

"Nah, the customer is too cranky and unmanageable," she said. "Besides, hair has never really been my bag."

"What would you like to do? I mean, beyond working at the shop, if you could do whatever you wanted?"

"I don't know. Well, if I could do whatever I wanted, I'd travel all the time and see what I could see. But in the practical career sense, I never really decided. I've thought about owning a costume shop. I could make my own costumes and go around to thrift stores and garage sales and find cool stuff. I think that would be fun."

"Really? That's cool. I wish I knew what I was doing . . . where I was going . . . I haven't really looked much beyond the comics store."

Jeane pulled my bangs up, and I could feel her curling them back with her brush. She held them there, sprayed more Aussie on them, and turned on the blow dryer. When she had dried the bangs, she sprayed me again, this time all around my head, making sure one last time that the hair would stay fixed in place.

"Can I look now?"

"No . . . sit still."

She took the eyeliner pencil off the sink and crouched in front of me. She wet the tip of it with her tongue.

"Close your eyes," she said.

I closed them. I could feel her lean in, hear her breathing through her nose. It was gentle against my cheek. The pencil touched my right eyelid lightly and rolled across the bottom of it. Then she did the same for the other.

"Now, open your eyes," she said, "and look up."

The ceiling had a white glaze. I tried to focus on it, but as soon as I sensed the pencil coming near, I began to freak out. "Oh, God, I don't know," I said.

"What are you scared of? Don't you trust me? You think *I'd* poke your eye out?"

"No . . . but the pencil might."

"But would *I*? That's the question."

"No."

"Then look up. Think of something nice. Don't think about anything. It will all be over in a second."

I tried to relax, to do as she instructed. I thought of her, imagined her face painted into the ceiling above me. She finished the job in a few smooth strokes.

"All done," she said. "Now, look at me."

She held my chin in her hand and looked into my face. Licking her lips, she turned my head to the right and then to the left, examining her work. She squeezed my cheeks. "You're so cute," she said.

"And you're beautiful," I said.

"Shut up." She kissed my forehead.

I stood up and looked at myself in the mirror. She had combed all my hair back, creating one slick wave, except for the bangs, which stood straight out from my head, forming into a point an inch or so away. My eyes were outlined in black, and I blinked them, thinking that possibly they couldn't really be that way. "I don't recognize myself," I said.

"Do you like it?" Jeane asked.

I touched the tip of my bangs to see if they'd go anywhere. They didn't, and I cracked up. "So cool," I said. "I wish I could do stuff like this."

She put her arms around me and rested her chin on my shoulder. "Then what would you need me for?"

"To cook me breakfast and wash my clothes."

"Oh, yeah?" She squeezed me hard and giggled, and we looked at our reflection in the mirror for long moments. Jeane sighed, and I felt her breath against my neck as she buried her face into my shoulder. "Mason . . . you're not going to hurt me, are you?"

This surprised me. "I'm not planning on it," I said.

"I move too fast sometimes," she said. "*Usually*. I move too fast and I get scared." Her eyes were closed, and she was nuzzling her nose into my shirt. "It's just . . . it's just I fall in love too easily."

"You, me, and Frank Sinatra."

"I'm serious, Mason."

I leaned my head down, rested my cheek on her hair, soft and clean-smelling. "So am I," I said. "I'm the last person you should be scared of."

We stood together for a long time. I put my hands on hers and held them tight to my chest. I wanted that exact second to expand, like a sponge taking in water, time taking in the perfection of the embrace. I opened her arms, turned around, and kissed her. Our lips parted, but our noses and foreheads remained together. "I have to go," I said.

"I know," she whispered, and then she smiled. "Kick a few heads in down in the pit for me, okay?"

We kissed again and said good-bye.

I left and caught the bus on Wilshire, taking it up to Hollywood. Walking down Melrose, I saw Laine across the street by Retail Slut. She was hanging out with another girl, who had a face like a guppy—all puffy eyes and big, burgundy-painted lips. Laine was looking through a *L.A. Weekly* and twisting strands of her hair as if she were making a braid. She saw me and waved me over. I suddenly felt like a boy with the flu—empty and full of chills. I had hoped to pass without having to face up to her, but I was caught.

I stuck my hands in my pockets and guiltily crossed the street. A Volkswagen cut by me close, honking its horn, spitting exhaust on me as it went on. Someone shouted, "Nice hair, faggot!" I gave them the finger.

Laine was smiling. She swung her purple and blue shoulder bag around and hit me in the arm. "What's up, *Ma*son?" she asked. "Where ya been?"

"Nowhere, really," I said.

"Lookit your hair. Wow! What's going on?"

"Going to Social D. tonight."

"Yeah? We're going to *Rocky Horror*," she said, indicating her guppy friend, who flashed me a polite wave. "Too bad you're not sticking around. You could come along."

A black bra strap was peeking out from under her shirt, and she reached up to fix it. Under her knuckles, R-O-B was written in bloody scabs, a letter on each finger. They were thin and looked as if they had been carved with a safety pin. I wondered who Rob was and what had happened to Otto. It seemed obvious to me that it would never have been my name, I would have never inspired such an intense effort, and I couldn't think of anything to say to her.

"Well, I need to go," I said. "Jack's waiting for me."

"Okay. I'm glad I saw you. It's been a while. I've missed having you around. Call me some time, whydoncha?"

"I will," I lied, turning away.

I was saddened—sickened with myself—saying good-bye to her like that. I was angry that not too long ago I couldn't say enough to her, and today I couldn't say anything. Angry that not too long ago, all my thoughts were obsessed with how much I loved her, and now, until I had seen her standing there, I had completely forgotten that she had existed. I felt flaky. Fickle. She had done nothing to be so lightly cast off. I had no reason to silently turn away. She had never treated me badly or tried to hurt me. Her only crime was non-interest, which wasn't a crime at all. Only boys consider it to be a crime, because boys have egos that refuse to see the faults within themselves. Instead, they blame everybody else. I resented myself. I resented my fickle heart.

Looking back over my shoulder, I saw her laughing with the guppy girl. I decided my love for her hadn't disappeared. It had only lost its urgency. Or maybe its relevance. Then again, it probably wasn't really love at all. I tried to rationalize, to tell myself that I couldn't be blamed for the way I felt, that my desires had turned to Jeane. I had to follow love to where it lived, not keep knocking on a door that it never passed through. I had to move forward when the path grew up for my feet.

On the corner, William was leaning against a lamppost watching me, his fedora tilted down to shade his face. I was a little startled to see him. I felt as if he were spying on me, catching me doing something evil. When I got near him, I could smell clove cigarettes. I wanted to avoid him but felt it was impossible. "How you doing?" I asked, at a loss for anything else.

William just smiled his toothless smile. I kept walking.

I just wanted to get home.

Jack was asleep on the couch listening to The Birthday Party when I got in. His mouth was open, and he was snoring. I snuck over to him and slowly sat down on his stomach. He lifted me up and down with his breathing and coughed a little bit. I stuck my finger in his nose. He snorted and shook his head and then slapped himself, waking himself up. I was laughing pretty hard, and as soon as he became oriented, Jack grabbed me. He started tickling me and tried to pin me down on the couch. I squirmed out of his grip, landing on my feet on the floor.

Jack rubbed the gunk out of the corner of his eyes. "You little shit," he said.

"Grumpy Gus," I retorted.

He chuckled. "Some night I'll put my *paste* in your nose, then we'll see." He dropped his hands, letting them hang between his legs, and looked at me in that murky afterhaze naps create. Then, suddenly, he perked up. "Hey, check out the 'do, Magoo! What happened?"

"Jeane."

"Pretty snazzy. I guess since you have your own personal groomer now, I don't have to wait around while you primp and priss in the mirror."

"I'm all set to go if you are."

"Then let's . . ."

Steve's car waited for us out by the curb. We had opted to borrow it rather than try to take the bus all the way down to Irvine. I had to clear some cigarette butts and condom wrappers off of the passenger seat, and it smelled like someone had recently puked in it. We decided it might be best if we kept the windows down. We cranked up The Germs on the

stereo and shouted at each other over it and the wind. I told Jack about my
date, and he told me about ska night at NoWay with Gene Larkin's A Bum
and Sure Am, Sure Am. Jack had gotten really drunk and gone around the
street sticking rocks in people's tailpipes so that he could watch them
shoot out when they took off. We laughed so hard we almost crashed into
the freeway divider, but we didn't mind.

When we got to UCI, the parking lot was pretty empty. There were
some cars and a few people walking around carrying books and backpacks
and things like that, not at all what you'd expect for a Social D. concert.
We figured that they were students getting some weekend studying done
in the library or something. Most of the audience probably wouldn't show
up till it got dark, and a large part of that would be KROQ poseurs who
wouldn't really know what was up and who'd get thrashed in the pit. A
powder blue van with a Frazetta female barbarian painted on the side sat
in the center of the lot. Whoever was inside was listening to Dr. Know, and
it was turned up so loud that the vehicle was rocking from the sheer throb
of the speakers. A rollerblader weaved in and out of the cars and disappeared into the buildings.

We went to the nearest sidewalk and figured we'd walk around until
we found the theatre, and I hoped with all my might that we'd be the first
ones there. It was worth the couple of hours wait to be first in line, to
have dibs on front and center. I wanted to be right under Mike Ness'
microphone stand. I wanted to see every glob of spit and every drop of
sweat.

A blue El Camino rolled into the lot, playing some old country music.
As it passed, I looked in the window. A tough-looking guy with slick hair

and black sunglasses was in the passenger seat. He looked at me. I nodded to him. He nodded back. They drove out of sight.

"Holy shit, Mason," Jack said. "That was *fuckin'* Mike Ness."

It stuck me like a jab in the eye. He was right. It *was* Mike Ness!

"Oh, my God!" I exclaimed, grabbing Jack's sleeve. "I just nodded to Mike Ness. And he nodded back! Can you believe it?"

"Might as well go home now," Jack kidded. "Ain't no point seein' the show. Your head's gonna be kissing the clouds, and you're not even gonna notice anybody else is there."

"Mike Ness! I can't believe it!"

Just then, there was a burst of music. The van doors had been flung open. About ten beer cans spilled out, clanking hollowly against the pavement. A skinhead came tumbling out after them, followed by a second skinhead. The second guy was shirtless and had a dripping red gash across his chest. He had on black jeans and knee-high, goosestepping boots, which he used to kick the first skinhead in the stomach, the arms, the head. The

first one was trying to roll away, but the boots kept finding him. Each kick that hit, however, met only silence. The skinhead on the ground refused to cry or scream. He didn't even grunt.

Likewise, his attacker kicked on, cold and silent, unrelenting.

Then the first skinhead passed out, just lay there, lifeless and still. The one with the boots kept kicking him to make sure he was really out before dragging him by his shirt toward a concrete parking block. The shirt ripped halfway there, and the guy fell face first. His nose hit the cement and made a loud pop and squirted blood several feet, like a package of taco sauce under a bicycle tire. His friend picked him back up, grasping him under the armpits. He dragged him over to the block, the sleeping man's shoes scraping two lines over the asphalt.

The skinhead opened his unconscious friend's mouth and rested his top jaw on the block so that his teeth bit into it. He stepped back. He was going to curb him.

My stomach shrank into a raisin. The entire parking lot was frozen in mute horror. The students stood stock still in packs, staring in disbelief. Nothing seemed to move, not even the leaves on the trees.

The conscious skinhead lifted his boot up high and brought it down on the unconscious head of the other. Teeth splintered, creating an ivory snowstorm, and more blood gushed from his face.

But worst of all was the sound his head made. Like a water balloon breaking.

I turned away. Jack put his hands on my shoulders and gently pushed me along.

"Let's go," he whispered. We had seen enough fights to know it's best to get way before you become a part of it.

Behind us, a few more water balloons were let free.

DECEMBER
1990

13. I SMELL WINTER

We stayed up all night packing so that we could move during the day and screw around for New Year's. "A stupid thing like moving shouldn't stop us from getting out of our heads," Jack said.

We put off packing the stereo and music and played all of our thrash as loud as we could, drinking Jolt cola from the can to keep ourselves amped. We pogoed and screamed along with Suicidal Tendencies and M.O.D. and The Dickies. Our downstairs neighbor periodically pounded on his ceiling, and Jack would pick up my box of books and drop it in response. "Fuck 'em," he said. "What're they gonna do? Throw us out?"

Jack jumped around and slammed into the walls and howled like a madman.

We were almost done when the sun came up, only a few miscellaneous things waiting to be shoved into the small crevices remaining in already stuffed boxes or thrown in bags. Jeane came over to help us finish. "Why are none of the boxes marked?" she asked.

"We know they're ours," Jack said.

"But you don't know what's *in* them," she said.

"Stuff. Whatever fit."

"You just threw it all together?"

"Well, yeah," we said.

"Oh, *gawd*!"

She opened all the boxes and took out the plates, glasses, and other things that could get broken, including a blue ceramic soap dish shaped like a horny toad that Jack had found in the trash. She wrapped the dish in a Donald Duck towel and gently placed it inside a new box.

"What'd you get all fussy over *that* for?" Jack asked. "It's just a dumbass frog."

"But it's your frog," she replied, writing PERISHABLES on the box with a magic marker.

"You're much too serious at this business, Jeanie," he said. "Relax. If it breaks, it breaks. It was made to break. They all were. You just get new ones and move on."

Jack put on "Orgasm Addict," and we all danced and sang along.

Steve brought over Dean's truck, committing us to another night of lug work for Gene Larkin's A Bum. Phil came in Steve's car. I was surprised by his appearance, because his hair wasn't combed and he had let it grow long. His T-shirt was dirty, his jeans were ripped, and he reeked of hash and piss. Apparently, living with Steve was having its influence.

Jack told Jeane she could go home. "We appreciate your help," he said, "but it's all lifting and backwork from here."

"But you need someone to direct," she said, "to coordinate."

"Aw, shit!" Jack guffawed. He grabbed a box of records and carted it down to the truck.

"I don't mind if you hang around," I told her, "but he won't let you do anything."

"Well, jeez, why don't you stand up for my womanhood? Stare him down!"

"He's bigger than I am. He can kick my ass."

"Good reasons," she said, and she kissed me on my ear. "We still on for this evening?"

"I guess," I grinned. "Unless something better comes along."

She laughed. I watched her go down the stairs. She slid her fingers along the walls, and I imagined I could see the traces of their heat like red lines left behind on the paint.

We finished loading the truck and drove over to the new apartment, Phil and Steve following with some other stuff in the car. I fell asleep on the way over, a jerky sleep brought on by the all-nighter and the warmth in the cab. My head felt like it was in a pressure cooker. And I dreamed.

I was older. In bed. Rising. Awakened by nothing, but still having a purpose. I went to a desk and pulled out a gun.

Jack honked the horn and brought me out of it. "Damn idiot! Dozing at a green light!" he shouted.

A Dodge Dart was idling in front of us. Jack hit the horn again. The driver got startled and hit the gas real fast. His tires squealed, and a loud bang shot from his muffler. Jack stuck his arm out the window and bellowed his approval of the backfire. "Beautiful, baby!"

Our new place was only a couple of blocks away and still in walking distance of Melrose. It was a lot nicer, but a little pretentious—all white with big blue letters on the front saying "Ocean Crest," as if it was some

sort of beachfront pad or resort hotel. The rent was a little more than the old apartment , but it had an outside pool and an air cooler in the living room. The carpet was nice and clean. It was green, and the marks from the shampoo machine were still visible.

We unloaded, and Jack kept singing the theme from "The Jeffersons." We stacked all the boxes in the living room, figuring to get all the stuff moved and inside before unpacking.

As we were leaving to go get the second load from our old home, we saw our neighbors going into their apartment next door. They were a middle-aged couple. He wore Bermuda shorts and a shirt with pineapple halves tumbling down the front of it. She wore a polka dot sundress, and her cheeks and breasts were red from the sun. They saw us and did a double-take. She looked confused. He sneered.

"There more of you around here?" Jack asked, slightly sad, slightly perturbed.

"All of us," the man replied, and they went inside.

"Fuck 'em," Jack said.

I felt a little shaky when we loaded the last of the boxes into the truck. I wasn't sure if it was my muscles going out from all the lifting or if I was just nervous about moving. I looked at the empty apartment, where Jack and I had lived for over a year, the first home of our own. Nobody here to tell us to cut it out when we were doing something retarded, or laugh when we got the bug to dye our hair green or neon blue or orange, nobody to say we needed new Vans just because the ones we wore had holes. We spent late nights here, lying on the floor in the dark, listening to The Sisters of Mercy and Peter Murphy and other equally moody bands, talking about whatever popped into our heads, no matter how personal or lame, like the first wet dream we had or times we thought we should take a razor or a bottle of pills and just cut the wires, switch off the power, end it. Jack had nursed me here, in the bathroom, when some jocks beat me up over by Fairfax High, cleaning out and bandaging my wounds, putting me to bed. I thought I would never stop bleeding, that you wouldn't be able to even see it was me through the bruises and scabs. Jack said I'd heal. "Like a snake," he said, "one skin will fall off and you'll be even better lookin' than before."

All that, here on the ugly brown carpet, staring at the cracked and dirty walls.

Everything.

Here.

And the new place, already a bad move.

Tomorrow the wrecking balls and dynamite and more than a year gone.

Before we left, I got the mail for the last time. There were some pizza coupons, a farewell note from the building manager—generic, made on a computer—and a card from my mom.

A few weeks before, Jeane and I had gone to the Santa Monica Mall, cooling off after hanging out on the pier. We'd gotten some corn dogs and strolled along looking in the shops. Outside a toy store, I saw my mom up ahead, and she was coming straight for us. She was small, with bleached blonde hair that looked as if someone had dumped a bucket of water on it. Her shirt and shorts matched—white with red horizontal stripes—and she was clutching her purse to her chest like she thought someone might steal it. Luckily, she was paying more attention to the stores beside her than what was in front of her, the sharp hook of her nose clear to me in the fluorescent light. She didn't see me.

I yelped and ducked back into a health-nut store, hiding behind a rack of sweatpants. Jeane came in after me, her brow raised. "Mason, what the hell's going on?"

I peeked over the clothes and saw my mother waddle past.

"My mom," I whispered. "She's outside."

"What? Where? I want to see."

"Oh, no. I haven't even talked to her since I moved out."

"C'mon, we'll just follow behind. We won't let her see us. I just want to know what she looks like."

I came out from behind the pants and, grabbing her hand, led Jeane out. We moved cautiously through the crowd until she came into sight. Now that we were behind her, I noticed that there was a slump in her step, like she couldn't see too straight, and I thought maybe her orange juice had been especially wonky that morning.

"Up there," I said. "Red stripes. Big ass."

"*Her?!?*"

"The very one."

"Oh . . ."

My mom turned left into a stationary shop. A sign in the window said "CLEARANCE — EVERYTHING 75% OFF" in huge red letters.

Now, thinking back about that day, I started to feel angry. I looked at the envelope in my hand, holding it slightly to the side so Jack couldn't see it. I was sure the card was from the close-out store. She would have never spent full price. She didn't have it in her.

Steve was yelling at me from the street. "Come on, Jailbate! Let's go! I can't wait all fuckin' day on your ass!"

127

I went out to the truck, aiming a steady middle finger in Steve's direction.

In the truck, I cursed the clear skies and wished we lived in a place where winter was real. I wanted to live in a place where it snowed, covering the ground in white, so I could really feel the finality of it all, feel how cold it really was. Things died in the fall. Leaves changed their faces and fell, and there was a sense of loss, but snow, snow would make it all seem real. I'd lie down in it all and feel the ice and think of the snow as one big shroud, keeping all the corpses warm—be it leaves or hibernating bears or humans.

The image changed, and I was on my back, a gun in my hand, a puddle of blood under my head, staining the snow like spilled fruit punch.

It would be lucky if we ever got rain.

I opened the envelope and took out the card. It was white with a small picture drawn with wavy lines in the top half. The lines were purple and blue. It was a woman sitting at a table, looking sad, holding a coffee cup. The cup was colored yellow. Next to her was an empty chair.

Inside, she had written "Dear Mason" with a black pen above the printed message, which was also in black.

> *No matter how hard*
> *they try sometimes,*
> *everybody makes mistakes.*
> *I made a mistake this time,*
> *and I'm sorry.*

You're so special to me,
and I would
never hurt you on purpose.

Underneath, she had written, "Love, Mother."

A letter was also inside, typed on cheap carbon paper. It said:

"December 28, 1990

Dear Mason,

I thought I'd drop you a few lines to maybe clear a few things up. I'd rather talk to you in person but that doesn't seem possible so this is my only alternative.

I am so upset and confused I don't know what to do. I have been since you left which I don't know why. IF I WAS WRONG I APOLOGIZE. I never wanted y ou to be hurt.I loved you and still do.

I made a lot of mistakes after your father dissappeared but Mason I was going throughHell myself and didn't know many times <u>what</u> to do!! Unfortunately, the past cannot be changed. ALL of us were hurt! MY life the last 10 years has not been easy either. Could we all <u>finally</u> be friends?

I don't ask for much- Just your forgiveness and a small part of your life. I don't even ask for your love. I'm sorry you hadto live with me those years. I know how much you loved your Father and would <u>never</u> try to change that! I hurt too but if I could change things I would. Mothers are not perfect but we are humans with faults and we mess up. but I've always loved you and been proud of you,If I made a mistake I didn't do it intentionally.

I have nothing more to lose by telling you this and probably nothing to gain either but at least I have said it. I have no reason to lie at this point. Weall lost something through this mess but if you think about it you'll see I lost the most as I Lost Everyone!!!!

Anyway, I'm sorry you were hurt. I never would have done that to you. I hope someday you'll understand and put the past behind you."

It was signed, as well, "Love, Mother."

I began to feel sick. I decided to blame it on reading in a moving vehicle, which always bothered me, rather than giving her credit for still being able to affect me.

14. WATCH THAT GRANDAD GO

We left the unpacking for the new year. We had brought clothes for the night in our duffel bags, as well as soap and toothbrushes and all that junk.

The shower in our new bathroom wasn't very good. Our old shower put the water out at a high velocity so that it was hard against my skin, and when I turned the temperature up real hot, it was almost like getting a massage. I would stand there forever, forgetting where I was or anything I had to do. Sometimes, when I had put a particularly good tape in the player, I would be in there for an hour or more, sliding across the tub and drawing pictures on the walls with soap. It always seemed like time had ceased to operate.

But in the new shower, the water came out soft and didn't have any weight. It didn't have the strength to move over me. Rather, it just fell against my back and let gravity take it wherever. I could no longer conquer time and the forces controlling it, but became subject to them.

I was ready before Jack, so I ate a bagel with some peanut butter in the kitchen. The former tenant had left a telephone book in one of the kitchen drawers. I opened it up and started reading through the As, seeing if I could find someone I knew. After five pages, I had read a couple hundred names and didn't recognize a single one. It suddenly occurred to me that the world was a huge thing, and I didn't even know an inch of it. I found that depressing, so I put the book back.

When Jack was cleaned up, we drove the truck back over to Dean's. We were hoping he'd give us a ride to Steve's, but he had connected himself to his bong and was too content to be removed. We took the bus instead.

We could hear Black Flag blasting out of Steve's apartment from the street. An old lady was out walking her mutt, and she looked up towards his window with a disgusted look on her face. Jack laughed and flicked a pebble at her dog. The mongrel had a tail that stuck up in the air and curled over like a question mark, and the rock hit its exposed butt. The dog jumped off the ground and yelped.

"What in heavens . . .?"

"Dog must have fleas, ma'am," Jack said innocently. "Probably should give it a good bathing."

The lady looked frightened. She clutched the end of the dog's leash to her chest and backed away, not taking her eyes off of us until she was around the corner. We burst out laughing. Jack did an imitation of her face, folding his bottom lip down and sticking out his top teeth. His eyes were as big as eggs, and he crossed them.

Upstairs, Steve and Phil were sitting in a haze of cigarette smoke and drinking Plain Wrap beer. Phil was wearing Steve's Christian Death T-shirt, and I had to laugh. It was bad enough to live with the guy, but to wear his clothes! And for Phil, for whom clothes had been everything! Unbelievable.

The music was deafening, but neither Phil nor Steve seemed to notice. There was a potted plant on top of the stereo. Not very healthy, but alive nonetheless. The music was causing it to vibrate, and with each snap of the drum, it scooted a little closer to the edge.

"Shit," Steve said, "is it time to go to Lenny's already?"

"We got a little while," Jack said.

Steve's chin fell down to his chest. "Good," he said. "Let's just chill a bit. I've got to sober up some."

We kicked aside some magazines and dirty clothes and sat down on the floor. Down close to the carpet, it smelled like old refried beans.

Phil's eyelids kept fluttering, and his head slumped back. He was falling asleep, but the jerk of his head kept waking him up. He was right by the stereo, and I watched the plant inch closer to the drop-off point. Finally, it reached the edge and fell off with a loud crash, scattering dirt in a circle on the carpet. Phil leaped out of the chair and looked around, his mouth open, his face blank. "Wh'th'fuck?"

We all about died laughing at him. He sat back down and scowled at me, as if I were the only one who had done it. It didn't bother me, though. Let him be mad. Fuck him.

The record ended, and we all got up to leave. Phil had mellowed by then. His scowl had metamorphosed into an empty daze. "You okay, man?" Jack asked him.

"Huh? Oh . . . yeah . . . sure . . ."

I got to sit with Phil in the back seat of the car. At first, he just sat there with his hands hanging between his legs and his forehead against the window. After about five minutes, though, he started pressing his hands against his crotch and opening and closing his legs, like he had to go to the bathroom. Then he began shaking all over and letting out high-pitched moans through his nose. Steve looked at him in the rearview mirror. "Hey, you all right back there?" he asked.

"Holy jeez . . ." Phil whined, almost crying.

"Ohhhhhh, dude, you didn't take those tabs o' acid, did you?"

"Whu—no, no, man, I didn't . . ."

"You dirty fuck, you did! Bastard! Those were for later . . . and half of them were mine. I hope you trip bad, *motherfucker!*"

"Unghhhh . . ."

It was all pretty ridiculous, but I tried not to let it bother me. I was pretty stoked to be going to Lenny's. The fact that he had invited us over to his place to hang out made me feel like we weren't like all the other ratty punks he saw at NoWay Home. His seal of approval made me feel important, like I wasn't just a poseur. He was old school and knew his shit. Plus, I knew I would be seeing Jeane later, and that really made Phil and Steve's stupidity seem especially unimportant.

Lenny lived in an old warehouse downtown. Its outside walls were gunmetal gray and the windows were all made of yellow glass. There were bars over each one, and a barred gate protected the front door, but the gate and the door were open, and we went inside.

Lenny had put up walls in an octagon shape all around the inside perimeter of the warehouse. Inside the octagon, he built his living quarters and a bunch of other rooms that he would loan out to bands to rehearse in. The walls were only about eight feet high, and the actual ceiling of the warehouse was much, much higher. Several people suggested that Lenny should put a ceiling on his octagon and build a second floor, but he said that would box him in too much, and the point of life was to stay out of the box as much as possible, wasn't it? Besides, the upper part of the warehouse was sectioned into an intricate pattern by beams and pipes and steel-grate catwalks, holdovers from whatever operation centered itself there before Lenny bought it. This would have made building any higher extremely difficult, not to mention the fact that the whole industrial vibe would have been destroyed.

We didn't know our way around, and Lenny wasn't in sight, so Steve shouted, "Hey, Lenny! Where the hell are ya?"

"Hang on!" Lenny called back from somewhere inside the octagon. "I'll come out and get you!"

Phil looked up at all the beams and pipes. "Jeez-*us*," he said. He put two fingers together in the shape of an X and held them up above his head, closing one eye, trying to line the X up with the criss-cross design of the pipes. "Damn."

Lenny came out. He walked with his head held even and his back straight, eyes forward and focused on what was directly in front of him. He was wearing a plain white T-shirt with the sleeves rolled and black jeans with the legs pegged. He didn't have any shoes on, just white socks with a blue stripe across the toes. "What's up, guys?" he said, smiling. Laugh lines appeared at the corners of his mouth and around his eyes, the only real signs of his age. Lenny was pushing forty or so, yet none of us would have dared to call him old. He was still as hardcore as they came and could probably take us all at once. Even Jack, who just about equaled Lenny in size, looked upon him with reverence. As Jack always said, there's something about a tough guy who doesn't have an attitude about it; he just *is*.

Lenny went out and shut the gate. The hinges squeaked, and the sound made me shudder. Then he closed the front door. The slam echoed through the entire warehouse.

Phil was still attempting to align his fingers with the pipes, moving around in little circles, trying to get it just right. "What's with him?" Lenny asked.

"He's a friend of Steve's," Jack said. "He's fried."

Lenny guffawed. "No kidding."

He led us around the octagon and into a door on the other side of it. We went through a practice room that still had some band's equipment in it. The floor was bare concrete and the walls were unpainted sheetrock. There was a yellow bucket on wheels in one corner. A mop was stuck into it and there was a sign taped to its side. It was written with magic marker and some of the letters were all wobbly from getting wet. It said, "CLEAN YOUR OWN HURL."

Phil jumped on the drum kit and started pounding randomly. "Will you leave that thing alone?" Steve moaned. "Jeez, you stupid fuck . . ."

"Ah, let him be," Lenny said. "It'll keep him out of our hair."

The next room was Lenny's library. It was narrow, only one body's width, and about fifteen feet long. It had nice, red shag carpet that went up to my ankles. The two long walls weren't walls at all, but bookshelves filled with books. They were mainly on philosophy and Eastern religions, stuff that made Lenny think. He said he needed downtime from the harsh in-your-faceness of punk, which was strictly an Artaudian experience. Whatever that meant.

The next room was where Lenny had been relaxing when we showed up. Some vanilla incense was burning, the stick poking out of a green Buddha's bellybutton. Next to it was a copy of *The Portable Nietzche* and some pieces of lined paper that Lenny had been making notes on. His reading glasses were folded closed and set on the cover of the book.

The floor had smooth carpet the color of orange bricks, similar to what they have in doctor's waiting rooms. There were two or three bean-bags around the room. A blue one next to Lenny's book had a large inden-tation in it—from Lenny, of course. There were posters on the walls, and there was a lamp sitting on a cardboard box, single-handedly lighting the entire room. The lamp was fake porcelain, painted a dark green, with primitive drawings of naked people dancing on it. It looked like some knock-off from a museum or something. The bodies had no detail, no genitals. Not even faces. The only details were extraneous to them—the leafy crowns they wore on their heads and the pan pipes one or two of them were playing. I thought it was a strange thing for Lenny to have.

"Why don't you give us some music, Mason," Lenny said, pointing to an old record player in the corner. There was a plastic tube in the center of the turntable, and three stacks of seven-inch singles beside it. "You know how to work a 45 set, don't you?"

"Uh-huh."

"Well, go to it, and I'll get the beer."

He left through the library.

I went to the records and started sorting through them. Some were ancient. Things like Bill Haley and the original version of "Summertime Blues." Also, really old punk stuff, like The Plugz and Patti Smith. I threw The Germs' "Forming" on first, and then started building my selection from there, making a tower of vinyl on the plastic tube. The incense was floating right into my face, and it was making me feel light-headed.

Lenny returned with a case of Budweiser and four bottles of Jägermeister. Steve immediately grabbed one of the Jägers. "Eager, huh?" Lenny laughed.

Jack took a Bud and plopped down on a black beanbag against the wall. Above his head was a poster of James Dean with his sweater pulled up over half of his face. Someone had written "WHY?" in black across his forehead. Jack took a sip of his beer and looked down at his shoes. Lenny sat down on the blue beanbag, directly across from Jack. He sat cross-legged, with his back straight, blocking some of the light. His shadow fell on Jack, landing almost squarely on him, like it was Jack's own outline.

I finished stacking the records and laid on my stomach, my legs up in the air, clicking my feet together to the beat. Lenny motioned to the beer. "No thanks," I said.

"Jailbate's goin' out with his chick," Steve said. "He don't want to get

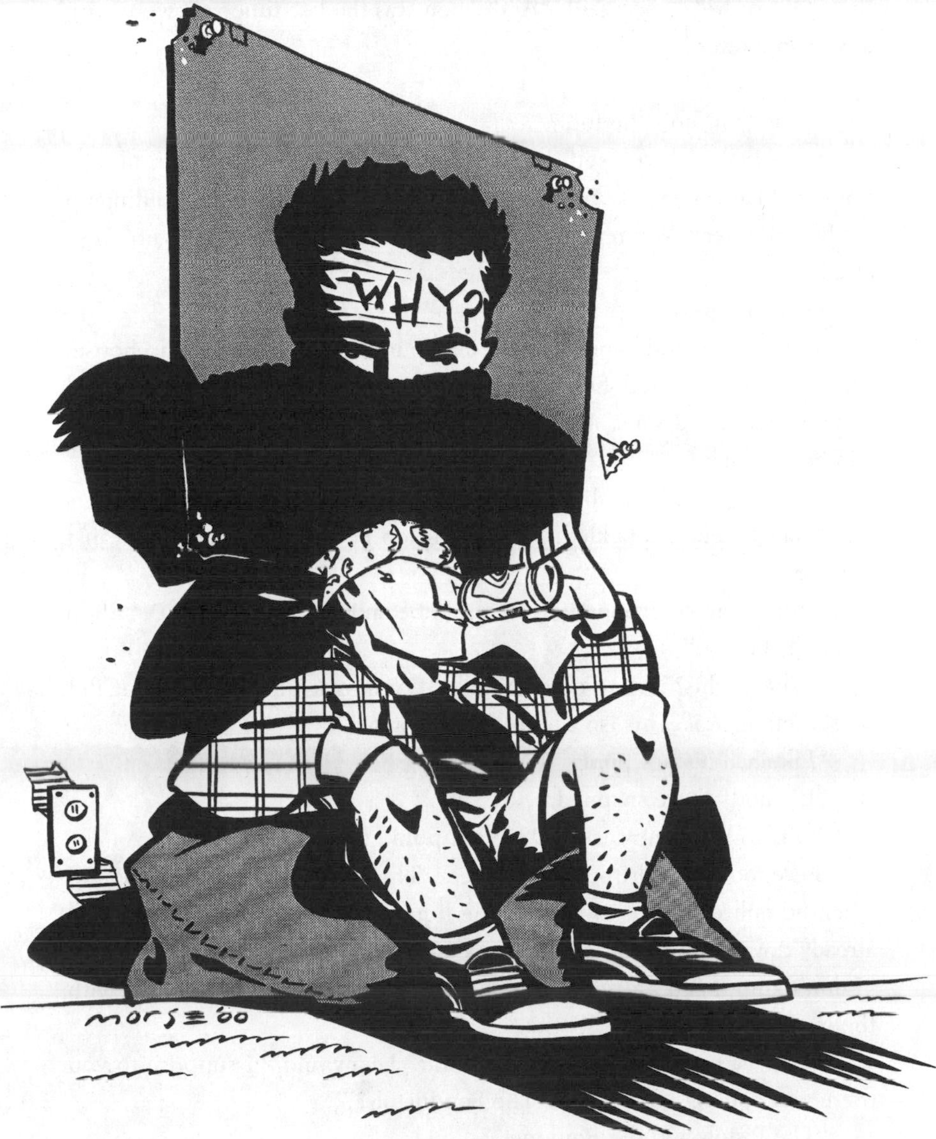
WHY?
MORSE '00

drunk 'cause he knows he'll make a big enough fool of himself without the booze."

"Oh, yeah?" Lenny said. "And when was the last time you were with a woman, Steve?"

"What?"

"Exactly. Who's the fool?"

Steve looked perplexed. I smiled at Lenny, but he didn't act like he noticed. "How many of these you had, Big Len'?" Steve asked, holding up his Jägermeister. "You must've had a lot, 'cause you ain't making no sense at all."

Lenny laughed.

There was a loud banging above us, up in the rafters of the warehouse. Then someone started howling. I hadn't noticed before, but Phil had stopped playing drums. He must have found one of the ladders and climbed up there.

"Idiot's gonna break his damn neck!" Steve exclaimed.

"Naw," Lenny chuckled, "the condition he's in, if he falls, he'll just bounce."

Another single dropped down the tube and started playing. Pet Shop Boys' "Suburbia."

"What is this?" Steve complained. "Damn machine music, man! Put on something *real*. This isn't punk. This is weak."

"Like hell it's not punk," Lenny said.

"It's not!" Steve snapped.

"Oh, yeah?" Lenny asked. "Define punk, then."

Steve took a big drink from his beer. The bottle made a hollow sound when he pulled his lips away, and the liquid sloshed around inside. He'd already downed over half of it. "Punk is . . ." he began. Then he paused. "I don't know . . . it's attitude. It's guitars and drums. Punk's anything with the word 'fuck' in it."

"That's a pretty limited view of it all," Lenny said. "I suppose to you there was nothing punk before The Sex Pistols?"

"The Pistols and the Ramones."

"The Holy Trinity. Sid Vicious was Christ, Joey Ramone was God, and the Spirit was the big punk thing itself, right? Or was Sid God?"

"Are you saying something different?" Steve sounded cocky. He looked at Lenny like he was ready to fight him, like Lenny was going to have to prove it.

"I was born in 1951," Lenny said. "How about you?"

Steve didn't answer.

"'71," I said. "Just like me."

"Okay," Lenny continued. "So, let's establish the fact that you haven't been around very long. No, scratch that. Neither of us has been around very long. I've just been around longer than you. And I'm not implying that age automatically makes me smarter or anything, just that I've seen more of what we're going to talk about first hand. It's true, for you punk maybe *did* start with The Pistols. That's the earliest thing you would know, though you probably even got that after the fact. The thing is, it goes farther back . . .

"It was already there when I was born. I didn't know it. Not many people realized what it was, but there was a music of rebellion and it was undermining the Hit Parade and sanitized pop. Be-bop jazz and blues was the stuff of punk. It's no different. It's disaffection, anger, and despair. It's the destruction of accepted forms. It's the destruction of the Platonic concepts of art, and it need not be confined to music. It's everywhere.

"It was cool having an older brother around because he brought home all kinds of music. A lot of it was stuff that our parents told us we couldn't listen to. They called it 'colored music' at the time, not getting how great that term was. If that music was colored, then the other music was obviously bland and sterile. They didn't know that they could have called it punk, but it was punk. An oppressed people were expressing themselves in music, the very same thing everybody says The Pistols and The Ramones did. Only here, it was more life-threatening. The '70s punks fought against prog rock and institutionalized boredom. So many people before them were just trying to live without being terrorized by a lynch mob in the middle of the night. You could just hear the heartbreak in the voices of Billie Holiday and Nina Simone, the despair in Coltrane's sax, or the rush of freedom breaking out when Little Richard pounded on his piano."

"How much difference is there between boredom and slavery?" Jack asked.

"Exactly."

I rolled over onto my back. The incense had made me a little sick. I thought I might pass out. The room was silent except for the record player. I could hear the disc go around. It had changed to The The's "The Beat[en] Generation": " . . . *but can you still walk back to happiness when there's nowhere left to run?*"

"I remember the first time George brought home a Johnny Cash record," Lenny continued. "I was stunned. Here was a guy who knew what it was like to be kicked around for no reason except for the place you lived in and the fact that you had no money. I was getting in fights every day and getting the shit knocked out of me in most of them, just because I had poor clothes and a bad, home haircut. I hated all of the bastards. And here's Johnny Cash. He's taken a few punches, he's done some time, but he's not accepting it anymore."

"Blow me!" Steve interrupted. "Johnny Cash is goddamn country!"

"Don't be an ass," Lenny said. "They call him 'the original man in black' for a reason. All you little pissants think The Cure and Depressed Mood were the first, but I'm telling you, Johnny Cash and I were wearing nothing *but* black before there was a single hair on your collective heads. We were busting the skulls of cops and jocks before Doc Marten made boots for it. So, don't come steppin' up and telling me that Johnny Cash is country. He's more hardcore than you'll ever be."

Phil screamed like an ambulance from the rafters.

"You don't think punk's roots suck from the country wellspring? What about X? I'm sorry, but Billy Zoom's guitar riffs are country. And The Stray Cats? Hell, Social Distortion has been playing 'Ring of Fire' in their show for years, and The Sisters of Mercy do Dolly Parton's 'Jolene.' How come they know and you don't?"

"All right, already," Steve said, grabbing another beer. "I give up. I'm a dumbshit. Get on with it."

"Fine," Lenny said. "So, I heard that first J.C. record. The sleeve had a picture of him on it. He had on his black jeans and black shirt and that dark, dark pompadour. Nobody at school had hair like that. Nobody was that cool. Best of all, though, was the look on Johnny's face. He stared out at you with these challenging eyes, just daring you to go ahead and mess with him. I hung the picture up in the back of my closet where my parents couldn't see, and I'd stare at it for hours, practicing making that face. I'd go out in the mornings before school and rub coal all over my clothes and in my hair, trying to make them as black as possible. I looked awful and got into more fights, but I didn't lose much anymore. I even started some.

"There was punk in that. You call it something else, so did we. My mom called it 'trying to be a bad apple,' but it was punk. It was punk just as The Who would be punk, and The Doors and The Stones. They took things and they shook 'em up. They made rock 'n' roll unconventional."

"The Rolling Stones unconventional?" I asked.

"You scoff," Lenny answered, "because now they *are* the convention. Sure, they became the standard that rock is measured against, but when *Satanic Majesties Request* and *Let it Bleed* and all that other stuff came out, it was *new*. No one had heard that before. Like Elvis. You look at him now and you say, 'Oh, Elvis, what a bloated cliché.' Go back to '56, who else was there? Who had clothes like that, moves like that, sang like that? And I tell you, nobody but no one had that hair."

"It's the hair that does it!" I exclaimed. "There's your defining point, Steve. Punk is bad hair."

Phil barked in agreement from somewhere.

"Punk is revolutionary," Lenny went on. "Like The Who, taking the idea of traditional opera and throwing it in with rock 'n' roll. That's damn revolutionary! Punk is the only thing that can change art. Art becomes static, becomes fixed, and it takes punk to energize it again. Things like dada or pop art. Now, 90% of what Andy Warhol did was shit, but he changed the way people looked at art."

"And the Underground," Steve said.

"Now, wait," Lenny said. I could tell by the tone of his voice that he was zeroing in for the kill and was relishing it. "You say it all began with 'Blitzkrieg Bop,' but then you acknowledge The Velvet Underground? I don't get it."

"Oh, shit, I don't know . . ." Steve gulped some beer.

I laughed at him.

"Fuck off, Jailbate!" he said.

Lenny jumped in. "Don't shirk the question. What's up with this?"

141

"I said, 'I don't know.'" Steve was being snippy. I could tell he had probably started arguing just to argue, and now he was in over his head. "They were ahead of their time or something, I guess."

"There would be no music of worth today if it weren't for The Velvet Underground. No Pistols, no Sonic Youth, no Jesus and Mary Chain, nothing. Music would have died. They took sound and pushed it as far as it could go. They were the John Cage of rock 'n' roll, and there's no getting past them. No getting past the Underground, no getting past MC5, no getting past The Stooges, no getting past Bowie's odder theatrics. It's an ancestry, a family tree. You can't eat one apple without acknowledging the other bad apples that came before and gave the seeds.

"You may not recognize the foundation, but I assure you that the bands you're listening to do. That's why punk keeps metamorphosing, retracting, building. The Ramones knew rock. They just made it faster, clenched the fist a little tighter. The Jam not only covered The Who, but they also covered the songs The Who *covered*. Or there's Bauhaus, who certainly have their music based firmly in tradition—consciously, mind you. They took their name from an architectural movement, they cross-referenced The Spiders From Mars with Bram Stoker and Salvador Dali—it's undeniable. They took that history and made a new product. Gothic rock began with them."

"And ended," I interjected. "Nobody's ever come close. I mean, The Cure and Siouxsie are good and all that, but it's not the same thing as Bauhaus. It's not right that they're lumped into the same category. And all that other Batcave shit is just cartoons."

"Art is like a stalagmite—little drips piled on one another," Lenny said. "It's only logical that a new drip would eventually get curious and look to see what's underneath. That's why punk exploded and splintered off in so many different directions. It only makes sense that The Smiths would resurrect the pop melody, that Blondie would re-interpret surfer music, that The Stone Roses and Primal Scream would rediscover dance and psychedelic acid rock and put them together. You've got to know what you're standing on, what the ground is like."

"So then grunge is punk?" Steve asked. "It's all ripped off from Zeppelin and all that shit."

"No," Lenny replied, "grunge isn't punk. Zeppelin and all that '70s crotch rock is part of the boredom. Robert Plant and Jimmy Page got stoned and flowed with the *ennui* rather than reacting to it. Same with this SubPop stuff. These bands live in Seattle, a shit dull town, have nothing but dull records to listen to, and so they create dull music. Something that was dead fifteen years ago can't be resuscitated now. It was part of the *status quo* then and is part of the *status quo* now. It doesn't shake anything up, change anything. That's not art. That's not punk. The song simply remains the same, and that song is bullshit.

"You see, you've got to know what came before, but you've also got to know how to make it new. Not only that, you've got to know what's ahead, to look at the stalactites above you, anticipate what you're growing into. That's how you got New Order and Kraftwerk and OMD. They looked to the future, saw technology as a prominent force, and incorporated it into their music. That's change. That's punk. It's not just throwing on a flannel shirt and saying, 'Lookit me, I'm an outcast.' You may be an outcast, but only because you're a slob with no hygiene.

"I know everyone is saying Seattle is the next big scene, and that's fine and good for them, but I'll be damned if I accept that dreck as anything new or worthwhile. There's nothing there. They might as well be holding cellophane up to a light bulb and claiming that it's movies. It's just a short flicker without any reality behind it. The undeniable truth is that rap is the new punk, bringing us full circle back to jazz and the fact that oppression breeds anger. When this anger is applied to some sort of creative outlet, you have punk. Rap completely breaks all forms. It devours sacred cows wherever they may exist. Supposed purists get all hot and bothered over sampling, but that's the greatest aspect of it. It's like going into a museum and cutting up all the paintings and throwing the pieces on the floor and calling it the best picture ever created. Just absolute dada randomness. Rap is taking the entire history of music and breaking it down to pure, absolute, fucking noise. That's exciting. That's absolutely fucking exciting!

"Rap is kicking over garbage cans in the ghetto, and the Pet Shop Boys are kicking them over in the suburbs, and they're both punk. They both prove that the structure is loose and ripe for manipulation. What separates them, what makes me think rap is the most suitable heir to the throne, is that rap has a deeper meaning. '80s music, what you guys suckled on, didn't always have a lot to say. It was more of a waiting period. Don't get me wrong, though. It's definitely cool stuff. It has energy. It has that kick that The Pistols and Clash and all those guys proved to be so necessary, but, at times, it's a kick misplaced. All it really does, if it's not about celebration and excess, is sit and whine about the fact that everything sucks, and it does so in a purely self-destructive manner. The Smiths and The Cure take the misery as a fault of their own and turn the frustration on themselves. You know, I saw it in the '70s, with all the fights and the kids getting mangled in the slam pits, but it was nothing like this overall depression that hangs over you guys. You come into NoWay, and it's like this blob of anxiety has squirmed into the place. You're so pessimistic, so beaten . . ."

Lenny stopped. He looked at us, his eyes red-rimmed, tears waiting on the edges. His breath sounded dry, like he was having trouble getting air. He took a drink of his beer and started up again.

"It just sucks, because I can see the whole lot of you being dead in the next couple of years. Or, at least, you'll be so mired down by this defeatist nature that you'll be stuck in some sort of suburban nightmare. Not dead, but lifeless. You have something to say, you just need to learn how to say it right. Like Johnny Cash and Paul Weller and Joe Strummer. Hurl that bile at the people who are fucking you over. Hurl it at your parents. Hurl it at all of us old bastards who gangbanged the world before you even had a chance to kiss it. That's what rap does. Do like they did in the '60s. They took the music of The Who, the music of The Doors, the music of The Beatles, and they used it, rechanneled it, and moved for social change. Civil rights. Vietnam. That energy had purpose. Yours doesn't."

"No," Jack spoke up, "that's not true at all." He looked at Lenny, whose shadow still engulfed him, giving his face an empty, sunken-in look. His eyes, particularly, looked eerie—all black, not a single trace of color. Only his teeth stood out, momentary flashes of white as he spoke, like sparks between two electrical wires.

"We've got a cause," he said, "and it's no different than any other cause that went before us. We're all just trying to save ourselves, to pull ourselves away from what's dragging us down. Only reason we seem aimless is because the Love Generation pooched it, became bitter, and spawned us—fighters beaten before we even stepped into the ring. So much failure has been heaped upon us, we never had a chance to stand. You all want to ignore the fact that your big social consciousness did absolutely nothing, and the best way to do it is to make us seem worse than you. You thought your cause was wider somehow, but really, when it comes down to it, it's just as slim. You just want to save your own asses.

"We're all the same," Jack continued. "Nothing ever changes. Our music isn't so special or different. It's just like all the old music, which wasn't all that unique, either. No one ever says anything new. They never even say it in new ways. When you read something and it really connects, when it really says something to you, you say, 'Wow, that's just what I was thinking but didn't know how to put it,' so it's really not that new at all. It's normal. It will always be normal. You can't change things. They go on, no matter how hard you try. *'But I will always exist, because I always exist. Damn good, too.'"*

Lenny and Jack stared at each other for a few seconds, each blank. Then Jack put his head down on his knees, James Dean still asking "WHY?" above his head. I was glad Jack wasn't really drinking his beer, because it seemed like one of those nights where he could get depressed really fast, and what with the move and all, I thought it would be too easy for something bad to happen.

The last record on the stack finished playing, and the sound of the needle reaching the end was like an explosion. We sat in silence. The dancers on the lamp were still frozen. Nothing had changed for them. I wondered if they even thought about breaking free.

"Hey," Steve said, "what the hell happened to Phil?"

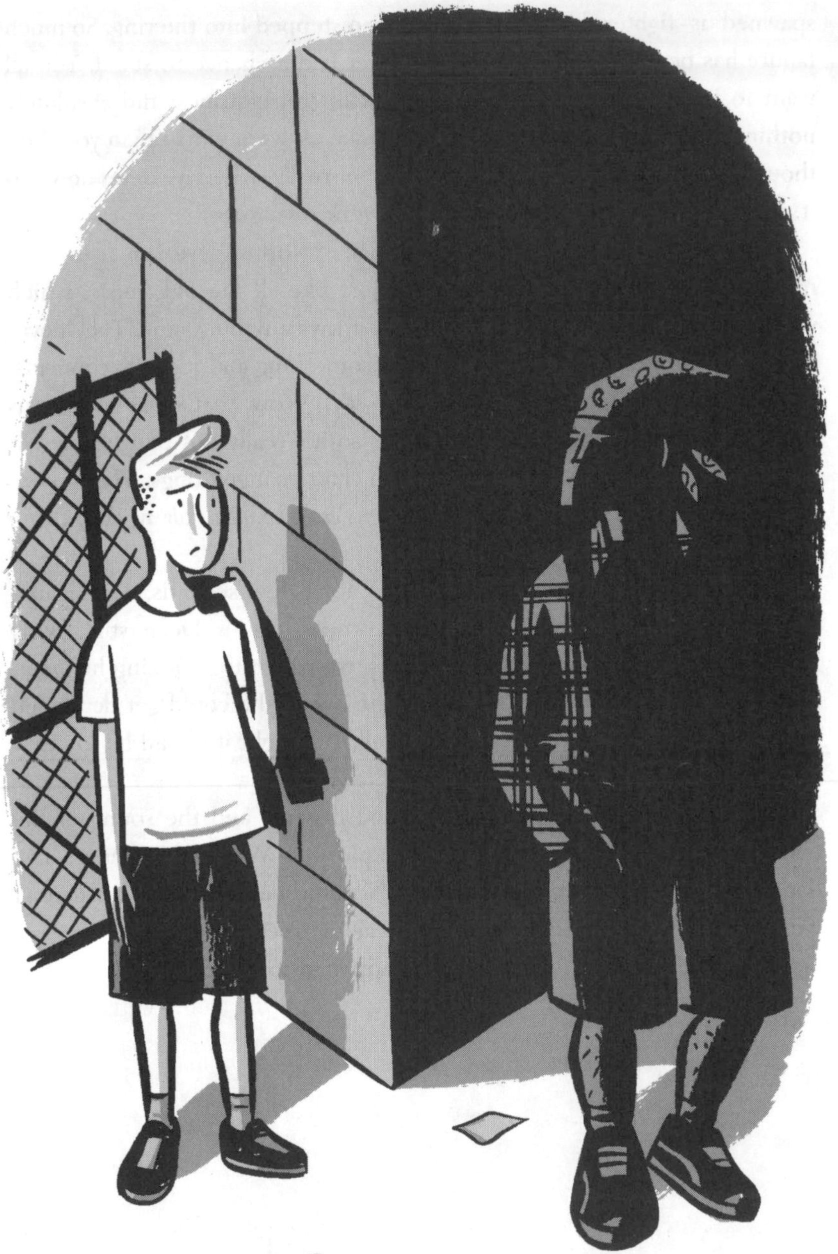

15. DO YOU WANNA HOLD ME?

We found Phil when the guys were walking me out. He had climbed down from the rafters and was sprawled out at the foot of the ladder. Gray puke was all over the front of his shirt, and he was asleep. "At least he didn't up-chuck on the floor," Lenny said.

"Yeah, but the fucker's wearing my shirt!" Steve whined.

They picked Phil up and carried him into the octagon.

"Well," Jack said, "I guess you gotta go, huh?"

"Yeah."

"Can't be late. Don't ever be late. It's not worth it in the long run. You add up all those lost seconds, it comes out to quite a lot. 's why I always pick up pennies. They build up, y'know?"

"Yeah . . . I'll see you in the New Year, okay?"

"Have fun tonight. Tomorrow's another day, and it ain't worth frettin' over till this one is done."

Jack was really confusing me. I couldn't read his mood. He was smiling a small smile, but his eyes were dark.

"What're you looking at?" he asked.

"You're not getting melancholy on me, are you?"

"Will you get the hell outta here? Christ! Go on. Let the men get drunk in peace. You can be my nanny in the morning."

I turned and started out.

"Hey!"

I stopped.

"Give Jean Genie a big 1991 wet one for me, whydoncha?" His smile had grown considerably larger.

"No sweat."

He laughed. "See ya, Ma. I'm a big boy now, and it's time . . ."

"So long."

It was cold outside. My cheeks immediately started to sting from the wind, and I was sure they were totally red. I figured Jack, too, would be red-faced by the end of the night, all filled up with booze, a vague imitation of W.C. Fields with a taste for The Damned. The sky was clear and full of stars. I looked for my patron, and it was in its usual place—off by itself, out on the rim of the sky. I wished on it—star light, star bright. I wished continued happiness for all of us—me, Jeane, Jack—and felt better for it.

I grabbed the first bus that came along and rode it down to a couple of blocks away from NoWay Home. Like A Dog was supposed to be playing a midnight show. They had been in hiding since The Garden. No one knew why—though I'm sure it had something to do with the second gig in a row ending violently. Outside the brawl, however, the Garden performance had been a smashing success. From what I'd heard, they had made a profit even after paying for the damage.

Unfortunately, with the band's exile in effect, I'd never been able to introduce Jeane to Tristan. This was going to be her first time as part of the Like A Dog experience. I was a little nervous. She had heard the demo and thought it was cool, but I was still scared she might not like it overall.

Jeane was waiting in the parking lot, sitting in her car and listening to Ride. I could hear the muffled crunch of hard guitars coming from inside the club, as well as a lot of shouting. It sounded as if it was packed.

She didn't see me come up. She was playing drums on her steering wheel and swirling her hair in half-circles, keeping time with Ride's shimmering sound. I knocked on the window, and she jumped. Jeane looked at me with wide eyes, gasping for breath, her hand on her throat.

"Sorry," I said, chuckling.

Jeane started laughing, too. "Oh, God, you dick!"

"Hey, hey," I protested, "no need for that."

I opened the door and grabbed her hand. She stepped out. We kissed. When we finished and she moved her head back, I leaned in and kissed her again. "From Jack," I said.

"I think I like that one better than the rest," Jeane laughed. "Maybe I'm going out with the wrong chap."

"Wouldn't surprise me. I hear size matters."

She flicked my nose.

"Bad news," she said.

"What?" I asked.

"Like A Dog cancelled. All-night dancing instead of a concert."

"No."

"Yep."

"That *blows*."

"Sorry."

"Isn't your fault."

"I know," she said, "but I'm sorry anyway. Shall we dance?"

"Would you like to?"

"We can always go home if it sucks . . ."

It seemed like a very small consolation. It had been so very long, and I was really looking forward to showing Jeane the band. A few other disgruntled Doggies were sitting on the curb outside NoWay. One, a boy of

no more than sixteen, had his head in his hands and a bouquet of lilies at his feet. The water in the gutter washed over their petals, turning them brown. The Smiths' "Unhappy Birthday" was playing inside.

As I had thought, NoWay was wall-to-wall full. The tune had changed to Aztec Camera's "Oblivious," and people were finding its draw irresistible. Or perhaps it was an already existent urge to get lost that drove them to the dance floor. Only a small group of hardcore punks seemed to be having a lousy time. They stood in a pack on the edge, probably upset that the song's poppiness didn't really make itself available to slam dancing. They jeered and spit at the dancers, who pretty much ignored them.

Steam rose off of the crowd, and the air was sweltering. Just entering the room was enough to make you start dripping. Jeane took hold of my hand and leaned into my ear, saying, "You want to get something to drink first or go straight to dancing?"

"I don't care!" I shouted back.

It really *didn't* matter to me. I was bummed and didn't much care what happened at that point.

"Fine," Jeane said. "Let's dance. We can save our money for when we really need something to cool us off."

She pulled me out onto the floor, and she started to dance. At first, I just stood there, unsure of my desire to be involved. Jeane grabbed my hand again and swung my arm back and forth. "Come on," she said. "Let's have a good time."

I felt bad. I didn't want to bring her down, too. So, I put what little effort I could muster into it, stepping lamely back and forth to the beat and moving my arms around. The DJ put on Ministry's early single, "Work for Love," and I couldn't help but laugh at how bad it was. Jeane smiled.

Things quickly ended, though. The next record was Nitzer Ebb's "Hearts and Minds." The bored group of punks got excited by the hard-driving industrial vibe and jumped into the crowd. They didn't seem to notice or care that it wasn't a pit, wasn't their scene. People fell two or three on top of each other, and one guy got a fist waved into his face, making him bite his lip. He stepped back and felt it with his fingers. He seemed shocked to see blood on them, though we could see it pouring down his chin from across the room.

Most everyone started to get off the floor and crowd into the bar. Jeane and I were on the edge and had no trouble getting out of the way. We decided to wait and see if it would calm down, if maybe the slamming would be isolated to a pit or the DJ would go back to tamer material.

The next selection was The Misfits, and it was greeted with raised fists and shouts of approval.

We wasted no time in leaving.

People had spilled outside. They were smoking cigarettes and chilling out. The Doggies had vacated the curb and presumably gone to a safer place. Jeane's neck glistened with sweat, and she unsnapped her choker, pulling it away from her pale skin. "That's better," she said. "God, was it hot in there."

"Sorry I wasn't into it at first," I said. "I was just a little upset that Dog didn't show. I wanted you to meet Tristan."

Jeane took my left hand and lifted it up. She took her choker and wrapped it twice around my wrist, snapping it shut. She looked me straight in the eyes, a clever smile on her lips. "Shall we go to my place?" she asked.

I nodded.

In the car, Jeane replaced Ride with Social Distortion's *Prison Bound*, I think in an attempt to keep me cheered. As usual, I found it hard to resist thrashing along, which was good, since it meant I wouldn't have to fake it to make sure her gesture didn't meet with disappointment.

Her apartment was dark, and when she went to turn on the lights, I told her not to. "Let's leave it like this," I said.

"All right."

The lights from the street made a patch of white on the carpet in the center of the room, with the shadow of where the window split in the middle. I sat down in the light, cross-legged. "You know," I said, "I don't think I ever asked you what your favorite album is."

"Hmmm, no, you haven't," Jeane said. "Very neglectful of you." She was still in the dark of the room.

"Well . . . it's . . .?"

"New Order's *Power, Corruption, & Lies*. Big shock, huh?"

"Put it on. Let's listen to it."

She moved to the stereo and crouched down. Her records were in the hollow of the crate supporting the system. She began shuffling through them. I imagined that her fingers were moving in the darkness like the legs of a running spider, and she didn't really look where they were going or instruct them. They just knew the terrain. I could hear the sleeves *flap flap flap* against each other as Jeane passed through them.

I took out a piece of mint Wrigley's. "You want half my gum?" I asked.

"Uh-huh . . ." She had found the right album and was putting it on the turntable. The speakers hissed and the needle touched vinyl and the familiar crackle of that initial groove filled the room. With CDs and tapes, you don't get that, and I think the experience is a little less for it. There will never be anything quite as stunning as the anticipation held within those seconds.

Jeane came over and sat down next to me. I tore the gum stick in half and passed hers to her. I popped mine in my mouth. It made my breath feel cool.

Jeane swayed slightly to the melody of the music, her eyes half-closed, lips half-moving to the words. "If you had to pick only one song off this album, and it could be the only song you could listen to ever again, which would it be?" I asked.

"'Leave Me Alone,'" she said, without skipping a beat.

"Is that a hint?"

She slapped my chest and laughed. "What about you? What song couldn't you live without?"

"I don't know. Maybe something by The Smiths, like 'Back to the Old House.'"

"Really? You surprise me. I thought it would be Social D. 'Sick Boys' or something."

"Yeah, I know. Most of that's just posing, though. More attitude than feeling. It makes me thrash, but I guess I was trying to pick something that gets me in a different way." I stretched out on my stomach, pressing my face into the carpet. I put my hand in the shadow of the window split and slid it back and forth, watching the black move over my skin. "I guess you could say Social D. is my weapon," I said, "while The Smiths and stuff like that are my friends."

Jeane stretched out next to me. "I understand," she said. "It's kind of like me with Bow Wow Wow. I was really into that, but it was more fun than anything. When I first heard New Order, it was like there was something more . . . It was the first music I heard that I could dive into. There're so many textures to it. The reason I like to work with fabric is because I like to feel all the different kinds, how soft and how special they all are. New Order was like fabric for my ears. It was startling."

I turned my gaze to her. She had her chin on the floor, near the edge of the light. She seemed to be staring at something. Or maybe it was just the look she got from losing herself to music. She seemed all serious and sad, yet really content. The bass line resembled a dirge, and Bernard Sumner's voice cracked and seemed to drone. Still, it felt energizing and compelling and pushed on us. It promised something.

"You've captured me," I said.

She turned her head to me. "What?" she asked.

"I love you," I said.

"You do?"

"Yes."

She smiled. "Well, that's a good thing. That makes it an even swap. I love you, too."

We kissed. It was soft and cold from the gum.

"*Our love is like the flowers,*" Jeane said. "*The rain, the sea, and the hours.*"

We kissed.

People in the street began screaming, and there was a loud pop, like a firecracker, that shook us apart. Jeane started laughing. "Scared you, huh?" she said.

"Oh, like it didn't you!"

She laughed again, loud, and kicked her feet. "All the shouting," she said, "must mean it's midnight."

"'s a safe bet." I felt the choker on my wrist and was glad it was still there.

"Happy New Year's, Mason."

"Happy New Year's."

1991

16. I LOVE LIVING IN THE CITY

When I got home, Jack was already in bed. I figured he was probably smashed, and it'd be best if he got some sleep rather than listen to me babble. He was snoring awfully loud, which was usually a sign that his slumber was alcohol inspired. I just shut his door and went to my room.

I was a little worked up over the night with Jeane. Though I felt absolutely exhausted, I couldn't help going over it in my mind, to the point where I was madly in need of sleep. I plugged in the stereo and put on my record of The Smiths *Louder Than Bombs* to give myself something else to concentrate on. When "Asleep" began, I knew that was the end. It was guaranteed that if I put that song on while in bed, I would never hear it fade out.

In the morning–late, late morning–when I got up, Jack was gone. Burton was coming back on winter break. Jack and Steve were supposed to pick him up at the bus station. Surprisingly, Jack had rolled up his sleeping bag and neatly placed it in the corner, his pillow resting on top. He must not have been very hungover. Either that, or he was doing penance by cleaning.

I ate some more peanut butter and bagels and decided to give "Asleep" another listen while I was awake. It seemed like it was an okay thing to do. It's always bedtime for *some*body in the world, and The Smiths always needed their due.

It was getting around 1:00, and the guys still hadn't come back. I was bored. I called Jeane. She wasn't home. The message on her answering machine was the first verse of New Order's "Every Little Counts," followed by her saying, "Your call counts especially, so leave a message or be hanged."

I said, "'*Heavy words are so lightly thrown, but still I'd leap in front of a flying bullet for you,*'" and hung up.

I went downstairs and waited on the steps. Cars rumbled by every few minutes, but not nearly as many as at our old place. I wondered how we'd survive without all the noise.

About half an hour later, Burton came strolling down the sidewalk. I barely recognized him. He was wearing Dockers, Penny Loafers, and a blue Oxford shirt. In the shirt's lapel, he had stuck a fraternity pin. His hair was combed to one side, parted evenly, and his skin was tan. I almost said, "Boy, have *you* become a square," but thought better of it.

"Where're the boys?" I asked.

"You tell me, Jailbate," he said. "Nobody was at the station to pick me up."

"That's weird," I said.

"Luckily, a fraternity brother came down, too. His mom took me to your old place. What's up? The whole building is empty. If your landlord didn't hold his dick so tight, he'd probably've left, too, and there'd 've been no one to tell me where to go."

"He sold the place and booted us out," I said. "I don't get it. Jack and Steve have been gone for hours. They said they were going to get you last I heard. I don't know why they wouldn't be there."

Before I could really think about it, I saw Steve stumbling up the block. Something grabbed my spine and squeezed, and it yanked me off the steps. I ran up to Steve. He was soaked with dank sweat and shaking all over. His shirt was covered in caked splotches the color of a basketball. His eyes were wide as fists, but he wouldn't look at me. "What's wrong?" I asked. "What's going on?"

Burton came over. "Where the fuck have you been, asshole?" he asked. "I practically had to walk."

Steve looked at him as if he couldn't believe Burton was there. "Burt," he said. "They shot him, Burt. They shot him, man."

"What the hell are you talking about, 'shot him'?" Burton laughed. "You strung out or what?"

I reached behind me and got a handful of Burton's shirt. His frat pin was poking in my skin. I was shaking my head back and forth. *no uh-uh no*

"Jack's fuckin' been shot!" Steve screamed. "Fuck you, man! Fuckin' walk! He's been *shot*!"

I was confused. It seemed oddly unreal. I tried to tell myself my imagination had taken over, but I could smell the sweat and the blood (*blood? how did I know it was blood?*) on Steve and I knew it had to be real. Only I wished it wasn't. I was *wishing* . . .

"What do you mean?" Burton fumbled. "Shot? How could he have been *shot*? Like with a *gun*?!"

"Yeah, with a gun!" Steve was starting to bawl. "What the fuck?"

"By who?" Burton asked.

"I don't know . . . some fuckin' guys. Some gangbangers."

"What? This makes no sense. Where *were* you guys?"

"Downtown. I had a hook-up there. Jack went with me. We were gonna do that, and then we were gonna get you. It wasn't gonna be no big deal. Happens all the time. We'd get the shit, then we'd get you."

"Yeah?"

"Some guys came in this big car . We were in the middle. Jack took it in the . . ."

Steve's voice trailed off. I wasn't there. I wasn't hearing. They argued, but not with me.

I was *there*.

I was where it happened.

And I could see it to perfection.

I imagined myself leaning against a big tree, hands in pockets, casual. Just watching. Steve and Jack were talking to some *cholos*. Well, just Steve. Jack is only with him and has no interest. Jack is only there because Steve begged him. Steve was too scared to go it alone. Steve is arguing price or something stupid, prolonging it. Jack's looking around, watching some leaves blow by or a cat. He doesn't notice the car coming. No one does. I do.

It's a big, brown Caddy. It slides down the street in silence. The radio is turned off, no one inside speaks, the engine barely even hums. As it rolls over the asphalt, coming closer, the back window, driver's side, rolls down. Behind it is a guy in sunglasses, blue bandanna, hat turned backwards. He doesn't have a face. No color. Nothing distinguishing. Except a rifle. He pulls it up and leans out the window with it. I think to scream, but then think again. I'm not even there.

One shot is fired. It hits no one. Buckshot is buried in the paneling of the neighbor's house.

Jack turns. He just heard the noise. The loud BANG! He probably thinks it's a car backfiring and is turning to cheer it on. It's not.

Jack turns straight into the second shot. He takes it full on. The *cholos* probably dive out of the way. Steve is too dumb to, but Jack falls on him and shields him from the third shot, like he'd shield me from a boot in a concert. He takes the fourth shot, too. His face looks as if he is trying to find something but doesn't know where to begin.

Tires squeal. The Caddy is gone. Only the smell of rubber and smoke remains. And me—I'm left standing there. I'm left looking at him as he bleeds and stops breathing and dies. The smell changes to rotten meat. Jack is dead.

"No-no-no," I cried. "He's not. He's not."

"Take it easy, Mason," Burton said. "Take it easy."

"You . . . you . . . He wasn't supposed to be there. Why'd you take him? He doesn't do drugs. He didn't be*long* there . . ."

"I'm sorry, Mason," Steve said. "I had no idea. I mean, of course I didn't know, right? Why would I fuckin' know? I never would have gone."

My fist slammed against his cheek. The skin was soft and rubbery, but the teeth behind it were hard. I felt it jar him, and the shock shot back through my whole body. I was on him, pounding him. I was crying and screaming, "He wasn't supposed to be there, he wasn't supposed to be there, he wasn't supposed to be there. You stupid, stupid fuck. I hate you.

Fuck you. Fuck you. You should be dead. No one was supposed to be there."

Burton grabbed me and pulled me off. He was yelling my name. I kept hitting and kicking at the air, but I couldn't feel it around me. "— he wasn't supposed to be there, he wasn't supposed to be there —"

My elbow caught Burton in the neck, and he dropped me. I moved to kick Steve. I wanted to kick him in the stomach, to knock the wind out of him and stop him breathing, but he was all crumpled up on the sidewalk, sobbing, and I couldn't.

I ran away.

Burton called me. I didn't stop.

Now it was me trying to find something. Now it was me not knowing where to begin.

If only it were me that was dead.

17. STRAIGHT TO HELL

In high school, after I became friends with Jack, I spent lunchtime with him and his friends, a small pocket of the larger group of punks and freaks. We all hung out behind the gym, away from the cafeteria, acting like we were exiled and being snotty. I was mostly quiet and stayed close to Jack.

One day, a guy from one of the other cliques saw me sitting there. He had a big, green rooster cut and was as tall as Jack, but thin. He said, "Hey, Jack, what're you hanging out with that jailbait for?"

At the time, Jack was not only very protective of me, but even more eager to fight than when we were out of school. The comment was minor, but it was enough. Jack lunged at the guy, grabbing him by his jacket, saying, "You better take that back. Take it back."

"Fuck you, Jack, I got mine," the guy replied.

Jack pushed him away and lifted his fists, ready to brawl. A bunch of other kids quickly got between the two, knowing if they let them fight it would mean trouble for everybody. The guy's friends grabbed hold of him and dragged him across campus, telling him it was better if he just got out of there. Steve told Jack, "Fuck him. Let him run like a pussy. Whatta you care?"

It wasn't enough for Jack, though. He had to be sure he had the last word. During one of his classes, he got a bathroom pass and went to the dude's locker. With a fat marker, he wrote on the door, "Jail*bate* says Piss Off."

Everyone saw it after the next bell rang and thought it was a pretty humiliating blow to the other punk. Steve liked the name and started calling me that all the time. Soon, other people picked it up. Jack, in his haste to defend me, had tagged me, misspelling and all, for good.

Long after (it seems), Jack stands on the sidewalk, his back to the big car coming down the street. This time, I scream. I scream and scream and scream as loud as I can, but it's no good. Before I can do anything more, before I can make myself heard, I'm under Jack, being smothered by his body. I feel the jerk as the bullets hit him. I scream more, but only get a mouth full of flannel and blood.

I went straight to the hospital after I found out. I asked to see Jack. They told me he was dead. They said, "He didn't make it." They said it just like that. As if he was trying to catch a plane.

"Well, let me see the body, then," I demanded.

"We can't," they said. "His family has to come and make a positive I.D. first."

"What's going on? Where are they? What're you going to do to him?"

"We're sorry," they said. "We have to talk to his family first."

"What the fuck am I?" I asked them. "Huh? What am I?"

"Don't argue," they said. "Once we have final word from his next of kin, we'll let you know what's happening."

"Yeah, fuck yourselves!"

I sat in the waiting room and watched soap operas. The chair was too small. I felt pinched, and I couldn't get comfortable. A guy came in screaming. His hand was cut off, and they had wrapped a towel around the stump. It was all red, and blood was pouring down his arm. I wanted to stop him and ask, "Is that it? Is that all you got? That's absolutely fucking nothing!" Even after he was gone, I thought I could hear him sobbing from somewhere inside.

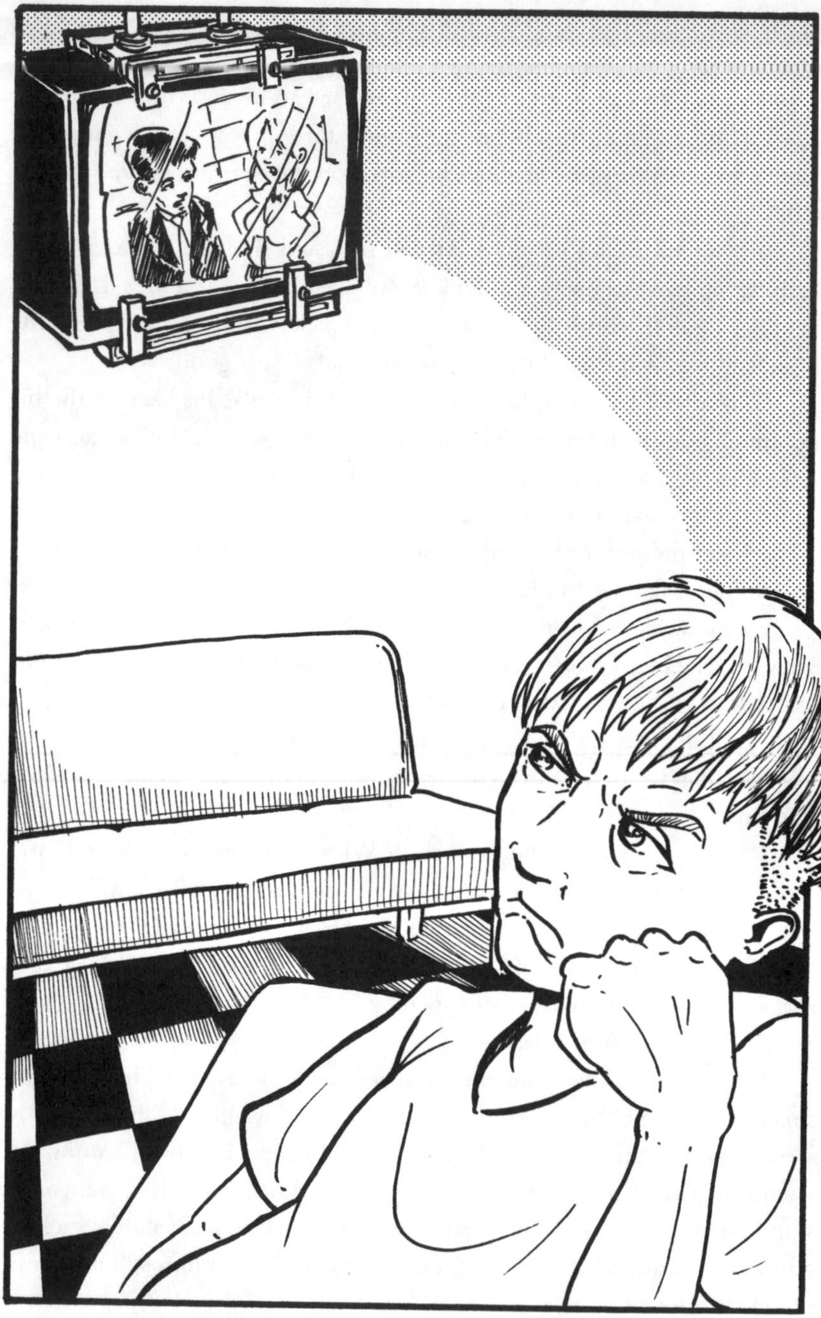

And then I thought of Jack.

"Please, lady," I begged the nurse. "You've got to tell me something. I'm going nuts just sitting there!"

"We've been over this fifteen times," she said. "I can't tell you anything other than what I've already told you."

I sat back down. I tried to think of things I could do. I thought of throwing my chair through the TV. Or setting fire to their magazines. I couldn't come up with anything that had any meaning. I felt like I'd been pushed out of it.

I had to do something. I wanted to be effective.

If you are there for the act, you can react.

I'd been pushed out.

I wanted something that would let me feel.

A poster on the wall said, "Friends don't let friends . . ." and that was all I could stand to read. I got up and went walking around. The front entrance was uncommonly bright. The sun was right above us, and it hurt my eyes. A baby was crying, real loud, and his mother slapped him. She told him, "Shut up, or I'll strangle you."

I bought a copy of a science-fiction magazine from the gift shop and tried to wade through it. I figured if I could give myself something fantastic to latch on to, this whole scene wouldn't seem so outrageous anymore. I mean, if I could believe stories about aliens and spaceships, how far-fetched would this all seem?

But it didn't work. I kept seeing Jack, turning, turning into the gunfire. Over and over. It was all too real. Play, rewind. Play, rewind. I started to cry.

I imagined Jack's funeral. Everyone was standing around. All the guys, his parents, sister, even his dead grandmother. I wore a trenchcoat and dark sunglasses. I was smoking a cigarette. The casket was closed, but then it didn't really need to be opened. Even if we saw his face, would we remember who he was? His grandmother looked at me, and then she mouthed the words, "That poor boy," to no one in particular. I blew smoke in her direction. I was imagining myself enjoying the misery. It made me sick.

A doctor came into the room. "Are you all right?" he asked.

I wiped my eyes and nodded.

"Are you the one who was asking about Mr. Kostler?" he inquired.

"Jack? Yeah, that was me."

My guts were all twisted up like barbed wire.

"I'm afraid we have something of a problem," he said. "Now, you are . . .?"

"Mason," I said. "I'm his roommate, um, his best friend."

"Well, Mason, you would be familiar with Mr. Kostler's family?"

"Yeah. Why?"

"We called his parents, and they have refused to come down to see the body."

"You're kidding me? Those assholes. Those stupid fucking assholes. Don't they . . .?"

"Would you consent to serve as Mr. Kostler's next of kin?"

"Why do you keep calling him that?" I snapped. "That's not him. He's Jack. Jack, goddamnit! Doesn't anyone even give a damn?"

"I'm sorry, Mason. I didn't mean—"

"Yes," I said. "I'll do whatever you need."

He took me back into the hospital. The hallways smelled like medicine. They smelled like sick. They smelled like the rancid cotton in your mouth after having teeth pulled. The lights made my eyes burn, like I'd been swimming all day, so I kept them almost completely shut. I didn't want to look or pay attention to where I was going anyway. I didn't want to see the walls or the rooms or anything. I was scared I'd be looking at the insides of death. I kept my eyes open just enough so that I could see and follow the doctor. He took me to a place way far back in the building. When we got there, I thought maybe it would have been wise to drop breadcrumbs along the way. What if I never found my way out?

The doctor had taken me to a small room with a single overhead light. There was a table in the center. A cold metal slab with a body covered in a sheet. The figure was small. My head got light, and I thought I was going to fall down. The doctor put his hand on my shoulder. "Are you doing all right?"

It was the second time he had asked me that. Again, I nodded.

"Let me see," I said.

"Are you sure you're ready?"

"I want to see."

A lie. I didn't.

I wanted to get the hell out of there and go hide somewhere. Go somewhere dark where no one knew me and just hide until I could forget. I wanted to go where Jack was going. I wanted to enter the impossible.

The doctor pulled the sheet forward. Jack's body rested underneath. He had no clothes on. His eyes were closed. His skin was a very odd, very pale color. His lips were blue. He seemed like he was made of wax.

"Is this John Kostler?" the doctor asked.

"John? You mean Jack?"

"Is this your friend?"

I didn't recognize him. I didn't want to say yes. I didn't want to admit that the thing lying there was Jack. Everything I knew about Jack was alive. This person was dead. It couldn't be him. Nothing dead could be Jack.

"Yes," I said. "That's him."

For all intents and purposes.

I touched the body's hand. It didn't return the grasp. It didn't even yield to mine. It only remained as it was.

The doctor pulled the sheet back up.

It felt as if there was *nothing* alive in the room. I thought perhaps I was in the stomach of death after all.

"Thank you, Mason," the doctor said.

They gave me a bag with his belongings in it and sent me on my way. I bought a blank postcard in the gift shop. I addressed it to Jack's parents. I wrote on it, "FUCK SHIT AND DIE!"

Outside, it was a clear, sunny day. There were no clouds, there was no rain. I expected there to be at least a drizzle. It seemed only right. But then, nothing else was, so why should the weather be any different?

I took a bus back into West Hollywood and got off about five blocks from the apartment. I walked back slowly. I didn't particularly want to get there. I looked in shop windows, stopped to pet a cat, did whatever I could to slow myself down. Unfortunately, nothing short of running in the opposite direction would stop me getting there.

When I finally arrived, the double glass doors in the front weren't familiar to me. I had to stop and think whether I had to push or pull to get them open. When I stepped on the stairs, they made a hollow noise, like they were saying, "Go away. You don't belong here." I even had to look at the numbers on the apartment doors to make sure I was going to the right one. It wasn't home. It was just a place I'd crashed for a night.

When I put the key in the lock, I suddenly felt hopeful. I thought maybe Jack would be behind the door. I don't know where the idea came from, but it seemed like the only possible truth. He wasn't gone at all, that really wasn't him spread out on the slab. Jack was on the other side of the door waiting for me to get back. "Where ya been, Mason? I'm hungry. Let's go eat." He was there. All I had to do was look.

I turned the key as quick as I could, threw the door open, shouted, "Hey, it's me! I'm back!"

There was no answer. The only thing behind the door was a stack of boxes. Boxes with cold, blank faces. We hadn't even unpacked. I looked around the room, around the entire apartment, for anything that was his, for anything that said Jack. There was nothing. His whole life had been packed away, put into boxes. He had been put away.

I sat down on the floor, in the middle of everything. The airless feeling—like at the hospital, back in the bowels of it with the doctor—returned. With all the boxes around, I felt there was very little room for me. I felt like an intruder. I felt alone.

Nothing was so impossible anymore.

I dumped out the bag of stuff from the hospital. His shirts, bandanna, old boots, and wallet. I looked in the wallet. Up front was a picture of us, in black-and-white, taken in a photo booth. We were seventeen. I was close to the camera, a big, dumb grin on my face. I had a terrible bowl haircut, forced on me by my mom. Later that day, we'd shave it all off, swearing if I couldn't have the hair I wanted, I'd have none at all. It was Jack's idea. In the photo, he was behind me, leaning against the back of the booth. He was sticking his tongue out and pulling down the corner of his eye so that the nasty, squishy rim was showing. Alive. Screwing around. The Jack I knew. The Jack I recognized.

I pressed my face into the carpet and cried.

This was a bad move.

18. THE WEEPING SONG

They buried Jack two days later.

I was contacted by someone I didn't know. Probably someone from the mortuary. He left a message on my machine, telling me where and when. I wasn't answering the phone. I didn't want to talk to anyone.

When I heard it, I said to myself, "I can't believe he's just leaving this on my machine." *My* machine. Just like that. Jack and I had bought it together. It had been *our* machine, but now he was dead, so it was mine. Too easy.

Jeane called twice. She said Steve told her. She kept asking if I was there and saying to pick up if I was. I sat on the floor with all the boxes and listened to her. I didn't care that she was there. I didn't care anything about the phone. I just wanted Jack to come out of the bedroom and laugh at me and say, "What? Are you deaf?" I wanted him to answer the phone, to say to her, "Yeah, he's here, but what's it to you?"

I got out all of Jack's Birthday Party and Nick Cave records. I thought maybe it would make it seem like he was there. I knew if he was there, he'd be listening to Nick Cave. I put on *The Good Son*. The only time I'd ever seen Jack nervous was when he met Nick Cave after the concert for that album. Jack could barely speak. He tried to hand his CD to him, but his hands were shaking so badly, he dropped it and the case shattered. Nick was very nice about it. He picked it up for Jack and signed the booklet. The music made me remember that, but it didn't make him come back. It just made memories come back, which was no good, because memories were just reminders of the truth. Memories were the past. Jack was the past.

I put on Depeche Mode's *Black Celebration* and drank some Peppermint Schnapps. Around midnight, I threw up and passed out on the bathroom floor.

I woke up in a puddle. It was late in the morning. I had to hurry if I wanted to make it on time. I threw on my leather jacket and splashed some water on my face. It was going to have to be enough.

When I opened the door, I found Jeane. She was sitting with her back against it, her knees to her chest, her face buried in her knees. She looked at me. "Mason," she said.

"Hi," I said.

Jeane stood up. "I've been knocking all morning. Why didn't you answer?"

"I was asleep," I said. "Guess I couldn't hear back in my room. Sorry."

"It's all right. I've been waiting to talk to you. I'm worried. Are you doing okay?"

"Yeah. Sure."

"Really? You don't look it. Are you really all ri—"

"Look, how do you think I feel?" I snapped. "My best friend was just murdered. Jesus!"

Tears filled Jeane's eyes. "Sorry," she said. "I'm just worried, that's all. And sad. I don't know how else I can approach you."

I looked away. I wanted to say, "It's not your fault," but I swallowed it.

"Where are you going?" she asked.

She knew. "The funeral," I said. But she knew.

"Yeah? Need a ride?"

"Sure," I said. "I'd probably be late otherwise."

"Okay." She smiled. She made a move toward me, but stopped, didn't know if she should. Then she moved again, reached out, and hugged me. I tried to give back, but I couldn't make my arms go around her. I felt like a crash test dummy who'd already hit the brick wall.

We went down to the car. I told her where we were going and got in.

"Any tape preferences?" Jeane asked.

"No."

I watched the passing buildings as we drove. And light posts. They went by so quickly, one after the other, that they all looked alike. Sometimes, in the quick flash, I thought maybe I saw Jack standing there, leaning against a pole, but then we'd be to the next one and he was gone. I could still see him in my head. He was just standing there, paying attention to nothing. The car is coming down the street. The big brown Caddy. The guy leans out the window with the shotgun. The face—that blank face—has grown a moustache. I don't know why. I was there, too. This time, I've got a pistol. I point it straight at the killer—his blank face with a moustache. Now there is a line-thin smile and two dot eyes, like pencil drawings on cardboard. I pull the trigger. The chamber clicks. Nothing. I pull again and again. Each time, I come up empty. The gangster aims at Jack and fires. I scream and jump in front of Jack. The bullets blast right through me. They don't touch me at all, but when I turn around, Jack's down, blood seeping out all around him, forming a large puddle on the ground. Like he's a piece of melting ice.

And I can't see him so clearly anymore. It's him, but I can't see his face. It's almost like he no longer has one.

I put the gun to my own head and pull the trigger. Click. Nothing.

Jeane pulled into the mortuary parking lot. There was a small, run-down building. Its outside walls were stucco. It was crumbling and full of holes.

We went in through double wooden doors the color of mud. They made a crackling sound. Inside was a short Mexican man with a beard and damp hair. "Hello," he said, "are you here for the Kostler service?"

"Yes," I said.

He pointed down a hallway. "The main room is down that way. We'll be moving to the cemetery at ten. You can spend some time with the deceased until then. There won't be any ceremony."

I nodded and went to where he was indicating. Jeane thanked the man and came after me.

The room was large and full of folding wooden chairs. They were all empty. No one was there. It smelled like dust. A plain coffin was all by itself up front. It was closed. "What time is it?" I asked Jeane.

"Five till."

"Nine?"

"No, ten."

I walked down the center aisle, hitting my hand on each chair as I passed. The slap was loud. It echoed in the empty room. Up above the coffin was a large crucifix, brown except for the bleeding from Christ's hands and head. The red of the blood was chipping, showing white underneath.

I knocked on the coffin. Silence. I laughed. Then I felt bad. I could feel Jeane behind me. Had she heard me? I didn't want to look.

I opened the lid. Inside was the body, stretched out on burgundy velvet. It was supposed to be Jack's body, but it didn't seem like it. The skin of his face was a deep, powdery pink. His lips and cheeks were practically red, the color on the latter applied in sloppy circles. The last time I saw him he had been purple. I guess this was meant to be more natural. Dead was as natural as you could get. He didn't look dead. More like he was in a cabaret.

Jack's long hair was cut off in the back. What was left was nicely combed, slicked back, very clean. He was wearing a blue suit. I laughed again. I couldn't help it. Jack in a suit. I laughed loud. It was very funny. I had to sit down I was laughing so hard.

I sat down and cried.

The Mexican from the entrance came into the room with a few other men. They closed the coffin lid and lifted it off its platform. "If you're ready," the Mexican said, "we'll move to the cemetery now."

"Wait," Jeane said. "Shouldn't we hang on until everyone else gets here?"

The Mexican stammered. "W-w-well . . ."

"No," I said. "No one else is coming."

"Mason!" Jeane was shocked. She put her hands against her chest, like she was scared I was going to hit her or something.

I know she didn't think that, but that's what it looked like.

"This is most likely it, Miss" the man explained to her, and it almost sounded like an apology. "All the arrangements were made over the phone, and they didn't seem to care all too much about it. They said make it as cheap as possible—but no cremations. They don't believe in them or something."

"No one else is coming," I said. "Nobody gives a fuck."

The Mexican motioned for his men to continue. We followed them out. The Mexican locked the front door behind us. The coffin was put in a big, black hearse. They slammed the door and locked it, as well. The handle on the door squeaked.

"You can follow us, if that's okay?" the Mexican asked. We said that was fine, and he got into the hearse.

We followed behind in Jeane's car. She turned the radio off. Neither of us talked. The only sound was the engine, and I ignored it. It felt like we were underwater. The farther down the road we went, the greater the depth. I kept waiting for the pressure to crush us like a peanut between two headbutting trains. I kept waiting for my skull to cave in. We were sinking.

I would shoot myself in the head and put blood all over the windshield.

The graveyard was a small grass field in the middle of the city. It was surrounded by a dirty wall of white bricks with black spikes on top. Next door was a warehouse outlet selling unfinished wood furniture. All the tombstones were flat on the ground. Plaques, really. *In honor of your recent achievement in the field of dying* . . .

The men took the coffin and put it in a cradle straddling an already dug hole.

A priest came in a separate car. It was a small blue hatchback driven by a woman with white hair. The priest himself was bald. He came up and asked, "Are we ready?" The Mexican said yes. "Then let us begin."

He delivered a speech about God's ultimate plan for us. He said, "However brief our time on earth, we were here for something. Even in our end, there is meaning, and Jesus has built a home in His kingdom where we can be safe and happy and free from harm." I wanted to ask him what I should do until I get there. If my home is so far way, where do I stay now?

When the priest finished speaking, he asked if there was anyone who wished to say a few words about the deceased, almost like he was pretending that there was more than just us there. Jeane looked at me. I was staring down into the hole, into the dirt. It was dark down there. It was empty. There were no words for that.

The priest said a prayer, and the men began to lower the coffin into the ground. The cradle's winch made a shrill noise that hurt my ears. The box began to disappear beneath the edge of the hole. It would be the last time I would see it, I thought. I screamed out, "Wait! Stop!"

The coffin jerked and froze in the air. The men looked at me. The Mexican, the priest, Jeane, the white-haired lady—they all looked at me. I went to the edge of the hole, knelt down. I stretched my arm and grabbed the lid of the box and opened it. There was Jack, still trapped inside with no hair, covered in cheap make-up, and wearing some other man's suit. I could see now that the jacket was too small and his bare wrists were sticking out. His eyes were closed, like he was only sleeping. But I had seen him sleeping a million times, and this was nothing like any of them. When Jack was sleeping, I could look at his eyes and know he was dreaming in there. There were no dreams behind that face. None. I wanted to be able to open his eyes. I wanted him to look at the sky one last time. I wanted him to look alive, to be alive, even if it was just pretend. I wanted it to be like a game of war on the playground. "I shot you." "Uh-*uh*. Missed!"

But Jack was dead.

I spit on the corpse. I could see it, white and shiny on his powdered nose. "Fuck you," I said. "No sell out."

I kicked the coffin. It shook on its cradle. Everyone was stock still with open mouths and wide eyes. They were stunned. Like freeze tag. Good. Back to the playground. I slammed the lid, turned, and walked away.

"Wait, Mason," Jeane called after me. "Let me dri—"

I flipped her off behind my back. I didn't even look at her. My feet were on grass, but outside was the street. It would take me to where I needed to go.

Wherever that was.

19. DAMAGED

I started to work a lot more. The boss was glad to have someone go full-time during the week. He was hoping to get a lot more day customers, take advantage of the Melrose traffic. This was all fine with me. I needed something to do.

Jeane came in once. She started to ask if I was okay, which I was pretty damn sick of people asking me, and I cut her off. "You can't come in here," I snapped. "I keep getting in trouble for having friends in here, so get the hell out before someone sees you." It was a total lie, but I hoped the way I said it would give her the hint.

Nights, I would leave by the back exit so I wouldn't see her or her store. I went back to the apartment and drank and listened to music. I was buying a lot of gothic records I would have made fun of before, and I would play them and burn candles. By two or three in the morning, I'd be really drunk and pass out. The alarm would wake me up, and the whole thing would start all over again.

One night, I was in the middle of a binge, and I got the idea that it would be really funny to call a suicide hotline. I found the number in the back of the phonebook. Some guy answered.

"Hello. Hotline. This is Brad. You want to talk?"

"No, you fuck, I dialed for my health."

"In a manner of speaking... yes, you did."

"..."

"What's going on, man?"

"What do you think? I'm gonna kill myself."

"Uh-huh."

"That's it?! That's all you got to say? 'Uh-huh'?! Fuck you, Brad!"

"What do you want me to say?"

"'Don't do it.' That'd be a good start."

"Why would you listen to me? You're not listening to yourself."

"What?"

"Well, if you want me to tell you not to, then really, you're telling yourself not to. If you're not going to listen to *You*, what chance do I have?"

"What the hell kind of shit is that?"

"Hey, man, what's your name anyhow?"

"Shouldn't this be anon'mous?"

"If you like. Have you been drinking?"

"My name's fuckin' Lee Majors, and I'm fuckin' gone, man!"

"No, Lee, you're not gone yet."

"Listen, Brad, you wanna know how I'm gonna do it?"

"If it'll make you feel better, Lee, sure, but it's really not impor—"

"I got this gun, see? A real nice pistol."

"Where'd you get it from?"

"What the hell's that matter? Some guy was sellin' them out of the back of a van on the street. You could get a gun or a good deal on speakers. Your choice. Big fuckin' noise either way. *Now*, you wanna hear how I'm gonna go out or not?"

"Go ahead, Lee, I'm listening."

"My name's not Lee, you asshole!"

"I'm sorry. What is it then?"

"Uh . . . hell if I know . . ."

"That's okay."

"It's Tom Bosley. That's it! Now, you wanna know how I'm gonna do it or should I hang up?"

"Please, tell me, Tom."

"I'm gonna blow my brains out, asshole. I'm gonna walk right out in the middle of the street, and in the middle of rush hour, I'm going to put my brains all over some cunt's Volvo. What the hell you think of that, smart guy?"

"Sounds kind of gross to me."

"That's 'cause you got no heart, you fuck. It's shits like you, you can't kill yourself, you ain't got no guts, so all you can do is talk other guys outta it and force them to live your shame."

"Doesn't it take more guts to keep going, Tom?"

"Fuck you! My name's not Tom."

"I'm sorry. What is your name, then?"

"Ah, fuck it."

I hung up. I took some sleeping pills I'd gotten from a connection of Steve's I knew and went to bed. Had a horrible dream where I wanted to buy a rifle and the guy wouldn't sell me one. I kept telling him he had to, it was the law. He pulled out an uzi and pointed it at me. I tried to run, but I couldn't get my legs to move. It was agony, just trying to get to the door. I kept waiting for him to blast me, but he never did.

I don't remember days too well. I remember nights. But not the order. They're mostly the same. The days are the same, too. Different from the nights, but the same as each other. The days I had off, I slept away the last night's drunk. That's if I could sleep.

Jeane called occasionally. I still wasn't answering the phone. I just let the machine record her little message bombs in between alarm call beeps.

"* . . . Hi, it's Jeane. Just want to know how you're doing. Call me, all right? . . . *"

"* . . . Mason . . . I'm worried . . . Can you pick up? Are you there?

. . . Call . . . *"

"* . . . Look, you don't have to talk to me. I just need to know you're okay. I just need to know what's going on. You can just call, say 'I'm fine,' and hang up. Please, do something . . .*"

"* . . . Fuck you, Mason. Go to hell! You shut me out, so fuck off . . .*"

"* . . . I'm sorry, Mason. I love you. I meant it when I said I *needed* to hear from you. Call anytime. I love you . . .*"

I ignored them.

Well, I didn't *ignore* them. I just didn't call back.

February came around. The day before Valentine's day, things begin to start to come back together. I remember that day. That day is the brick wall. All the other days stop tumbling and SLAM!

That day, heart-shaped pieces of paper were everywhere. Plastered to newspaper machines, on the ground, stapled to telephone poles. A stack of them was in the comics store. They were blue, and on them was a line drawing of a man's head—long face, triangle chin, heavy eyes. They said, "FOR THOSE ALONE ON VALENTINE'S DAY – **LIKE A DOG** – Ritalin 8pm – w/DiscoTents – (also 2/13)."

I took one and pinned it to my sleeve.

That night, when I got off work, I made my usual stop at the liquor store for a bottle of Schnapps. It was becoming so routine, I didn't even have to show the old man my fake I.D. I made angry faces at the surveillance camera, looking out of the corner of my eye to see myself on the moni-

see myself on the monitor. The old man saw me doing it. He ran his fingers through his greasy white beard. "Video is the wave of the future," he said.

"Is that so?" I asked.

"Yeah, yeah," he said. He licked his lips. "The gov'ment is putting cameras in people's television sets. When you watch TV, they watch you back."

"Get out of here."

"Serious. They got it going on down in Atlanta. That's their test site."

"They just go into people's houses and stick cameras in their TVs?"

"Yeah," he said. "People know about it. Like me, I read it in the free press, you know? Everyone is just scared of the gov'ment, so they pretend it's not there. Who can blame 'em? When your own home is dangerous . . . Jimmy Carter, he's bankrolling a lot of it. You're probably too young to remember Jimmy Carter, huh?"

"How much I owe you, man?" I asked.

"The warning is free, but the bottle is four bucks."

I gave him the money. He handed me back change. His fingernails had dirt caked underneath them.

"Don't tell no one I tol' you," the old man said. "Just you and me know, right? People–those people–they'll get you if they think you know, you know? Nowhere is safe. They'll get you."

"I'll throw out my TV right away," I said and waved him off.

Jeane was waiting for me when I got to the apartment. She was kneeling down, petting a neighbor's cat. She didn't see me. I contemplated backing down the stairs and getting out of there, but I froze. Jeane looked up. She smiled. "Hi," she said. Her voice was low.

I stomped to the door and unlocked it. I was going to go in and slam it on her. She grabbed the back of my shirt.

"Wait," she said. "Don't do this to me." She almost sounded like she was growling. Her face was all tensed up.

"What do you want?" I asked.

She took a deep breath. Her face settled. "Can I come in?"

"Sure, why not."

I opened the door for her, and Jeane went in. She looked around at the unpacked boxes and the trash on the floor. I sat against the wall, wedged between boxes.

"So, how have you been, Mason?" she asked.

"How do you think?"

"I suppose it's been pretty tough." She kept her voice even. "You don't look so hot. You haven't shaved, or . . ."

I didn't say anything.

"What have you been doing?" She sat down on a box.

"Don't sit on that!" I exclaimed.

She jumped up. "What? What?" She was confused.

"That's Jack's clothes," I said.

"I'm sorry, I — "

"I've been working a lot. If I want to keep this place, I've gotta make rent."

"You know, if you need a place—"

"I'm doing fine here."

Jeane nodded. There was a silence. She looked around. I watched her.

"Mason . . ." she began.

"Save it."

"No, Mason. You don't have to do this. You don't have to go it alone."

"Ahhh . . ."

"I understand how you feel. A lot of people go through it."

"No! You don't! Don't tell me . . . you don't understand. A lot of people don't understand. They're not *me*. They'll never know how *I* feel. You'll never know how it feels to be me and to have nothing, okay? I am here. I am by myself. When the lights are out, it's just me, and you can't know that."

I got up and walked past her into the kitchen. I didn't want to see her eyes get all glassy and full of tears.

"That's so much crap, Mason," she said. "You may like to think you're alone, but it's not that way at all. I may not be able to know everything and give you all that's necessary in life, but at least I can hold your hand and make you smile and just be around. You need that. *I* need that. I may not get to know you completely, but give me a chance to see how close I can get."

I didn't say anything. I didn't even look at her. I kept my back turned. I couldn't look at those eyes.

"You've got a responsibility to other people. When you've started something, you've got a responsibility to stay with it. You can't just build a house and when a light bulb burns out decide you don't want to live there anymore. You started something with me. Like it or not, you did. The least you could do is own up to it. You owe me that."

I turned on her. "Owe you?" I said. "Fuck you! My responsibility is me. I'm all I got. I don't owe anyone nothin'."

She stood completely still. "Really?" she asked, staring into my face. "Regardless of what you do to other people? You don't care about that?"

"Just me, baby. That's it."

She nodded, but still remained motionless. "It seems everyone I run into is with you on that one," she said. "A bunch of selfish pricks. You know, my mother didn't care I was there. She was too busy trying to hide from things she knew had died. She spent hours working on her face and chasing guys she knew were going nowhere just to try and pretend that youth and love hadn't passed her by. She didn't want to admit they were gone. That's your problem. You're too scared to look at those of us who are alive, because you know if you do, you'll notice who isn't there. You're scared of a dead man, Mason."

"I walk with the dead. Nothing about the dead holds any fear for me."

Jeane began to cry. The tears wouldn't hold any longer. She tried to wipe them away before they could move down her face, but there were too many of them. "Look," she said, her head down, "why don't we just calm down, we can get something to eat—"

"Why don't you just get out?"

She looked up at me. Her eyes were as round as cannonballs. I bit my lip and prayed my face would hold, that I could look like I meant it.

Without saying another word, Jeane left.

I took the bottle out of my pocket and put it on the counter. I looked at the seal on the cap, and it seemed like the only thing that mattered in the world was breaking it. I removed my jacket. Something scraped on the inside of the sleeve.

The paper heart was still pinned to my shirt.

"Go to hell, Mason," I said. "Go to hell."

20. I WANNA BE ADORED

The sky was clear, but the air was cold. The apartment reminded me of Jack and my own rotten self, and Jeane's perfume remained and reminded me of her, so I had to leave. I couldn't stay and get drunk again. Not that night.

I walked down Melrose and looked at all the people on the sidewalk. I had never done that before. I was always in the middle of it, and I never cared about who I was there with. Now, I saw faces—long faces, fat faces, ugly faces. No one looked back at me. They all looked down to their feet or in shop windows. No one saw my face. The exhibits never view the tourist.

I stopped in briefly at NoWay. FreakWent and Sure Am, Sure Am were sharing a bill with On Your Last Nerve opening. There wasn't much of a crowd. I moved on.

Ritalin was up on Sunset, so I caught a bus on Fairfax rather than walk. The bus was almost empty. Just the driver, an old woman with her groceries, and a business man. The old woman had her face down in her grocery bag, but I could see her eyes. She was watching me. I stared at her as

I walked past. I scowled. Trying to get as far away from her as I could, I sat in the back, but I could still feel her old lady eyes on me. They felt like spiders on my skin. I wanted to crush her.

The bus arrived at Sunset. I pulled the ripcord and left by the back door. Before I stepped down to the curb, I looked back at the old lady and stuck my tongue out.

It was a Monday night, but there were still a lot of people on the street. I put my hands in my jacket pockets and walked with my head down. I was going to blend in and be like everybody else. No more looking at faces that didn't belong to me. A disembodied voice called out to me. "Hey, buddy!" It was like steel wool.

I stopped, a little startled. I could see a figure in the darkness of an entryway, but no features. Just a shadow.

"I got anything you need," the voice said. "Just name it."

"That's okay," I said, following it up with a little nervous laugh. "I'm all right."

I moved on.

The club was a simple building, a black box with the word RITALIN painted in white on its front. There were no windows and no outside light except for in the solitary doorway on the end. There was a long line of people waiting to get in. Through the wall, I could hear the bass of a techno song. Next to the door, one of the heart-shaped flyers was taped to the brick. "**LIKE A DOG**."

I walked down the line, heading for the end, when someone called my name. "Mason!" I looked up and down the row of people, but I didn't recognize anyone. No one was looking at me, either. "Mason!"

I looked to the front of the line. There in the doorway . . . it was Jack. He had a big smile. He was wearing a black T-shirt and matching bandanna. He had his arms out, was reaching to me. My heart screeched to a halt, and then picked up a bizarre rhythm.

"Mason! My God, boy, where have you been?"

The voice.

It wasn't Jack at all. It was Lenny.

But the size, the bandanna, the booming call—it could have been Jack. For a second, just a second, it was.

"Jesus, Mason," he said. "I've been waiting for you to come by. I need your approval on the new place George has got here."

"I didn't recognize you," I said.

"Me?" Lenny laughed. "Look at you. Your hair's grown out, you've got a beard . . ."

Pause.

I could see it coming. Like the ground smashing into a suicide.

"Listen, man," Lenny said, "I'm sorry. I just heard a couple of days ago. It's the shits, man, it's the shits."

"Yeah, well . . ."

"You know, Mason, if I had known, I would have been there in a flash."

"I know, Lenny," I said, "I know."

But it seemed too easy. He approached it and went right on by. He got off too easy.

"Hey, it's good you're here," he said, trying to pick it up. "Seeing as you're a friend of mine, what say we bypass that line, huh?"

He stepped aside and motioned toward the door.

"Thanks, Lenny," I said.

"You got it. Any time."

The inside of Ritalin was massive. From the outside, it looked small, but that was very deceiving.

The dance floor itself was several feet below ground level. It was square and was located in the center of the club, with the stage at the back. The pit was packed with people, all throbbing and sweating in sync with the techno that filled the place. I couldn't see any speakers. It felt like the music was coming up out of the floor.

Beams of colored light shot from the corners of the dance floor, cutting through the crowd, disappearing somewhere near the outer edge. They were the only lights in the main room. The bar was up off the floor, near the entrance. It was fully lit so you would have no trouble finding it in the darkness. I headed straight for it.

As I walked along the wall, hugging close to it, letting it be my balance in the black, I noticed it was decorated with bamboo poles. They were each maybe a foot apart and ran perpendicular to the floor. The same design was on the walls all the way around the club. It looked like a cage.

I sat down at the bar. My initial impulse was to order a drink, but Lenny knew I was underage and wouldn't like me using a fake I.D. in his club. So, I ordered a Coke. While the bartender was serving it up, I looked at myself in the mirror that was on the wall behind his bottles. Lenny was right. I had to see who was standing next to me so I knew for sure which reflection was mine. My hair was all messed up, and the parts that had been buzzed were all grown out and shaggy. My eyes were deep and almost hollow looking, bags and circles underneath them like shadows. My skin was the color of dough. I was fucked.

The crowd was more mixed than I was used to seeing at NoWay. Apparently, the Sunset location had attracted more of the trendy club crowd. A guy in a suit came up to the bar and ordered a Sex On The Beach. He smelled like body odor and cologne. I watched him pull a wad of money held in a gold clip from his inside jacket pocket. He saw me looking and smiled. "Fuck yourself," I said, and turned away.

Near the edge of the dance floor, a goth in white-face approached a blonde in a skinny black dress. The death boy was smoking a tiny, hand-rolled cigarette, and the heat was bubbling the make-up on his upper lip. He leaned over and said something to the blonde, a sly smile on his face. She looked at him with disgust. He laughed out loud. She walked away.

The music went from techno to Crime & The City Solution to industrial to N.W.A.

Two skinhead girls were dancing close. Next to them, a curly headed guy in a college sweatshirt was with a girl in a leather jacket and miniskirt. She held a cocktail glass high above her head and kept her eyes closed. Behind her, a frail boy in a ruffled shirt danced alone.

From the far end of the floor, four guys with crew cuts started jumping up and down and pumping their fists in the air. They began working their way through the crowd in a weaving, snake-like fashion, grabbing other dancers as they went. Soon, it became a great path of people slithering through the mass, dancing with their fists raised to the ceiling, a grotesque bunny hop. The longer it went on, the longer it grew, snatching people up and making them a part of it, trapping them in movement, thrusting them forward, feeding the line.

They played the Mary Chain's "UV Ray," The Ramones' "Rock 'n'

Roll High School," De La Soul's "Magic Number," Bauhaus' "Telegram Sam," Erasure's "A Little Respect," Adam and the Ants' "Stand and Deliver."

And the mass kept moving, kept chugging along.

Then the DJ put on The Specials' "Ghost Town," and things began to slow down. Some took a rest, went to get a drink. Others just danced slower. Everyone started closing in on themselves. It became less of a crowd and more just isolated groups of people bunched together. The music settled into a subdued electronic groove. The club got quiet except for the beat.

I turned back and stared down at the bar. The wood was smooth with lacquer and stained a dark brown, and in the flow of the stain I saw the head of a cow. Then an old witch with a hooked nose. I would blink my eyes, and they'd be gone. I couldn't find them again.

The music stopped, and all I could hear was people talking and the clinking of ice in glasses. I focused in on a withered hand in the stain and waited, listened. Slowly, low, I could hear an acoustic guitar. Just barely. The people kept talking. I could hear one girl, her voice just a squeak. She was laughing out of control.

The guitar got a little louder, and underneath the strumming, I could hear drums. I was beginning to recognize the song. The Smiths' "Please Please Please Let Me Get What I Want." I turned on my stool.

Up on the stage, Eleanore was alone in the light, strumming her old, brown guitar. Mike was in the back, brushing the drums softly. Emery was off to the side, in the dark. Nobody seemed to take any notice of them.

Then Tristan stepped up and began singing. His voice was just a faint hum, lost in the crowd's babble. But as he sang each word, he got a little stronger, and the people began to fall beneath it. One by one, they stopped talking and turned and watched and listened.

Good times for a change
See, the luck I've had
would make a good man
turn bad
So please, please, please
let me, let me, let me
let me get what I want
this time

Haven't had a dream in a long time
See, the life I've had
would make a good man bad
So for once in my life
Let me get what I want
Lord knows it would be the first time
Lord knows it would be the first time

The audience was silent. Tristan's voice soared out above them. One hand held the microphone, the other moved with the words, moved with the emotion. It was on his face, too. The feeling.

He sang the second verse again, and there wasn't a sound in the club. Even the girl with the squeaky voice had stopped laughing. Only Tristan and Eleanore's guitar remained, the drums having slowly faded out. Two solitary birds flying their course. A girl in a suede shirt danced on top of a table, slow, almost like she was with a lover. I closed my eyes and leaned against the bar and forgot the stools next to me weren't empty. Solitary birds.

Eleanore and Tristan—guitar and voice—ended together. In triumph. The audience clapped and cheered and whistled. Tears were running down my face. I was sobbing uncontrollably.

Tristan smiled shyly. "Hello," he said. "This is 'When You're Lonely.'"

Mike hit his sticks together, counting three. He began the song with a slow beat. Emery came in on bass, picking the tempo up just a little. And then Eleanore, beautiful and plush and full . . . Jeane would have said it sounded like crushed velvet.

Jeane . . .

Damn . . .

Life is long
Life is so very long
when you're all alone

And is it wrong
not to be strong
not to be a stone
Life is so very long
when you're alone

Every day
a new film of dust
on my window
pushes me away
further away
further from normal
Life is long
so very long
I'm all alone.

They played for an hour. In that hour, I forgot. The music swirled around me and held me and smoothed out the bad ripples in my memory.

For an hour, I wasn't Mason. For an hour, Mason was lost. For an hour, I was part of something, something whole. I was part of music. There was energy in my body.

When the band finished and left the stage, it was all over. I was jetti-

soned again. I was another guy at a bar with a dead friend. I ordered another Coke and went back to remembering.

Like A Dog came out of a door near the bar. They didn't see me,
which I thought was probably better for all of us. The bartender had their
drinks ready for them, and they took them eagerly. Eleanore looked particularly exhausted. She swallowed her mineral water in one gulp.

Emery took two bottles of beer in his hand. He sucked on one, tilting
his head back, and when he brought the bottle down from his mouth, he
noticed me sitting there. He spit a mouthful of beer back into the bottle.
"Holy . . ." he said. "Is *that* Mason?"

The rest of the band looked. Tristan got a big grin on his face.
Eleanore came over and hugged me. She smelled like sweat and peaches.
"How are you?" she asked. "I can't believe you're here."

"Are you kidding?" I said. "Nothing would make me miss this. You
guys were fabulous tonight. I-I . . . the new stuff . . . just amazing."

"Thanks, Mason," Tristan said. "It's good to see you."

"Yeah," Emery said, "but what's with the beard? You trying to look
like a man?"

"Shut up, Emery." Eleanore shot him a nasty glare.

I said nothing. But I didn't take my eyes off of him.

Emery took another drink. With his tongue, he flicked a little spit at
me. "Well, I'm leaving," he announced. "More action out there." He
motioned with his head to the dance floor. "Oh, by the way, Jailbate . . .
sorry to hear about Jack. Real shame." He snorted.

I slammed my glass down on top of his bottle. The beer foamed up
and spilled out of the bottle onto his hands and the floor. "Ah, shit," he
said, holding the bottle away from his body. "You asswipe!"

I jumped up off of the barstool, my fists clenched, the right one tight
around my glass. "Say another word, fucker, just one more, and I'm going
to smash this up against your fucking head."

Emery's eyes burned. He stepped closer to me, closing his fists.

"Do it," I said, "and I'll kill you. Just another inch, and I'll crack your
bones."

Emery took another step forward and I began to pull back to hit him,
but Eleanore jumped between us. She put a hand on my chest and an arm

against Emery's. She put her face right up to his. "Back off," she snarled. "*Now.*"

Emery pushed against her. Sean jumped behind him and pulled his arms behind his back. Tristan took the beers from him. "Go take it out on someone else," he said, putting the bottles down on the bar.

Emery loosened. "Fine," he said. "Another time, maybe." He shook Sean off and disappeared into the crowd.

"I'm going to keep an eye on him," Sean said, and he too disappeared.

I sat back down. "Sorry," I said.

"Don't mention it." Eleanore smiled.

"It was nothing," Tristan added.

I turned on my stool and went back to looking at the wood stain on the bar.

"Mike and I are going to finish packing the equipment," Eleanore said. "You take it easy, okay, Mason?"

I swung back around. I hugged Eleanore again. "Thanks," I said.

"Yeah . . . sure . . ." She went out through the door by the bar. Mike followed.

I sat down again and cursed myself. I just gave Eleanore more than I gave Jeane. Her choker was still on my wrist, and it burned my skin. I scratched under it. There was a crimson indentation in the skin all the way around my wrist, and it made my bones and my veins appear to be closer to the surface. I looked in the wood stain and saw myself dead on an old notebook.

Tristan sat down on the stool to my left. "Emery's a bastard," he said. "I'm sorry."

"Happens," I replied.

He took a sip from his cream soda. "I heard about Jack, too," he said.

I nodded.

"That really guts me," he said. "Lenny told me. I had no idea. When did it happen?"

"New Year's. But it's over now."

"I guess."

No, it's not over, I thought, *I don't know if it ever will be.*

"I meant it when I said you guys were really good tonight," I told him.

"I think the best I've seen you."

"Thanks," Tristan said, "it means a lot. We've been working hard. I think it was good to start with the Smiths cover. I was nervous about it. I just wanted to give everyone something to latch on to, something they knew. Win them over and *then* hit them with the unfamiliar, you know?"

"Hey, what happened to you guys New Year's Eve? I was down there with Jeane . . ." I stopped. Jeane.

"Oh, God," he said. "I guess I haven't talked to you in a while."

"No."

"In October, I went to England. I stayed with some pen pals and roamed around. I went to a lot of shows. I got to meet Tim Booth from James and this guy Frank Read. He's in this really great new band called The Trash Can Sinatras. You have to check them out. I went to Manchester and saw Morrissey's house, which was a thrill. I even saw him once. He was driving around in a Cabriolet.

"I went to Ireland and Scotland, and I hopped over to France and saw some of Europe. I went to Oscar Wilde's grave and the Rodin museum and the Van Gogh . . . it was just incredible. I wrote a lot of poetry and really started to think about what to do with Like A Dog. It may be the turning point for us. I see big things.

"Anyway, I came back on Christmas Eve. Eleanore booked us at NoWay, but with all the new songs and time off, we decided it would be better to wait. We wanted to get polished and start off really fresh. I think we're the tightest we've ever been."

"I agree," I said. "The songs sound wonderful, too. Especially that second one."

"Yeah? The lyrics are a bit of a riff off of 'The Queen is Dead.' I wrote it outside Morrissey's house. I got his gardener to take it inside and give it to him. Well, supposedly he gave it to him. Just the possibility is enough."

"That's fantastic."

I finished my Coke. A whale surfaced in the stain.

"Are you sure you're all right, Mason?" Tristan asked. "I know this time must have been tough. I can't really imagine . . ."

"Don't worry about it," I said. "I'm doing fine. You don't need to waste your time on me."

"I'm your friend, Mason."

"Man, things sound like they're going the right way for you. I'm glad. You deserve it."

Tristan blushed and looked away. I ordered another drink.

Tristan cleared his throat. "I need to go, Mason," he said with some trepidation. "I have to help with the equipment."

"No sweat."

"It was good seeing you again."

"Yeah."

He headed for the door. A firefly too bright and fast to be captured by my grasp.

"Tristan!" I called after him.

He stopped.

I smiled. "'*When you're dancing and laughing and finally living, hear my voice in your head and think of me kindly.*'"

Tristan laughed and vanished behind the door. I felt I was at the bottom of the ocean watching him walk across the surface of the water above me.

And I saw Jack. Standing on a lonely sidewalk. A shotgun ballet. The blast hit him in the face. It wiped his features clean away. I couldn't even tell it was him.

I gulped down the rest of my drink. I needed something stronger. I had to leave.

I went to the bathroom. One of the light bulbs was burnt out, and it was dark and empty. It was like a cave.

Completing my business, I went to go wash my hands. William was waiting there. I was taken by surprise. He was sitting on the sink. He was smiling without showing any teeth.

"William?"

He nodded.

"How're things, William? I haven't seen you around lately."

He shrugged. He only smiled.

I stared at him hard. He only smiled.

I was frightened and angry and I could feel my face and hands get hot. I rushed forward and grabbed William by the collar. I pulled him off the sink, threw him up against the wall, shoved my face into his. From the

corner of my eye, I could see our reflections in the mirror. They multi-
plied in my head to a million reflections. They went on forever without
stopping. Everything went on and on, and I wanted there to be a stop.

"Why are you here?" I said, my voice like a tight and trembling guitar
string. "What are you doing hanging around? What are you doing always
hanging around?!"

William's smile narrowed. "I know you," he said.

"What?"

He didn't say anything more. Only smiled and looked at me. His face
was hollow. His eyes and mouth were deep, black holes. I began to shake.
I threw him aside and ran from the club.

21. OVER RISING

In the morning, I hopped a Greyhound and set out for San Diego. Jack and I had gotten tickets for The Charlatans at the university. We'd planned to visit Burton and go to the concert. It was supposed to be a blast. Then lots of things became a blast.

I needed escape. I needed out. Alcohol didn't do it. Music had let me go. Like A Dog could do me right, but records couldn't. Records kept me confined. They kept me in the apartment. I had to keep running.

I still had the paper heart pinned to my sleeve. I still had Jeane's choker on my wrist. I was running, but I wanted my demons in tow.

I forgot to bring food, and by noon, I was starving. A middle-aged couple and their daughter had the seats across the aisle from mine. The woman had frosted hair and wore a white T-shirt and khaki shorts. Her husband sat next to her. He had a bad hairpiece that he held onto his head by wedging his sunglasses over his skull. The woman had a bucket of chicken in her lap.

Their little girl—she wasn't more than eight—was in the seat in front of them. She had on a red dress with a white apron over it. Her shoes were

black with coppery buckles. She
had ribbons in her hair.
Standing on her seat, the
little girl reached over
and took a drum-
stick from the
bucket. When
she ate it, she
got the grease
all over her
hands, but she
bit into the meat
carefully so as not to get
any on her face. When she
was done, she put the bone back in
the bucket. The girl then held out her hands and let her mother wipe the
grease off of them with a wetwipe. I could smell the lemon soap. Her
mother cleaned each finger, one at a time, with soft strokes, and when she
finished each hand, she kissed the girl's palm. She then daintily wiped the
girl's lips—just dabbing at them, really—and then kissed them. "All done,"
the woman said.

The mother put the lid back on the bucket and put it under her seat.
I looked at it down there, and my stomach seemed to grow even more
empty. I couldn't stand it anymore. I leaned over and said, "Excuse me?"

The woman and the man looked simultaneously. Out of the corner of
my eye, I could see the little girl peeking around the side of her seat. I
could see her ribbons.

"I'm sorry," I said, "but I didn't think to bring any food. I was wondering if I might have some of your chicken?"

The woman smiled. Like adults do when talking to a child. "Nooooo,"
she said. "There's not enough."

"I would just need a piece," I begged. "I'd pay you."

"No. I apologize."

"Thank you. Apologies are mine."

I turned back and stared out the window. I took the collar of my leather jacket into my mouth and sucked on it. It was sour.

At Oceanside, the family got off. The little girl took the bucket of chicken and ran over to a planter where a bunch of pigeons and sparrows were. She took the lid off and began pulling scraps out and throwing them to the birds.

The bus moved on.

On the back of the seat in front of me, I wrote with a black pen, *I got the teenage depression. It's becoming an obsession.*

The bus let me off near the college campus. A guy at a gas station gave me directions for the rest of the way, and I walked. It was bright outside, and the air smelled of fish. Guys walked around with shorts and no shirt on. Girls wore tank tops and had their hair pulled back. I was sweating in my leather.

I found the campus all right but realized I had no idea where anything was on it. I stood on the sidewalk outside and stared into it. The place looked gigantic and fake. It was almost like I was looking at a huge bill-board. I expected it to say, "Come . . . Escape Inside," in big red letters. Or maybe it would say, "Run While You Still Can."

I opted to get a burger at the Jack-In-The-Box down the block before actually going onto the campus. I sat alone in a corner booth. The table and the seats and the walls were all red. I felt like a dark splotch on them. A tan guy with long blonde hair came in. He was smiling and several people said, "Hello," and, "What's up?" and I thought it didn't matter if they knew him, they'd say it to him anyway. Some guys are just like that. I imagined a gun in my hand and knew it was a way to make my colors match everything around me.

I threw my trash away and went on campus. There wasn't any litter on the ground and no graffiti on the walls. The place was pristine. I wanted to write **FUCK** real big in bright spray paint on something. I wanted to cut it into the lawn. Great big scars. F. U. C. K. Fuck fuck fuck. At the very least, I wanted to chew a piece of gum and spit it on the sidewalk for somebody to step in.

People walked by wearing sweatshirts with school or fraternity letters on them. They were all in groups of two or three, sometimes more. I don't know what they were talking about, but they all seemed to be smiling. They seemed so happy that I thought there wouldn't be any problem with asking them where the concert was. I tried to stop a couple of guys. "Excuse me," I said. "Could you tell me . . . hey, excuse—"

They kept walking.

I went up to some girls at a picnic table. They were laughing. I was going to tap one on the shoulder, but chickened out. I stood behind them and hoped they would notice me, but they kept talking and laughing and didn't turn around once.

So, I wandered around some more. Something honked twice behind me, and I turned just in time to see an orange cart coming straight at me. I jumped out of the way. A janitor was driving. He had two big trashcans on the back. If he hadn't honked I would have thought he didn't see me at all. I doubt he'd have stopped if he'd run me down. Just another assassin in a death machine. He owned the road.

He'd have written **FUCK** all over me if he could. Letters in tire tread.

Eventually, I found the ticket office. A girl was inside the booth. She was reading *Wuthering Heights*. "Excuse me, please," I said, "but where's the Charlatans concert at?"

The girl didn't look up. She just stretched out her hand and pointed off behind me. There was a charm bracelet around her wrist. A silver heart was hanging lower than all the other trinkets on it. Sunlight sparkled off of it, and it made me think of my heart—flat and made of paper—pinned to my sleeve. Then the girl pulled her hand away and turned a page in her book.

Over where she had pointed, a line of about twenty people was waiting. I went over and sat down at the end.

A circle of high school kids were sitting right in front of me. They were playing Go Fish. The guys wore baggy, striped sweatshirts and overalls. One of them had on a floppy terrycloth hat about two sizes too big and decorated in rainbow colors. He hadn't shaved in a while and had a scruffy beard. Next to him was an Arab kid with a rat face. He had buck teeth and freckles on his nose and his eyes were sunk part way inside his head. He had a bowl haircut and wore a blue sweater with red stripes around the neck and wrists. He didn't do much. He barely even held on to his cards, and he never said anything, just shook his head yes or no when asked if he had sevens or jacks. When it came around to him, he never asked for anything. He just took straight from the pile.

The girls in the circle were all blonde with white faces and red lips. One wore a baby doll dress with flowers all over it. Another wore a tight sweater with black horizontal stripes. They both smoked clove cigarettes.

"Does anybody have any E?" asked the guy in the terrycloth hat. "I could really use some E."

"Shut up," the girl in the dress said, flicking off some ash. "You've already taken some."

"But I want *more*," said the hat.

"You always want more," the dress snapped. "You're a pig!"

"I told you we shouldn't have brought him," complained the striped girl.

"I didn't want to fuckin' come!" the hat shouted. "I wanted to go to a rave or something underground, not with a bunch of tight chicks who won't give me no fuckin' E!"

"Oh, shut up," the striped girl said, tossing the butt of the cigarette in his direction.

Another guy and a girl came up. They were Asian. He had on a green shirt that went down to his knees. His hands disappeared in the sleeves. His pants had bellbottoms, and they covered most of his yellow hiking boots. Half his face was hidden under a jester's cap. I could only see his mouth, and it was expressionless.

The girl had long hair in pigtails, and she wore glasses and overalls. She had some Charlatans twelve-inch singles under her arm. "Hey, guys, what's up?" she said.

Everyone in the circle responded. "Hey, how are you?" "Hi." "What's goin' on, girl?" "Wanna play?"

Someone from up front called, "Hey, Cathy!" and the Asian girl waved to him and a few other people around him. The striped girl shouted back, "Why don't you mind your own business up there, asshole?" She laughed.

"Bitch," replied the guy up front. He laughed, too.

I wondered if I was the only one there who didn't know anybody else in line.

It got dark, and the little group put their cards away. The three girls started to sing "I'm Free." It ended with them giggling and falling all over each other because none of them could stay together. The boys sat in silence.

200

I watched a tall, skinny kid with wavy blonde hair and a white dress shirt walk across a faraway lawn and come toward us. He had his hands in his pockets and kept kicking at things in the grass, but I never saw any of the things he was knocking away. He was whistling.

The kid strolled along the edge of the line, waving to the occasional person that called out to him. He was getting closer, and I wondered when he was going to stop, just where he thought his place was. It wouldn't have surprised me if he walked to the front of the line and just sat down and made himself first. He got right up next to me and looked down. He grinned. "Hello, neighbor," he said.

I was about to tell him to piss himself, when the girl in the dress jumped up and ran to him. "Ronald! Omigod, what're you doing here?"

"I broke out!" Ronald replied.

"No!"

"Yeah," Ronald laughed, "not even bars on the windows can keep me inside. Anybody got a butt?"

"Aren't you supposed to be clean?" the dress asked.

"I am! They haven't taken my piss for a week. No worries. I'm fully recovered."

Everyone laughed. "Fuckin' Ronald," the terrycloth hat said, and he snorted.

Ronald sat down in the circle, and the dress sat next to him, her head on his shoulder. The jester boy passed a pack of Marlboro reds over to Ronald, and he took one. The striped-girl flipped the top off her Zippo and reached it over. The cigarette caught fire and burned orange. Ronald exhaled through his nose, which was long and curved like a bird's beak.

When he breathed, his cheeks sucked in and out. His skin looked like a wet paper towel draped over his skull. His arms and legs were thin as telephone wires. He was a scarecrow.

Or maybe it was a skeleton he reminded me of.

I know skeletons.

"Hey, did anybody see '120 Minutes' on Sunday?" Ronald asked.

"I did," the dress said.

"Did you see the video for The High?" he asked.

"I don't remember," the dress giggled. "I *was* high."

"Hey, man, you get MTV in the clinic?" the velvet hat asked.

"Shit, I get whatever I want," Ronald replied. "A happy boy is a sober boy. No one saw the video?"

Everyone shook their heads and mumbled, "No."

"I *told* you guys. Watch out for The High. I told you they'd be big, and now they're on '120 Minutes.'"

"What the hell are you talking about?" the striped girl asked, grinding a cigarette out on the sole of her shoe.

"The *High*. They're a new band from Manchester."

"What do they sound like?" the dress asked.

"The Stone Roses, kind of. You see, the leader of The High," Ronald explained, putting a cupped hand in the air to signify the leader, "was in The Stone Roses." He put up his other hand, this one being the Roses, and then put the two hands together—the guy from The High in the Roses. "He left The Stone Roses and formed The High." He pulled the hands apart again. "He helped create The Stone Roses' sound. I'm telling you, they're going to be huge."

"I watched '120,'" the hat said, "but I didn't see those guys. I saw some Morrissey video. They said his new album is going to be called *Grandfather, Beat Me* or *Beat Me, Grandfather* or something weird like that."

Ronald laughed and spit off to the side. "Now we know where *his* manic depression comes from," he said. "Spent too much time in the back room with the old man."

Everyone laughed.

"Morrissey . . ." Ronald went on, "why does he even come out with stuff anymore? Shit, if you're so depressed, why don't you just die? Morrissey! What the fuck? He don't matter none."

I glared at them. "Since when?" I asked.

"Hey, neighbor," Ronald said. "Do you wear black on the outside because black is how you feel on the inside?"

"Maybe," I answered.

"Ignore Ronald," the girl in the dress said. "He's a jerk."

"Yeah, ignore me." Ronald smirked.

"He was away two months and didn't write or call once. Doesn't that sound like a jerk to you?" the dress asked.

"I wouldn't know," I said, and looked away.

"Are you here by yourself?" she asked.

"Yeah."

"That sucks."

"I do everything by myself these days."

"Ohhhh . . ." the dress moaned.

"Ah, fuck," Ronald said.

"We all have friends here, and he doesn't," the dress said. "It's sad."

"He's sad," Ronald said, and they laughed, and that was the end of it.

After a while, they opened the doors. It was dark, and the line disappeared around the side of the building. At the entrance, they were frisking people, and when someone got through, they ran into the club at full speed to get their spot. The girl in the dress and the one in stripes ran in screaming and waving their hands. Ronald just strolled casually, like he knew there'd be a spot waiting for him.

I was frisked and was all ready to go through, when the guard said, "You have to take those out."

He was pointing at the safety pins stuck in my pants.

"What?" I asked. "You've got to be kidding . . ."

"Nope. You have to take those pins out."

"But I've been to hundreds of shows, no one has made me take them out."

"You ain't been to this show. This show is different. Take them out or don't go in. I don't care which."

He moved me to the side. I hurried and pulled the pins out and shoved them in my pocket. I showed the guard my bare pant leg. "Okay?"

"Go on in," he said.

I sprinted into the club. All the people were crowding in at the stage. I joined them at the side, finding an open hole one person away from the barricade. A techno song was on the sound system. It had a steady, droning beat. As people packed in, it got hot. The heat and the constant drumming made me tired. I began to sweat, and soon my shirt was soaked through. The air was thick. I felt like when I was hiding under the covers as a kid, hiding from my parents, who would be in the other room. They'd be fighting. Screaming at each other. I'd hide under my blanket and wait and wait and wait, wait to fall through the mattress and go on into the world beneath my bed where only kids lived and no one ever shouted. I'd wait and it would get hot and the air would get stale and I wouldn't be able to breathe. So, I'd stick my nose out the side of the sheet where the air was cool and fresh, knowing I might be breaking the magic. I thought of that in this crowd, standing on my tippy toes, sucking the sweet air above everybody's head. I was telling myself not to worry, there never was any magic.

Scratch it. A lie. A bullet. A little piece of magic. Boom. Abracadabra. You've disappeared.

Boom.

The opening band was atrocious barroom rock. More people piled in as they played, and everyone packed tighter together. I tried to come down off my toes, only to find I couldn't, there wasn't any more room for my feet. But my toes were beginning to cramp. Pain wracked my calves. I decided to fuck it and brought my heels down on some other guy's foot. He yelped. "Sorry," I said, giving a weak smile.

"It's not your fault."

"Really? It's about time something wasn't."

He laughed slightly.

The opening band finished, and the techno started again. Everyone groaned.

The lighting people started to test the lights. Occasionally, the house lights would blink off, and we'd all get excited, only to get disappointed when it would turn out to be a false alarm. Kids started pushing and getting in closer. Everyone started to get shuffled around, squeezed over as other people tried to move in. I attempted to stay where I was but couldn't for very long. I remembered putting little boats in streams when I was young. We lived in a place with lots of hills and stuff. The little boats were made out of wood, just scraps, and I'd paint them and stick on cardboard sails. I'd put the boats in the water, and the tiny currents would bounce them down the stream. Every once in a while, two rocks or some trash would present an obstacle, and the boats would be stopped for a second, but the pressure of the two objects would tighten the current, making it stronger. Pretty soon it was so strong it would shoot the boat out from the blockage and keep it moving.

And here I was. Unable to stand still. Pressed and shifted. I couldn't stop moving.

Later, after my dad cut out, we moved to the city. I used to sail boats in the gutter. Or I'd hop the fence and go into the sewer and wonder where the little vessels would go. Sometimes at the beach, I'd look and see if I could find them washed up on shore, but I don't think they ever made it that far. They were probably stuck somewhere in a nasty morass of algae and trash.

And here I was. I froze up. Still being pushed around, I froze. I couldn't move a muscle, not even a twitch. Like one of those boats. What the fuck was wrong with me? All these things I was thinking about . . . I was a kid then . . . I asked myself, *What am I now?*

The lights went out. The crowd roared and leaped as if a single beast, and the movement smashed against me. The music started. I could see the band in between people's heads and over their shoulders. I was trapped now, my face pressed into the back of someone tall. The air was old and sweaty and thick like motor oil. I was being jiggled back and forth, the crowd jumping to the rhythm, my face lodged in the spine of this person. He pulled me with him as he pushed away towards the front, my cheek stuck to the dank of his shirt. He was pulling me between other people—separating them for himself but letting them snap back and crush me. I was being wrung like an old towel.

Then the guy I was pressed against began shoving his butt back, trying to push me off. He did it about three times, but each time, the mass behind me just pushed me right back against him. He pushed me again, and then spun around to face me. It was Ronald. He bit his bottom lip and scowled at me. I somehow managed to stay steady, but the people behind me were threatening to shove me back into him.

"Can't I tie my fuckin' shoe?" he yelled, leaning in real close. Little flecks of spit launched off his lips.

"Sure," I shouted, "if there's room."

Ronald shoved me back again, a flat hand against my chest, and went down on one knee. His shoe wasn't untied at all, but he pulled on the bow and tightened it. He stood back up.

"Thanks!"

"Fuck you!" I shouted.

He turned around to face the stage again. I was going to punch him in the back of the neck, but before I could raise my fist, the crowd surged again. I was pushed off to the left, and as I went, I could see Ronald jumping into the air, using the guy in front of him as leverage, screaming out at the top of his voice.

Somehow, I became fixed, wedged in between all the people. My head hurt. I couldn't see right. It was like my eyes had been left behind two inches over to the right. I needed to breathe.

Suddenly, something slammed into me, and I relented to the force, my feet staying in place, me going over backwards, bending at the knees. Everyone continued to move, and I was swiveled around, still bent over, but now in the opposite direction. I tried to rise, to straighten myself up, but the people on either side of me came crashing together, trapping me between them like a mosquito between two giant hands.

It hurt.

Like I'd been caught beneath a collapsing building.

They pulled apart.

I felt dead.

"Fuck it," I said.

I turned toward the back of the hall and began to push my way out. "Coming through," I said. "Let me go."

A Mexican boy with a thin moustache refused to move. I tried to shove past him, but he pushed me back.

"Can I get by?" I asked.

He moved out of the way.

Near the back, the herd thinned out. People were standing and watching the band. I stopped and tried to breathe and cool down. There was a girl with a lace top on, and she had light brown hair in a ponytail. "Come *on*," she whined. "This sucks. I can't see *anything*. Let's go *up*." She looked about fifteen or sixteen.

Her boyfriend gave up and took her hand and dragged her into the mob. They were gone.

It occurred to me then.

The music wasn't mine anymore.

If it ever was.

Here I was. Yanked out of it. Hiding where it was safe. It wasn't mine anymore. If it ever was.

Fuck fuck fuck.

The music wasn't mine. *So, then, what was?*

I wrapped my arms around myself. My hand touched my sleeve. It was bare. I looked down. The paper heart had been ripped off.

22. DISINTEGRATION

I was in bed, sleeping. I was older. It was a small room with blue carpet, and the bed was just a mattress on the floor.

I opened my eyes. I was awake. There was nothing to wake me up so suddenly. I was just awake, like I had been anticipating the moment. I got up off the mattress. I was in my underwear. The room was dark.

There was a desk to the right of me. Above it was a window with blinds. I went to it and turned the control rod and opened the blinds. An intense, white light came in. It was an astounding light, and I could see myself fading into it, becoming just a silhouette against it. Outside the window, shapes moved, but they were distorted. They were like blobs, oozing across the surface of the light. I couldn't make out what they really were.

I reached down and pulled open a drawer on my left. I wasn't looking. My hand knew the way. It found a gun. Cold. My skin stuck to it. The gun was frozen. Steam rose off of it as I brought it into the light. I raised it to my head. I held it there.

The light blinked off for a second. It was black again.

Then I saw the leg of the desk, the floor. A pool of blood had formed there. More drops of blood steadily fell into the pool, exploding and fading into the liquid. There I was, bathed in it, my face down against the desk, my head cracked and leaking. My life was running out, soaking into papers and running off the edge of the desk. The gun was still in my hand. The light made it absolutely clear.

That was the end.

I woke up, and I was sprawled out on the hallway floor in the apartment. There was a spilt bottle next to my head, a soggy spot on the carpet. I pushed myself up, and my muscles ached and cracked and fought against the movement. I managed to turn myself over and sat with my back to the wall. I had my leather jacket on, and I was all sweaty. My hair felt like it had been dipped in grease. My skull throbbed.

A little bit of sunlight was coming through the windows. It looked as if the sun was on the other side of the building. That meant it was going down. It was evening, and I couldn't remember the last time I was awake, just that it had been dark. I didn't even know what day I was in.

There were six messages on the machine. One was from Jeane on Friday evening, another was Jeane on Saturday afternoon, and the rest were hang-ups. It was Saturday? Christ.

I peeled off my clothes and got into the shower. I started it off cold but quickly turned it to as hot as it could go. It just pissed on me with no real vigor, but it felt good. I watched the water slide down my body and rush into the drain. I stared at this for a long while. Then I imagined the water turning the color of blood. I got out.

I dug into my boxes for some clean clothes but found none. There were piles of clothes all through the apartment, so I went through those and picked out the best that I could find.

After I was dressed, I walked down to Melrose. Most of the places were closing up. It was dark, the moon was out. I went to Johnny Rocket's and ordered a burger. It wasn't enough, so I got a second one and some fries. I didn't even realize how hungry I was until I started putting the food in my mouth. I had probably been running on fumes and alcohol for days. The reality of it all escapes me.

When I was done, I went back out on the street. It was cold. I zipped up my jacket and went over to a sidewalk newsstand. I looked to see who was on the cover of *NME* and *Melody Maker* that week and checked out what old comics they had in their racks. They had a really old back-issue of *Playboy* from the mid-eighties with Sybil Danning, a bad b-movie actress, on the cover. I had seen her on TV when I was a kid, and I thought she was sexy. When the magazine had come out a few months later, I had really wanted to see it, but I was always too scared I'd get caught sneaking a peek and get arrested or something. I figured better late than never, so I picked it up and thumbed through it. There were pictures of her just naked and pictures of her touching herself and close-ups of her face with pink lips pressed in a pout or a moan. I was turned on. There was a whole rack of similar mags, old and new. So, I kept looking.

The next magazine was much more explicit. The women were pressing their breasts together and spreading their legs. They stuck their tongues out and were bending over with their butts in the air.

A third magazine had women together, licking and feeling each other.

I didn't know *what* I was thinking. My stomach felt like it could growl at any moment, like it was ready to rumble. None of it made sense, but I kept looking, searching through the racks for worse ones. I wanted them to be sleazier, not some cheap, sweaty fantasy from when I was in diapers.

The man who ran the place came over to me. "Hey, kid," he said, "are you going to buy any of those?"

"I don't know," I said. Women stared out at me from the covers, with taglines like "Hot and Waiting for YOU!" and "More Double-D Action!" I began to feel stupid. "Kid, I don't even think you're old enough for those magazines. That beard ain't fooling nobody. You don't want me to get in trouble, do you? Why don't you take off and go play at the park or something."

"Fuck you," I said.

"Don't be like that, kid, I—"

I hurled the magazine at his face. He tried to catch it, but it went through his hands. I took off.

"You little shit!" he yelled. "I'll remember you. Don't be coming back around here, you got that?"

I gave him the finger over my shoulder and kept going.

Only, I didn't know *where* I was going.

I walked up and down the block a couple of times and finally decided to go down to NoWay Home. It was dark on the street outside. Someone had busted out the streetlight. People were in the parking lot, smoking and drinking, gathering in packs and whispering. I saw a couple wrestling in a VW bug. His pants were around his knees, her underwear over the headrest of the front seat.

I looked in the door of the club. The place was three-quarters empty. A thrash band was on the stage. The singer had long hair and no shirt. Big, bulging veins stood out on his neck when he screamed. A group of six or seven guys tried to get a pit going, but as I watched, an elbow went into somebody's eye and the two guys tried to fight. The group separated them and everyone went to opposite sides of the room, leaving the dance floor empty.

At one of the tables, sitting all alone, I saw Steve. He was staring straight ahead. He didn't blink or swallow or anything. He just sat there, completely still. He looked skinny. His face was sunken in. He looked like a rotting piece of fruit.

The bouncer came over from the bar. "Are you coming in, or what?" he asked.

I didn't say anything. I just looked at his face. He looked familiar, but I couldn't think from where.

"Well . . .?" He had his arms crossed, and he was looking down at me. Then his eyes widened and a big, dumb grin came across his face. "Hey, you're that puny dick that used to come in here with that meathead guy . . . You're that Jailbate kid . . ."

I took a step back. It was all clear now.

"You little faggot," he said. "Lenny ain't here now. You thinkin' you're going to get through this door?"

"No."

"I'd like to see you try, queerbait."

"I don't want any trouble."

"Oh, yeah? Well, you're on my list of troublemakers. I keep it right here." He tapped on his temple. "Right at the top, it says, 'That little faggot kid, Jailbate.' What do you think of that?"

"Nothin'," I said, and I turned and ran. Right out of the parking lot without looking back.

In my mind, I kept seeing a gun. It was lifted to my head. A bright flash. And back to the gun.

I was fed up. There was no place for me around there. I bought a couple of bottles of Schnapps and went to a bus stop. I just figured I'd hop on the first bus and go wherever it was going. About fifteen minutes and half a bottle later, one pulled up. It was heading to Santa Monica. I got on.

The bus was empty except for an old black guy talking to himself. He smelled like pickles. I sat in the back.

I ended up down at the beach, a couple of blocks down from the pier. The street was quiet. The air was heavy with the smell of salt and sewage. A couple of homeless people were settling down for the night, huddling up against trees, going to sleep on the grass. I could hear the water off in the distance and see the white foam at the head of the waves. Beyond that, there was only blackness. Black all the way out, fading into the sky and the stars.

Some people were down at the pier. Couples sat close together on the benches and looked out into the night. I heard one guy whispering about how he'd love her forever, he wasn't like all them other guys, he was infinite. She smiled and yielded, and they started kissing. I went down to the end of the pier and sat on the edge, dangling my feet over the side. I took out a bottle. The water rushed in beneath me.

Jack and I used to ditch school and go out there. We'd play video games in the arcade. Or we'd go down to the water and throw sticks into the ocean and wait for them to come back. I kept hoping, too, that I'd find my boats. I kept hoping my boats would come sailing back.

Once, Jack got in a fight with his dad and ran out of the house. He was gone for two days. They couldn't find him anywhere. They kept calling my house and asking my mother if she was sure he wasn't there, if she was sure I didn't know where Jack was. She'd put down her drink and stumble into my room, saying, "Where is he? You know! Don't tell me you don't! Do you know where liars go?"

And I'd answer, "In the river of fire, Mom, and I haven't any idea where Jack's gone."

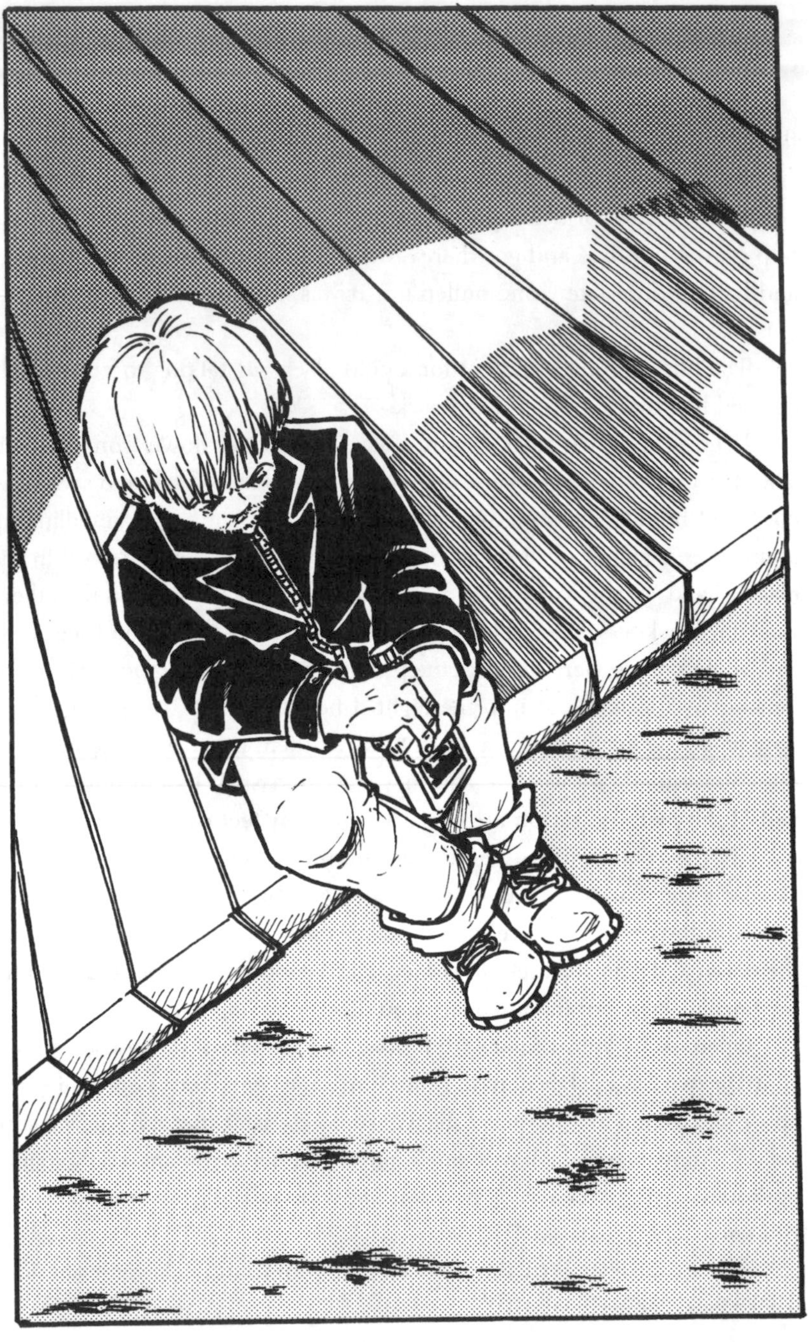

And she'd say, "Just remember what happens to liars."

It was the same threat I'd gotten all my life. By then, I figured hell was pretty much a safe bet. Only that time, I wasn't lying. I didn't actually know where Jack was, though I had a guess.

Instead of going to school, I went down to the pier. Jack was underneath it. All the support poles made the place look like a forest. Jack was sitting down there with his knees hugged to his chest, trying to stay warm. A bruise covered his whole right cheek. It was turning yellow. "The old man slugged me," he said. "I'm not leaving till I don't want to slug him back."

Jack started crying. It was three more days until he went home.

That was our one bad time at the pier. I always remember the bad times best.

It's hard to guess how long I sat there. I drank slowly and watched the water go in and out. I thought about drowning, being trapped beneath the water with nowhere to go. I thought about it a lot.

Except for an old woman sleeping on a bench, I was the last one out there. All the lovers went home or someplace else. They had someplace to go. I had another bottle. I started drinking it.

I walked several blocks with a vague understanding of where I was taking myself. The farther I got from the pier and the farther I got down the bottle, the clearer the idea became.

I walked back to the old place. Where my mother still lived. I stood out on the curb for a long while just staring at it. I looked at my old window, the second story on the right. There was a BB hole in the glass, left over from when some guy snapped, got a good idea, and shot up the town. I used to squirt water through the hole and get people on the street. Or I'd open the window and shout over the PA on my radio. I'd shout, "Hey!" and scare people. They would jump and look around for who was yelling at them. I'd say, "What're you looking for, asshole?" and just fall down laughing. I always had to quit by four, though, because my mom would be getting home from work. Usually, I'd leave and go kill time somewhere.

In the building's courtyard, they had a small garden. It was mainly rocks and cactus plants. The plants had gotten pretty tall since I had last been there. Tall enough that I could go sit down in the middle and nobody could see me. I sat there and stared up at the old door, sipping from my bottle, staring and waiting for the door to open or a light to come on. So many  times I had considered diving off the walkway of the second story. So many times I almost put a stop to it. A gray cat slinked in between the cacti, keeping one eye on me. I tried to get it to come over so I could pet it, but it ran away.

I kept waiting. After some time, I saw a small light in her window. It was a bluish color, and it flickered. She had gotten up and was watching TV. I stayed there, watching the flickering blue light. She was up there. My mother was up there watching TV, drinking something strong. Here we were, my mother and me, getting drunk together.

Then the light went out.

I began to shake. I could hear the air going in and out of my nose. My hands were moving side to side, trembling, moving like they wanted to do something but didn't know what. *I* wanted to do something but didn't know what. I became afraid.

"Fuck this!" I screamed, jumping up. "*Fuck this!*"

I held my bottle by its neck, and I threw it as hard as I could. It spun end over end and smashed against the ledge of the walkway, right under my mother's door. The glass rained down, little clear sparks struck off the stone.

"Fuck you! Don't you dare turn your back on me again! You can't just get up and walk off! You fucking bitch! You cunt! I'll kill you, you piece of shit! I'll rip your tits off and shove them down your fucking throat!

Cunt bitch!"

"Hey."

"I'll murder you, bitch!"

"Hey!"

"I'll kill you!"

"*Hey!*"

There was a man standing in the doorway behind me. He was in his underwear.

"What?!" I yelled.

"You better get out of here before I call the cops."

"Fuck you! Call 'em. I'll kill them, too. I'll kill *you*."

I grabbed a rock and held it over my head like I was going to throw it at him. He slammed his door shut. I looked around. Lights had come on all over the building. Except my mother's. Her window was still dark.

"Fuck every one of you!" I shrieked. I leaped from the cacti and ran out the front door. I turned and looked back in. The door was made of glass. The rock was still in my hand. I screamed as loud as I could and put the rock through the glass—a big, jagged hole in the middle.

Her light still didn't come on.

I hurried and went down the next street. I kept going and turning at every block, at every corner. I was crying and couldn't stop. I wanted to get lost. I wanted to be someplace I didn't know. Someplace I was new.

It was all familiar. Every street sign. Every driveway. It was old. I had been down the same sidewalks a hundred times. So, I decided if I couldn't get lost, I'd do the exact opposite and go somewhere familiar.

Two blocks over was Laine's house. There were no lights on inside. There were no lights on in any of the houses on the whole street. I was apparently the last person awake in the whole world. Everyone knew what it was like to be asleep but me.

I hopped over the wall into Laine's backyard. Her bedroom was there on the side of the house. Her curtains were closed. I tried to look through the crack between them, to see if she was inside, but the crack was too small. I sat down with my back against the wall. I looked at my hands in the moonlight. They seemed small, thin. Some nails were bitten down, others had grown long. These hands . . . they had nothing to do.

Jeane's choker was on my wrist. I sucked on my lip. I was lost. I was totally lost at last. I had no idea what I was doing there. None.

I lay down on the grass. It was soft and wet against my face. It smelled musty, like it had been left alone for a long time.

23. HIDEOUS TOWNS

The sun woke me up. It was just starting to rise, and its light roused me from my sleep. My face was pressed flat against the earth. The grass looked monstrous. Inches from my face, an ant was laboring with a rock it mistook for a crumb. I smiled.

I sat up. The two sides of my head suddenly smashed into each other, and I felt dizzy. There was dirt caked on my cheek and in my beard.

The night before rushed in on me, and I felt sick.

I quickly hopped back over Laine's wall and got out of there before anyone saw me. I had been stupid. Really stupid.

I walked to a nearby Denny's. I sat at the counter and ordered some coffee and scrambled eggs. Both made me ill, but I ate and drank anyway. My head lost a little of the pressure, and the world slowed its spinning.

An old man sat next to me and drank cup after cup of black coffee. His hands shook so much that he could barely get the cup to his mouth without spilling it all over the place. He drank in silence and looked straight ahead. The waitress kept coming over and refilling it. She never asked him if he wanted any, and he never said. She gave it to him anyway.

I whispered to her, "How do you know he wants more?"

"He comes in here every day," she said. "He always wants more. When he's done, he'll leave."

That struck me. *When he's done, he'll leave.* I couldn't think of anything that made more sense in the universe.

It was a gray morning. I decided not to take the bus and to see how long it would take to walk back to the apartment. I thought maybe being by myself for a while would be a nice thing. I mean, I'd been alone since Jack . . . I hadn't been by myself at all, though. Just alone.

After some time, I came to a church. It was a small brown building with a triangle roof and well-cut lawn, and it sat on the corner of the street. A sign out front said, "GOD ISN'T TO BLAME FOR THE ACTIONS OF HIS CREATURES – SERVICE 9-11AM – ALL WELCOME."

Inside, they were singing. I listened for a bit. It seemed weird. I wanted to go in but was distrusting of the sign. It had been a long time since I was part of the "ALL" that was "WELCOME." I couldn't imagine myself welcomed anywhere, but I guessed it was worth a shot.

I was greeted by a blonde guy in his mid-twenties. He was wearing a blue suit. He smelled like milk. "Hello," he said, extending his hand. "How are you this morning?"

His voice was even, his words measured out in exact tones. I shook his hand but felt myself draw back a little, like maybe he was going to come so close he'd hit me. "Okay . . . I guess," I said.

"Well, maybe we can help you be a little more sure about that," he said. "Can I show you to a seat?"

"Sure."

He led me into the main room. There was an aisle down the center, on either side of which were long benches. The singing had stopped, and all the people in the benches were praying along with the preacher. He was a balding man with glasses. He wore a charcoal suit and stood behind a podium on a stage at the front of the auditorium. On the podium's front, there was a yellow cross with lines coming out of it that were supposed to represent light. A larger version of the cross was on the wall behind him.

"Dear Lord," the preacher said, "bless us today with your presence. Look down on our worship and see that it . . ."

The blonde man motioned for me to follow him down the aisle. He took me all the way to the second row. There, he pointed at an empty spot in the middle, between a bunch of older men in suits. "Go right on in," the blonde man whispered. "My name is Brian. If you have any questions after the service, let me know."

I nodded.

The men stopped their praying and were now looking at me. I excused myself and squeezed down the aisle to the empty seat. I sat down and looked up at the man on my right. He was looking down at me. His mouth was tight, his arms were crossed, and he bowed his head in greeting. I smiled weakly and looked up to the preacher. I didn't want to look to my left because I could feel that man was watching me too. In fact, I was sure the whole group must have been looking at me, and maybe even the preacher himself. I was a dark spot, leather among tweed. Everyone was so nicely dressed. Their hair was combed and well-cut and all in place. I had slept on the ground all night.

I tried to listen and ignore everyone else. The preacher was beginning to talk now. He was saying, "John tells us the story of Lazarus. He is a friend of Jesus who has grown ill and who dies. When Jesus hears the news, he tells his disciples that they must return to Judea because, he says, 'Our friend Lazarus sleeps, but I go that I may wake him up.' The disciples hear the word 'sleep,' and like many of us, they assume he *means* sleep. They think by sleep he means slumber, rest, he's sleeping, dreaming, will get up in the morning. They don't think he means *dead*.

"How many times have you stumbled into work, groggy, cranky, looking for that cup of coffee? You're a mess. You tell everyone, 'Oh, give me a minute, I'm not awake yet.' You ever say that? You say, 'I'm not awake yet'?"

People responded with "Amen" and "Yes." I heard the man to my left shift. His suit made a rustling noise. I glanced at him. His face was solid. He nodded to me.

"In effect, what you are saying is, 'I am still asleep,'" the preacher continued. "Do you understand the basic concept of the words? You are telling everyone you are still asleep. You should be in bed, but you are up walking around. You go through your daily routine downtrodden, out of it.

221

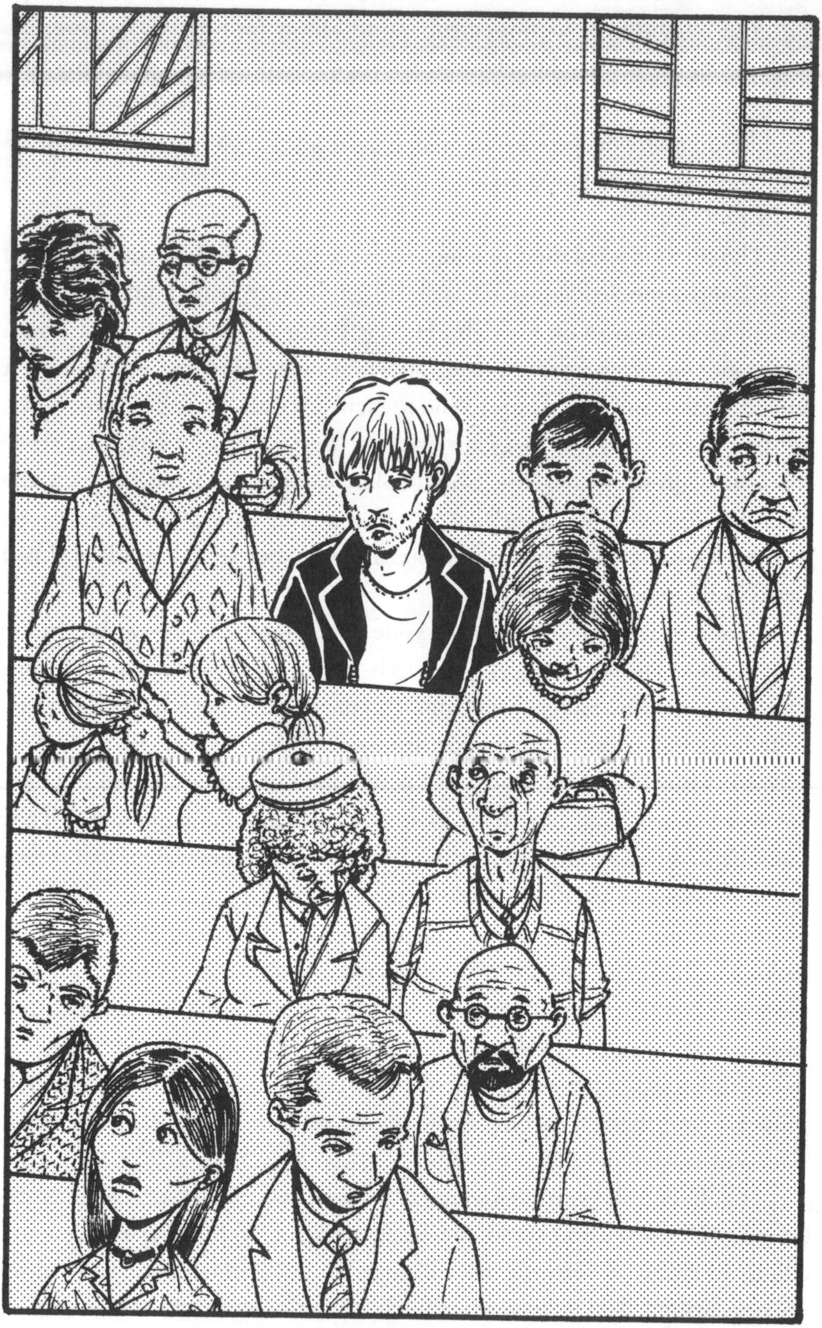

Not. Fully. Aware.

"So many people are like this. Asleep. Not there. Looking at life though half-opened eyes. Not seeing the full truth. But let me go on . . ."

People moved behind me. I could hear their clothes against the wood of the benches. The sound made my teeth ache. I wanted to turn around, but I didn't dare.

"So, Jesus returns to Judea to see Lazarus, who he already knows is dead. It's a done deal. They buried him. He's gone from the world. Jesus goes to visit him anyway.

"There, Jesus meets the sister, Martha, who comes to him, weeping, 'Oh, it's too late, it's too late.' She says, 'Lord, if You had been here, my brother would not have died. My brother. Would not. Have *died.*' If Jesus had been with him, if Lazarus had Jesus with him, he would be alive. He would be awake. Jesus wasn't there, though, and Lazarus is dead, and everyone has given up hope. They may be up and walking around, but they're just as dead as Lazarus is. Oh, Lord, give 'em a second, they need some time to wake up."

Everyone laughed. Except the guy on my right. He turned his head to look at me. I could hear his neck scrape against the collar of his shirt.

"So, Jesus, the greatest alarm clock known to man, says—and this is very important—He says, 'Your brother will rise again.' Understand? 'Your brother. Will rise. *Again.*' He will rise again. He will wake up. He is gone from this world, he has left this world. In *this* world, we are asleep. We're *dreaming* when we're in *this* world. When we leave it, *we wake up!*"

The crowd cheered and clapped and shouted, "Amen!" and "Hallelujah!" and their clothes rustled and they stared at me and I just couldn't listen anymore. I just couldn't listen at all.

I was going to get up and run out and never come back, but I stopped. In front of me, on the front bench, two little girls were sitting in their Sunday dresses. They had their feet on the bench and one had her back to the other. She was turned around so that her friend—or maybe it was her sister—could braid her hair. In her little hands, the friend held onto three sections of hair, three long bunches that she twisted around each other. When she finished, both girls turned around and faced the other direction. The girl who had her hair done was now doing it for the other, first making a braid on the left, then one on the right, giving her two braids, one on each side.

I watched them, and I started to weep. I stopped hearing the sermon. I stopped being aware of the people around me. There was just these two little girls sitting together and doing each other's hair.

An elbow nudged me. The man on my right was looking down at me. "You all right?" he asked.

I wiped the tears from my face and got up. I didn't say anything, but squeezed my way out and headed back up the aisle and away from there.

"You see, Lazarus didn't have to be dead. He *knew* death, but he didn't have to be dead. He was awake! *Awake!*"

Brian was leaning against the back wall, his hands clasped down by his waist. I hoped I could get by him and out the door, but he came after me and stopped me at the entrance. "Wait," he said, "is something wrong?"

"I need to go," I said. "I don't belong here."

"Everyone belongs here," Brian said.

"Not me," I replied.

"I'm sorry you feel that way. Could I maybe get you down on our mailing list? We could send you stuff, keep in touch until maybe you'd be more comfortable. Or maybe sometime I could come talk to you where you live?"

"I don't live anywhere, man," I said. "No place at all."

I left the church into the gray morning and started walking once more.

24. HAIRDRESSER ON FIRE

It was located next to a pawn shop. Across the street was a liquor store. The place didn't have a name. It just said "HAIRCUTS $5" in the window. The letters were large and red. The paint was chipping, especially the "A." If it weren't for the black outline, you wouldn't have known it was an "A" at all.

When I went in, a bell above the door jingled. The inside smelled like strong mouthwash. An old man was sitting in the barber's chair reading a newspaper. He had on tan pants and a white undershirt. The pants were held up by suspenders. His hair was white and combed to the back.

"Ya need a haircut, son?" he asked, looking at me over the top of his paper.

"Yes," I said.

The old man got up. "Have a seat," he said, motioning to the chair. "There's nobody in front of ya. I can do ya right up."

I took my jacket off and hung it on a coat rack by the door. The leather felt slick and greasy. When I ran my hands through my hair, it was the same way.

The chair was made of green vinyl. It squeaked when I sat down. "Do you do shaves, too?" I asked. "You know, like in the old movies?"

The barber smiled. The lacquer had rotted off one of his teeth, and it was blue. "Ya mean with a straight razor?"

"Uh-huh."

"Betcha I do," he laughed. "Usually, it's just the old timers that go for that, but nothin' says I can't do it on ya young fellas."

"Good."

He got out a white cape, and he wrapped it around my neck. "How's about we do the beard first?" he asked.

"However," I said.

He got out his scissors and leaned me back in the chair. "What's your name, son?" he asked.

"Mason."

"Mine's Joe. But ya probably guessed that. People say I look like a Joe." I laughed.

"Just relax, now, Mason, leave it up to Joe."

Joe started clipping hairs off my beard. The blades of the scissors were cold against the skin of my face. The sound they made each time he cut was sharp and clean. It was an anxious sound. It made me want to hit something or break a window.

"It's pretty thick, Mason, so I'm going to trim it down. Makes for an easier shave. How're ya going to want your hair?"

"Take it all off," I said.

"So, real short? Like army style?"

"No, I mean bald. I want no hair left on my head."

"Okay."

After he trimmed my beard, Joe sat me back up. "Might as well cut the hair off, then, while we're at it. Shave both spots at once."

He took a comb out of a glass canister filled with a blue liquid that I think was the stuff that made the place smell like mouthwash. He shook the comb off, and the liquid splattered on the tile floor. I imagined it was blood. Then I tried not to think about it.

Joe combed my hair back with long, strong strokes. He whistled as he did it. "Ya know that song?" he asked.

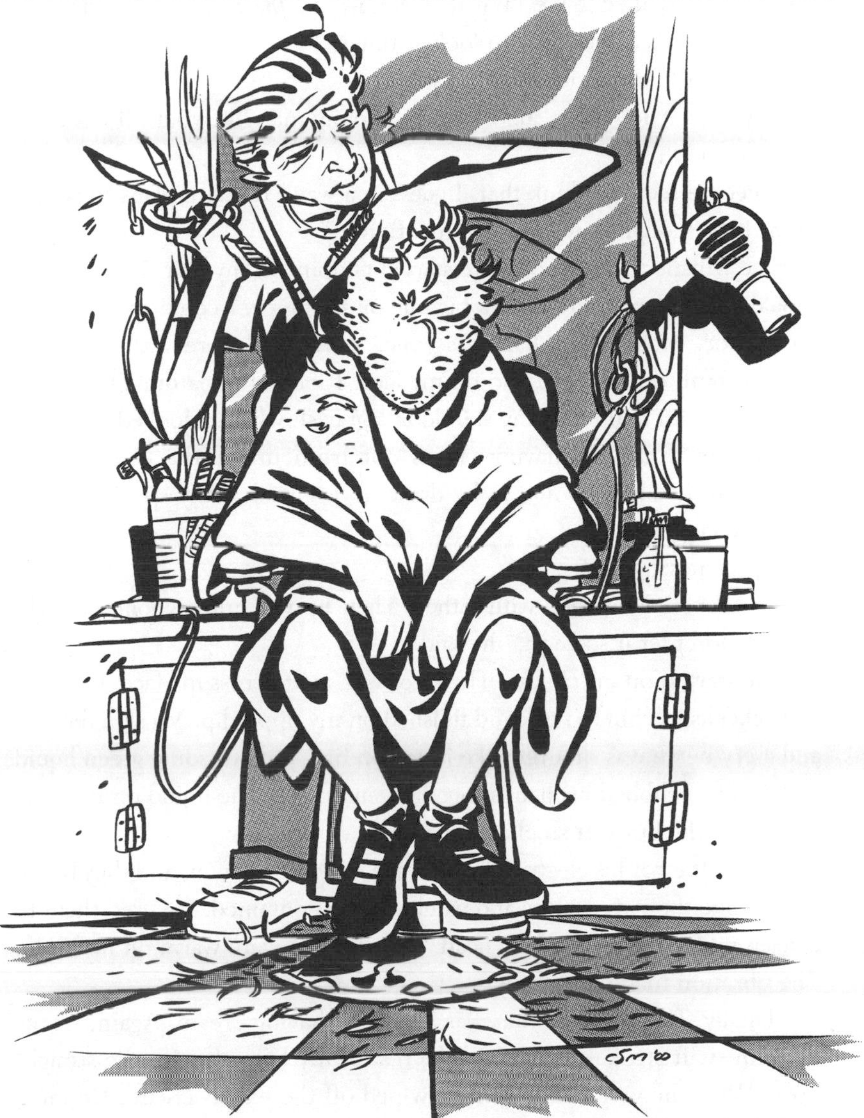

"No," I said.

"I'm not surprised," he said. "It's an old one. 'Accentuate the Positive,' it's called." He sang it. "'*Accen-tuate the positive, elim-inate the negative . . .*' It's a good way to look at things."

"I don't know about that," I said.

"Ah, it's true. 'Sides, ain't nothin' a young man like yourself has to be negative about."

"People seem to think that. I guess in a way I do have plans to get rid of the bad, though, now that you mention it."

Joe whistled some more. He started clipping at my hair. It fell on my shoulders and lap and formed a big pile on the floor. I could see myself in the mirror. Most of my hair was gone. What was there was in uneven patches—both on my head and on my face. I looked unnatural. The lights washed me out and made my skin look a grayish white. I looked sickly.

He got a can of shaving cream out from under the counter. He shook it up. "This is going to be drastic," Joe said. "Any special reason for the change?"

"Just moving on."

Joe covered my face with lather. Then he got out his long, straight razor. "Don't let it scare ya," he said.

He started on my cheeks. The razor was swift across my face. He went from cheeks to chin to neck and finished on my upper lip. My skin felt raw and every nerve was shouting like it was on fire. Joe put some green liquid in his palms, rubbed his hands together, and patted the liquid on my face. It soothed the burn. It smelled like trees.

Next, Joe got his electric clippers. He clicked them on, and they began to hum like they were angry and would not be contained. He used them to take even more hair off of my head. The clippers were warm on my scalp. The vibration made me sleepy.

Finally, Joe covered what was left with shaving cream. Again, working with swift strokes, he shaved the rest of my hair off with the straight razor. When he was all through, he wiped off the excess cream. He ran a washcloth under hot water in the sink and put it on my head to soothe the soft prickle. Joe finished it off with more aftershave, rubbing it all over my skull.

I barely recognized myself in the mirror. I reached my hand up to the top of my head in disbelief. The skin was smooth, bare.

Joe pulled the cape off, like a magician revealing the transformed object. "Is that what ya wanted?"

"Yeah," I said.

"Bare as a baby."

I paid Joe and stepped outside. The cool air felt good on my scalp. I rubbed both hands back over my skull, feeling the fresh skin.

25. THRUPENNY TEARS

I stand on a bridge. I have on a suit and a tie. It's windy, and my hair is blowing back over my head. Cars speed by underneath me. I can hear them in the space under the bridge. The sound is like when you put playing cards in the spokes of your bicycle tires.

I jump.

I'm on the pavement. It's silent. My body is broken, every limb at its own angle. Blood pours from my head, a river trickling over the road. My eyes and mouth are open. I look shocked that I made it to the bottom. It's silent.

That was my new dream.

It replaced the old one without me even noticing. It seemed to be the right one.

I was waiting out on the curb in front of Jeane's building. I was waiting for the flower truck to make my delivery. Three yellow roses and a card. It said, "WHY DOES IT TAKE THE TEARS OF A WOMAN TO SEE HOW MEN ARE?" I stole that from an Aztec Camera song. My creativity was occupied with something else.

The asphalt was covered in bumps. I could see blood flowing between them. I rubbed the toe of my shoe in the water in the gutter. It smelled like someone had been ill there.

When the delivery truck finally came, I felt my throat tighten. My fingers were locked together, and I squeezed them white. I had gone home and cleaned and changed. There was no message from her, and there were no hang-ups. Nothing Saturday night. Nothing Sunday. Nothing to wake me this morning.

The driver got out of the truck. He took the flowers from the back and went inside. Not too long after, he came back out without them. When the truck started, it belched a cloud of smoke out of its tailpipe. I watched it dissipate in the air—vertical ripples across the scenery. I timed five minutes on my watch, got up, and went inside.

As I walked towards her apartment, it seemed like the halls bent away from me. Like they were sickened by me.

Her name card was still on the door. JEANE with the little flower drawn next to it. I stared at it a long time and wondered if she was inside staring back at me through the peephole. If so, I was hoping she'd open the door, because I didn't think I could knock. There was no way I could knock. I was a fish stuck in an old bowl. Stuck in old water. Bumping my head against old glass. Who ever knew? Who ever asked? There's an end to suffering if there's an end to pain if there's an end to life if there's if there's if there's—there must be an end.

The door was hard against my knuckles. They stung and were pink.

The door opened slowly. Jeane leaned against the edge of it. She was trembling. Tears were smearing her mascara. Dark rivulets stained her cheeks.

"Hi," I said.

She didn't say a word.

"How are you?"

. . .

"I'm sorry," I said.

She laughed slightly. It sounded exhausted.

"Is that it?" she asked.

"I know."

231

"That doesn't even begin, Mason."

Jeane was looking directly at me. Her bottom lip was curled under her teeth. Her eyes were red and puffy. I felt small. I looked at the carpet. It was a dirty burgundy. I started to cry.

"I just . . . who . . . how was I supposed to know what to do? I didn't know. I just didn't know."

I felt her hands on my head. They were soft. The skin was still a little raw, but her fingers were cool and felt wonderful.

"What happened to your hair?" she asked. "It's all gone."

"I needed a change," I said. "Start something new. Do something drastic."

I looked into her face. It seemed like it was falling. It seemed like it was too tired to hold itself up.

"That's really moronic," she said.

I laughed. She didn't.

"Do you have any idea how I've felt?" she asked.

"No," I answered, "not exactly."

"Does it matter to you?"

"Yes. Very much."

Jeane turned away from me. She put her hand to her face, closed her eyes inside it.

"I ever tell you about the first fight I ever had?" I asked. "This kid, he picked on me all the time. It was fourth grade, I think, and he had ridden me since second grade. One day, I popped him, and we started going around. All the other kids, his friends who spit on me just as much as he did, were cheering *me* on, and I knew it was my time to move forward. But then *he* landed a punch, square on my nose. I started to bleed, and soon as that happened, I said right out loud, 'I gotta go. My nose is bleeding.' The other kids pleaded with me not to go, to stay and fight. 'He'll never mess with you again,' they said. But I went to the nurse's office."

She didn't open her eyes, she didn't even stir.

"I didn't mean to hurt you," I said.

"Yeah? No one wants to hurt anyone. But they do. All the time."

We stood there, neither looking at the other, neither saying anything. I tried to think of something. All I got was the same thing. There must be an end. There must be an end.

"Would you like me to go?" I asked, finally.

"Why? Are you thinking of staying this time?"

I stared at the dirty burgundy in the carpet.

"Look at me," she said. Her face was solid. Serious. "Are you going to stay?"

"I will."

"But?"

I was afraid to answer.

"I just have one thing left. I have one thing to do."

"What's that?"

"I can't tell you."

"Go to hell, Mason."

"If I tell you, if I say it out loud—"

"What?"

"I'm scared I won't be able to do it."

"*Pffff* . . ."

I took a step forward.

"Can you trust me?" I asked. "After all this, can you forgive me enough to trust me?"

"I can't *not* forgive you," she said.

"I need that," I said.

"You better be around, Mason. You can't do it again."

I didn't know what to say. I didn't want to tell her something that wouldn't make it true.

"Are you going to say anything?" Jeane asked.

233

"I have to get away," I said. "Just to get away, to just go, to find something, to find a place. Can you let me do that?"

I could hear her breathing. The air moved slow and heavy through her. "I have to," she said. "There's no other way I can know."

When we kissed good-bye, she held the back of my head tight, like she knew it was the last time but didn't want to admit it. When I walked out, the hallway caved in behind me.

She gave me a baseball cap to take with me. She said I might need it to protect my head. The hat was plain and black, and it smelled like a girl. It smelled like her. I smelled her perfume and thought about her the whole bus ride. I'd looked for her for so long. All the times I tried and failed—and we hadn't seemed to fail.

She hadn't.

I had.

And I owed her. I had to carry through. She deserved at least that.

I thought about her the whole way, fiddling with the choker on my wrist, wearing her hat. I saw her face and heard her laugh over each stretch of road—riding blindly, the bus taking one freeway after another. Every time we passed under a bridge, I saw myself tumbling down, falling in front of me, disappearing beneath me. One freeway leading into another, didn't matter to where, just as long as I kept going.

The bus pulled off and started on a road up a mountain. We followed that road until it didn't go anymore, took the next one that it faded into, and followed it until it too faded into the next one. The road became a spiral, circling around the edges of the mountain, taking me up, taking me to the top. I got off near a camping lodge and ran into the woods—through the trees, running, running, until I came to some rocks. They were big. Boulders. I sat down and stared at them. There was one that was larger than the others. Lines were cut deep into it, like wrinkles. There were several shallow holes. They made it look like a face. A big, blank face, staring back at me. I tried but could not see above it or around it.

So, I climbed it.

It only occurred to me on the way up that I was going to do it. I had thought about it, it was there, but now, I knew.

The stone ripped at my hands. The flesh was tearing, rolling off, but I had no feeling. My nerves and senses had shut down. No smell, no sound, no pain. A blank world. Blank and hollow like the face on the rock.

At the top, I stood in the emptiness, stood as tall as I could, and breathed. The air brought something back. My lungs burned with the deepness of it, with the effort it took to capture the thinness of it.

I stopped. I took my wallet out of my pocket. And a pen. Over my I.D., in fat letters, I wrote, "**THIS IS THE END OF ME. GOODBYE.**" I put it back in my pocket. My stomach was quivering. I couldn't open my mouth. Small steps.

I stepped lightly to the edge. Small steps. I peered over the side. As I did, my foot knocked off a tiny pebble. It crashed down below. Loud. Like a gunshot.

Or a car backfiring.

My senses came flooding back in. The sounds of the wind in the leaves, whistling between the boulders. The voices of people at the campground. All the colors. The blues and greens and golds. The crisp smell of pine and mountain air.

And looking down the face of the rock, seeing it curve under itself at its bottom, things suddenly became beautiful. I had thought I couldn't live anywhere, at least not on this earth, but suddenly the world was beautiful.

I sat down on the rock and let my feet dangle from it. I had been ready to slip off the side of life, but it all fell away.